PENGUIN BOOKS

ALL THE PRESIDENTS' LADIES

Born in Budapest, Peter Hay was raised in England, where he studied classical languages and English literature at Oxford. After working twelve years in Canadian theatre and publishing, he moved in 1980 to Los Angeles, where he has taught drama at the University of Southern California and the University of California at Los Angeles.

A recognized expert in script development, he has been working as a dramaturge and producer in theatre and film; he also helped found a nonprofit group, First Theatre, for the development of new scripts for theatre, film, and television.

Peter Hay is the author of *Ordinary Heroes*, which Warner Brothers and CBS are making into a miniseries. A lifelong collector of anecdote books (his personal library contains thousands of volumes, in several different languages, some dating back to the eighteenth century), he has compiled *Theatrical Anecdotes* and *A Book of Business Anecdotes*, and is currently at work on a book of legal anecdotes.

ALL THE
PRESIDENTS'
LADIES

*Anecdotes of the Women Behind the
Men in the White House*

PETER HAY

PENGUIN BOOKS

PENGUIN BOOKS

Published by the Penguin Group
Viking Penguin, a division of Penguin Books USA Inc.,
40 West 23rd Street, New York, New York 10010, U.S.A.
Penguin Books Ltd, 27 Wrights Lane,
London W8 5TZ, England
Penguin Books Australia Ltd, Ringwood,
Victoria, Australia
Penguin Books Canada Ltd, 2801 John Street,
Markham, Ontario, Canada L3R 1B4
Penguin Books (N.Z.) Ltd, 182–190 Wairau Road,
Auckland 10, New Zealand

Penguin Books Ltd, Registered Offices:
Harmondsworth, Middlesex, England

First published in the United States of America by Viking Penguin,
a division of Penguin Books USA Inc. 1988
Published in Penguin Books 1989

1   3   5   7   9   10   8   6   4   2

LIBRARY OF CONGRESS CATALOGING IN PUBLICATION DATA
Hay, Peter.
All the presidents' ladies: anecdotes of the women behind the men
in the White House/ Peter Hay.
p.   cm.
Bibliography: p.
Includes index.
ISBN 0 14 00.9755 4
1. Presidents—United States—Wives—Anecdotes.   I. Title.
[E176.2.H39   1989]
973′.09′92—dc19   89–30033

Printed in the United States of America
Set in Caslon 540
Designed by Susan Hood

For Richard Kahlenberg,
secret agent
and
unindicted co-conspirator,
in friendship
and with appreciation
for making many good things happen

ACKNOWLEDGMENTS

I want to thank Viking Penguin for suggesting the idea for this book, and my editors Dan Frank and Michael Millman for their expert guidance and patient help. I have been impressed with the professionalism of the whole Viking Penguin staff.

My friends Richard Kahlenberg, Oliver Muirhead, David Parrish, and John Sarantos have helped me with research and their suggestions. I am grateful for the assistance of many libraries, especially in Los Angeles: the librarians and collections at UCLA, USC (especially Anthony Anderson), Occidental College, and the public libraries of Pasadena and Glendale.

Since this is a book about First Ladies, I want to pay tribute to some of the great ladies in many countries whom I have admired over the years and whose friendships I have valued and enjoyed: Felicia and Jytte Allen, Laurence Ambrose, Dorothy Atwater, Polly Bak, Kati Benedek, Lia Benedetti, Nicole Blouin, Constance Brissenden, Alice Cahana, Jacqueline Crossland, Gisela D'Andrea, June Dragan, Marris Fehr and her daughters, Bella Feinsilber, Rebekah Finer, Mira Friedlander, Hermine Fuerst-Garcia, Alexandra Gerstein, Ursula Goldfinger, Jacqueline Green, Erna and Licci Habe, Julia and Leonora Hays, Donna Wong Juliani, Patricia Keeney, Agnes Kenyeres, the Kolosvarys (Agnes, Eva, Judy, and Julika), Carol Kranes, Bonnie Marranca, Elisabeth Marton, Hilda Mortimer, Miriam Neeman, Wendy Newman, Zsuzsanna Ozsvath, Miriam Pergament, Renee Paris, Nancy Perlman, Diana Quick, Kati Roth, Vivien Rothwell, Norma Ryga, Eve Tettemer Siegel, Loren Stephens, Kathleen

Acknowledgments

Szasz, Catherine and Ginnosra Szenes, Mariska Varga, Marina Warner, Yen-Lu Wong.

And as always, I want to express my love to the First Ladies in my life: my wife, Dorthea, and my mother, Eva, whose spirit continue to inspire and give me encouragement to write my books.

CONTENTS

Contents

INTRODUCTION: ANECDOTES AND HISTORY

If the Vice President is said (perhaps a bit too often) to be one heartbeat away from the presidency of the United States, then he still stands too far away from the President actually to hear that heartbeat. In fact, only when that heartbeat stops does the closeness matter. In every other than the constitutional sense, the President's wife—called for the past one hundred years the First Lady of the land—is in a much better position to listen to the presidential heartbeat, and to influence it in innumerable ways. Some Presidents have sought counsel from their spouses only privately; others have publicized the fact; still others received their wives' advice whether they wanted it or not. It is obvious to the power brokers in Washington that Nancy Reagan is the key ally needed to influence her husband. When Donald Regan ignored that wisdom and hung up the telephone on Mrs. Reagan, the White House Chief of Staff found out from the television news that the First Lady was interviewing his successor.

John Adams informed and consulted Abigail Adams on everything he did. Jimmy Carter scheduled regular working lunches with Rosalynn Carter. Eleanor Roosevelt was her husband's eyes and ears in her constant travels; she also campaigned hard to win FDR over to her humanitarian causes, which were often politically unpalatable. Nellie Taft was accused of scheming to put her husband into the White House (he would have preferred the Supreme Court); Warren Harding's "Duchess" openly boasted of having done just that. When Woodrow Wilson lay paralyzed for almost a year and a half, Edith Bolling ran the country, and insiders informally referred to her as the "Assistant President."

Some First Ladies have influenced the public policy of the United States more than others, but all of them have had significant impact on their husbands' careers. Whereas a vice-presidential running mate is selected—often with indecent haste in the smoke-filled rooms of political conventions—and many of them are relegated to deserved oblivion, the President's real mate is long courted and is chosen for life. She is wooed usually at an early, more obscure stage of the politician's career, when the influence is even greater. According to legend, Eliza McCartle taught her husband, Andrew Johnson, to read and write; another tailor, Millard Fillmore, had the good sense to marry a school-teacher, Abigail Powers, who laid out a four-year course of study for her ambitious husband. Widowers, such as Andrew Jackson and Chester Arthur, drew daily inspiration from their spouses' mementos.

But First Ladies have also, on the whole, embodied the most traditional ideas of a woman's place in the home and in American society. To Professor Lewis L. Gould's recent description of "hostesses and passive helpmates" one might add do-gooders and good troupers, following behind their men. Any departure from the stereotyped role has invited scorn and criticism. As Profesor Betty Boyd Caroli writes in her recent feminist study *First Ladies*:

> No matter how they performed their jobs, presidents' wives never lacked detractors. Critics pointed to their extravagance (Mary Lincoln), coarseness (Margaret Taylor), casual entertaining (Dolley Madison), elitism (Elizabeth Monroe), prudishness (Lucy Hayes), gaiety (Harriet Lane), excessive grief (Jane Pierce), advanced age (Martha Washington), and youth (Julia Tyler). When wives appeared to exert some influence on their husbands or on government, they were charged with exercising "petticoat government" (Edith Wilson), running their husband's careers (Florence Harding), putting words into the president's mouth (Eleanor Roosevelt), and "getting people fired" (Nancy Reagan).

Of the above, Eleanor Roosevelt came perhaps closest to having a separate career of her own, but she mostly saw it as built on her position as the spouse of FDR; she deeply admired and envied what her friend Lorena Hickok had achieved on her own. We have yet to see a presidential wife who, for example, refuses to move to Washington because of her job. Nancy Reagan was happy to sacrifice her career in Hollywood to devote herself to her husband; one wonders if Jane Wyman would have done the same. Elizabeth Taylor's brief marriage to Senator John Warner highlighted the problems an independent woman faces in a city ruled almost entirely by men.

As far back as 1774, Abigail Adams wrote in a famous letter to her husband: "Whilst you are proclaiming peace and goodwill to men, emancipating all nations, you insist on retaining absolute power over wives. If particular care and attention is not paid to the ladies, we are determined to foment a rebellion and will not hold ourselves bound by any laws in which we have no voice or representation." The women who became First Ladies did not as a rule set out to marry a future President (though Mary Todd Lincoln and Nellie Taft were notable exceptions); less ambitious politically than their husbands, many of them never imagined that they would end up in the White House. Unlike royalty, who are trained from birth to play public and ceremonial roles, or the presidential candidates tested in elected or appointed office and endlessly questioned by voters and the media through an increasingly tortuous process, the spouses are often thrust into the limelight without preparation and sometimes against their will. Many have resented this sudden change in their life, and made themselves sick, allowing others to play their public role. Some, like Dolley Madison or Louisa Adams, spent their entire life basking in the social life of the Capital, but others, like Pat Nixon—and, surprisingly, Jacqueline Kennedy—felt menaced in the public arena. Betty Ford, who found herself suddenly and unexpectedly in the White House, also rediscovered her real self in a publicly played-out identity crisis. What one of the Washington "cave-dwellers" observed upon Woodrow Wilson's second marriage in 1915 still holds up today:

Introduction: Anecdotes and History

When Edith Wilson first came to the White House she had to face many social problems. I really think there ought to be a training school for Presidents' wives that would give them a chance to try their fences. The long line of dead and gone wives who have graced this ancient house have set up standards, evolved codes, modified, expanded, duplicated, and generally left a position nominally very simple, but actually very complex.

Much that has been published by and about earlier First Ladies tends to reflect conventional aspects and criticism of a role model that relates less and less to the modern American woman. At the same time, the Office of the First Lady has become a political part of the White House, with a staff of some two dozen aides and with an agenda that has outgrown purely social functions. Presidential libraries now contain the separate archives of the First Lady, and there are conferences and scholarly studies about her role. But I have found that the anecdotist faces challenges distinct from those confronting the historian or the sociologist. For example, my other anecdotal books are built around the wide worlds of theatre, business, and the law. Each of these subjects boasts a long tradition spanning many centuries; they involve large professions in many countries. No profession exists for Presidents, let alone for their wives. First Ladies have numbered just three dozen, and have lived in the same country during a brief period of two hundred years. They are connected mainly by the accident that their husbands achieved or fell into the highest office of the land. Because First Ladies have been treated—or have regarded themselves—as appendages of their husbands, their personalities have been blunted and their abilities often restrained. This shows up clearly in the anecdotal tradition about the presidency, in which the wives form a background, rarely foils to their husbands' deeds and witty sayings.

Anecdotes tend to be preserved of those who are watched or listened to most. It is easier to be remembered in the daily melee of events when one is perceived as an author of them. The infancy of the American Republic happened to coincide with the age of Johnson and Boswell in England and with the great court gossipers on the Continent; booksellers of the late eighteenth century wanted the word "anecdote" in the title of every biography. Social life in Washington evolved around levees; its formality vied with the *bonhomie* that an elected President found useful to put people around him at ease and make them think that he was one of them. Since Franklin Roosevelt, the first modern media star in the White House, Presidents have been expected to be stand-up (or sit-down) comics; they least welcome competition in this regard from their wives. Consorts are meant to be seen not heard, and this dynamic held as true for the Washingtons as for the Kennedys.

On the other hand, the very facts that much of their lives and opinions have been hidden, that their influence is mostly kept secret, and that their deeds are largely considered too inconsequential by historians render the First Ladies ideal material for anecdotal treatment. Dr. Johnson took the Greek word "anecdote," usually denoting something unpublished, and enlarged it in his *Dictionary* to mean "a secret history. . . . It is now used, after the French," he added in a later edition, "for a biographical incident; a minute passage of private life." When Boswell, the supreme anecdotist, was leaving for Corsica, Johnson said to him: "Give us as many anecdotes as you can—I love anecdotes. I fancy mankind may come in time to write all aphoristically, except in narrative; grow weary of preparation and connection and illustration, and all those arts by which a big book is made." Isaac D'Israeli, the father of Benjamin, found Johnson's definition wanting. He remarked in his *Dissertation on Anecdotes* (1793): "This confines its signification merely to biography; but anecdotes are susceptible of a more enlarged application. This word is more justly defined in the Cyclopaedia, 'a term which denotes a relation of detached and interesting particulars.' We give anecdotes of the art as well as the Artist; of the war as well as the General; of the nation as well as the Monarch."

I have taken both Johnson's and D'Israeli's definitions to heart. By and large, this anecdotal anthology has omitted the wearisome preparation and connection, the footnotes, and all "those arts by which a big book is made." At the same time, I decided that, rather than devoting a biographical section systematically to each First Lady, I would make the "relation of detached and interesting particulars" my organizing principle. And to emphasize my anecdotal—as opposed to historical—approach, I also abandoned chronological order, which worked so well in Paul Boller Jr.'s two books of presidential anecdotes. While every President was historically important to some degree, many of the wives were not, or else they died before their husbands reached the White House. I wanted to avoid a great deal of repetition about wifely virtues and other hagiographic details in which the literature abounds. I felt no compunction about leaving out those women concerning whom no interesting stories were preserved, and to visit often with those who are well remembered. I was guided by what they did and thought, what was unusual rather than conventional about them, and yet I wanted to record how they retained their ordinary touch under extraordinary circumstances.

A British writer once defined "anecdote" as an expensive word for gossip. In selecting sources, I was drawn not only to "secret history" and to "minute passages of private life," but, quite frankly, also to malicious gossip. On November 22, 1987, *The New York Times* devoted an article to the raging debate on whether Thomas Jefferson's decades-long relationship with his slave Sally Hemings was historical fact or the successful product of British propaganda. From an anecdotist's point of view, the controversy—or even the historical truth—is only marginally interesting. What is relevant is that the story has endured for almost two hundred years, and that histories, biographies, novels, and plays are still being written about it. In the no-man's-land between fiction and nonfiction, anecdotes preserve only what continues to fascinate, and the way things might have been, as if life could always rival fiction. As in myth and in epics, what matters in an anecdote is the story and how it is spun. Reality as defined through painstaking historical reconstruction is suspended in favor of dramatic action. History becomes the footnote to the anecdote, instead of the other way around.

But I did try to achieve a different kind of authenticity by striving to preserve the reported words, rather than by rewriting my sources. With my background in the theatre, I was interested in the dramatic moment: wanting to find out and also trusting the reasons why some diplomat or backstairs maid took the trouble to keep alive the memory of little moments backstage or to capture a ludicrous personage or poignant event in a verbal snapshot. I was attracted to sources which I knew to be at times inaccurate, but which contained the dramatic ingredients of plot and climax, brevity and surprise, character and dialogue. This is the stuff of anecdotes also, and the reason why Sir Winston Churchill once called them "the gleaming toys of history." I was ready to play, and I hope that you, the reader, will come and join me.

Los Angeles
December 1, 1987

WHAT WERE THEY LIKE?

PORTRAITS

Temper

There is a tradition in Virginia that Mrs. Washington, with all her good qualities, was a little tart in her temper, and favored the General occasionally with nocturnal discourse. The story rests upon the slightest foundation, and it is safe to disregard it. Great housekeepers, however, are not usually noted for amiability of disposition, and ladies whose husbands are very famous are apt to be overrun with company, which is not conducive to domestic peace. Nor does it tend to curb the license of a woman's tongue to remember that, at her marriage, she brought her husband a vast increase, both of his estate and of his importance in the social system.

Neat as a Quaker

In about 1816 Dolley Madison was described as being a very gay lady, with much rouge on her cheeks, and always appearing in a turban. She was fond of bright colors and the elegances of the toilet; yet she generally wore inexpensive clothing, preserving always the neatness of a Quaker, with the elegance of a lady of taste.

Two plain ladies from the West, passing through Washington, determined to see Mrs. Madison; but as they reached there late at night, and were to leave early next day, they were much puzzled to know how the feat should be performed. Meeting in the street an old gentleman next morning, they timidly approached and asked him to show them the way to the President's House. Being an old acquaintance of Mrs. Madison, he took pleasure in conducting the strangers to the White House. The President's family were at breakfast when the party arrived, but Mrs. Madison good-naturedly went in to be seen by the curious old ladies, who were evidently much astonished to find so august a personage in a plain dark dress, with a linen handkerchief pinned about her neck. Her friendly welcome soon put them at ease, and rising to leave, after a visit never to be forgotten, one of them said: "P'rhaps you wouldn't mind if I jest kissed you, to tell my gals about." Mrs. Madison, not to be outdone by her guest's politeness, gracefully saluted each of the delighted old ladies, who adjusted their spectacles and, with evident admiration, departed.

Does She or Doesn't She?

The question of whether Dolley Madison used makeup seemed to agitate Washington society. One of its prominent hostesses, Mrs. William Seaton, remarked that "Mrs. Madison is said to rouge, but not evident to my eyes, and I do not think it true, as I am well assured I saw her color come and go at the naval ball, when the Macedonian flag was presented to her by young Lieutenant Hamilton." But there was another view:

A warm admirer of hers was trying to convince a friend that Mrs. Madison was not vain. "But," said the other, "you tell me she used rouge and powder." "Yes, yes, she did," he replied, "but it was to please and gratify those who were thrown with her, not because she was fond of admiration."

Plump Shoulders

No friend or acquaintance of Mrs. Madison's who came to Washington was neglected. Old and young, gentle and simple, Quaker and worldling, were bidden to the White House and made welcome there. This hospitable lady's great-nieces take pleasure in

4

telling how a Friend from Philadelphia, who was dining with the President, paid back the raillery of the gay hostess in her own coin.

As Mrs. Madison, looking very handsome in an evening gown that displayed her plump shoulders to great advantage, took her seat at table, she raised her wineglass to her lips and, bowing to her guest, said gayly: "Here's to thy absent broadrim, Friend Hallowell," to which the Quaker, nothing daunted, said, returning the bow of his hostess: "And here's to thy absent kerchief, Friend Dorothy!"

How Mrs. Madison and her sisters must have laughed over this clever rejoinder—those "Merry Wives of Windsor," as Washington Irving was wont to call them.

Puritan Frigidity

A nineteenth-century writer waxed classical (and pompous) in this paean to Abigail Adams:

Her lofty lineaments carried a trace of the Puritan severity. They were those of the helmed Minerva, and not of the caestus-girdled Venus. Her correspondence uniformly exhibits a didactic personage, a little inclined to assume a sermonizing attitude, as befitted the well-trained and self-reliant daughter of a New England country clergyman, and a little inclined, after the custom of her people, to return thanks that she had no lot or part in anything that was not of Massachusetts. Perhaps the masculineness of her understanding extended somewhat to the firmness of her temper. But, towering above, and obscuring these minor angularities, she possessed a strength of intellectual and moral character which commands our unqualified admiration. When her New England frigidity gave way and kindled into enthusiasm, it was not like light straw on fire, but red-hot steel.

A Daughter's Tribute

Six months before Martha Jefferson Randolph's death, Thomas Sully painted her portrait. According to her daughter:

I accompanied her to Mr. Sully's studio, and as she took her seat before him, she said playfully: "Mr. Sully, I shall never forgive you if you paint me with wrinkles."

I quickly interrupted, "Paint her just as she is, Mr. Sully, the picture is for me."

He said: "I shall paint you, Mrs. Randolph, as I remember you twenty years ago."

The picture does represent her younger—but failed to restore the expression of health and cheerful, ever-joyous vivacity that her countenance then habitually wore. My mother's face owed its greatest charm to its expressiveness, beaming, as it ever was, with kindness, good humor, gaiety, and wit. She was tall and very graceful; her complexion naturally fair, her hair of a dark chestnut color, very long and very abundant. Her manners were uncommonly attractive from their vivacity, amiability, and high breeding, and her conversation was charming.

Actress

John Tyler's first wife, Letitia, had suffered a stroke two years before her husband became President. The role of hostess fell to her daughter-in-law, Priscilla Cooper Tyler, who had worked as an actress in her father's company. She had a flair for self-dramatization and once said this about herself: "I am considered 'charmante' by the Frenchmen, 'lovely' by the Americans and 'really quite nice you know' by the English."

However, one of those Frenchmen stationed in Washington made a derogatory remark about a country where a woman could pass from being an actress to "what serves as a Republican throne."

Conspicuous by Her Presence

Mrs. Polk was tall, slender, and stately, with much dignity of bearing, and a manner said to resemble that of Mrs. Madison. The stateliness of her presence was conspicuous and so impressed an English lady that she declared that "not one of the three queens whom she had seen could compare with the truly feminine yet distinguished presence of Mrs. Polk."

Diamonds Are a Girl's Best Friend

Mrs. Roger Pryor, a Washington socialite, knew Harriet Lane in her glory days at the White House during the administration of her uncle James Buchanan. She remembered the bachelor President's niece across half a century, when she published her memoirs in 1904:

Miss Lane was very affable and agreeable, in an unemotional way—the proper manner, of course, for her. I imagine no one could take a liberty with her then, but I risked the experiment some years ago when we spent a summer together at Bar Harbor. A handsome widow, with silver hair, she was even more *distinguée* than she had been in the White House. I recalled, to her genuine amusement, two incidents of her life there. When she took her place as mistress of the Executive Mansion, the President had given her but one rule for her conduct: never under any circumstances to accept a present. "Think of my feelings," she had said to me, "when the lovely lacquered boxes and tables the Japanese Embassy brought me were turned from the door, to say nothing of the music-boxes and these fascinating sewing-machines they have just invented."

A party was once made up for a visit to Mount Vernon. Mr. Augustus Schell of New York accompanied Miss Lane. He was a fine-looking fellow and very much in love with her. As they walked along the banks of the Potomac, she picked up a handful of colored pebbles. Mr. Schell requested them of her and put them in his pocket. He took them to Tiffany, had them beautifully polished, set with diamonds, and linked together in a bracelet, and sent them as "a souvenir of Mount Vernon" to Miss Lane for a Christmas gift.

She carried them for a week in her pocket, trying to get her own consent to give them up. The more she looked at them, the better she liked them. One day the President was in fine spirits. He liked to rally her about Lord Lyons, which she did not fancy overmuch. But this time she humored him, and at last ventured to say, "Uncle Buchanan, if I have a few pretty pebbles given me, you do not object to my accepting them?"

"Oh, no, Miss Harriet! Keep your pebbles! Keep your pebbles," he exclaimed, in high good humor.

"You know," Miss Lane said, in telling me the story at the time, "diamonds *are* pebbles."

Typical Belle

At twenty-two, when she first set eyes on her future husband, Mary Todd Lincoln was a typical belle. Her sister Elizabeth described her as having "clear blue eyes, long lashes, light brown hair with a glint of bronze, and a lovely complexion. Her figure was beautiful, and no Old Master ever modeled a more perfect arm and hand."

And Elizabeth's husband, Ninian Edwards, remarked of his sister-in-law: "Mary could make a bishop forget his prayers."

Careworn

When Andrew Johnson occupied the White House, Mrs. Johnson had been an invalid for twenty years, and although she could not go into society on account of her ill health, her pride was amply gratified in the advancement of her husband, whom she had taught to read when he was a village tailor and had won her heart. Her only appearance in public at the White House was at a party given to her grandchildren. She then remained seated, and as the young guests were presented to her, she would say, "My dears, I am an invalid," which was fully proven by her careworn, pale face, and her sunken eyes.

Reticence

Mrs. Lucretia Garfield, familiarly called by her husband "Crete," held four successive receptions of invited guests immediately after the inauguration, at which her deportment and dress met with the heartiest commendation of society. Ladylike, sweet voiced, unruffled, well-informed, and always appropriately dressed, she was eminently fitted to be "the First Lady in the land," and she quietly yet firmly repelled any patronizing attempts to direct her movements. She had a natural aversion to publicity but was anxious to entertain the thousands who flocked to the White House. To a stranger she appeared reticent and rather too retiring to make him feel at home, but the second and third time he saw her he began to appreciate her sterling, womanlike qualities and to like her.

Everydayish

Florence Harding was natural to the point of being naive. There was something sweet and distinctly feminine about the way in which she conducted her first shopping tour to New York after she became our First Lady. It was almost as if she had brought a bit of Main Street and plunked it down right into Peacock Alley at the Waldorf! But it was so human and everydayish that everybody liked it when she showed her new clothes to the reporters and had her picture taken right in the midst of it.

Mrs. Harding was always proud of being a small-town woman. She never wanted to be anything else. She remembered when she didn't have things. When roses and carnations were four or five dollars, a bouquet from the White House, with a gracious message, expressed the understanding of a woman who once knew what it was to make ends meet, and who liked flowers at her party.

Mrs. Harding understood the small-town curiosity and the value of the close-up of the high spots in the Capital when a visitor was relating adventures in Washington back in the home-town. "Wouldn't you like to go up and see the other rooms in the White House?" she asked a middle western woman one day. "I know how curious I used to be about it all," she admitted frankly.

Looking as She Should

J. B. West, Chief Usher at the White House from 1941 until 1969, painted this portrait of the quintessential small-town woman who is suddenly thrust into the middle of high society:

There was very little glamour to Bess Truman. Like most midwestern women I'd known, her values went deeper than cosmetics and color schemes. She was matronly and comfortable, often wearing gray to complement her soft gray hair. I don't think it ever occurred to her to tint her hair—it might end up purple, like that of so many of the berouged Washington ladies who came through our reception lines.

"She looks exactly as a woman her age should look," Harry Truman said proudly.

As a young girl, she had been considered a beauty; at sixty, she wore her age gracefully and naturally. Her clothes were tailored—two-piece suits with hat and gloves for outside, simple dresses at home. In the evening, she wore long gowns cut with straight lines, usually with one strand of pearls. And I never saw her wrinkled or rumpled. She was always impeccably groomed.

Her eyes were her single most engaging feature. Her warm, expressive smile began with a twinkle there. But her eyes could freeze you with their steel-blue glint.

CLOTHES

Recycling

Mrs. Washington was extremely plain in her dress and displayed little taste for those luxurious ornaments deemed appropriate for the wealthy and great. In her own home the spinning wheels and looms were kept constantly going, and her dresses were, many times, woven by her servants. General Washington wore at his inauguration a full suit of fine cloth, the handiwork of his own household. At a ball given in New Jersey in honor to herself, Mrs. Washington wore a simple russet gown, and white handkerchief about her neck, thereby setting an example to the women of the Revolution, who could ill afford to spend their time or means as lavishly as they might have desired.

President Washington wrote to his friend Mrs. Macaulay: "Mrs. Washington's ideas coincide with my own as to simplicity of dress, and everything which can tends to support propriety of character without partaking of the follies of luxury and ostentation." On one occasion she gave the best proof of her success in domestic manufactures by the exhibition of two of her dresses, which were composed of cotton, striped with silk, and entirely homemade. The silk stripes in the fabric were woven from the ravelings of brown silk stockings and old crimson chair covers.

Bird of Paradise

Following James Madison's inauguration, at a ball which was given at Davis's Hotel in the evening—the first inaugural ball in Washington of which there is any record—it is said that "upwards of four hundred persons graced the scene, which was not a little enlivened by the handsome display of female fashion and beauty." The "Lady Presidentess," who was the center of all eyes, was resplendent in a gown of yellow velvet, her neck and arms hung with pearls and her head surmounted by a Parisian turban from which nodded a bird-of-paradise plume.

Exit the Bustle

Like royalty, First Ladies exercise a great deal of influence on fashion. In this story, Frances Cleveland followed rather than led the trend:

In those days, Congress didn't spend so much time in session, and newspapermen from other states, reluctant to return to their hometowns during the recess, resorted to every trick to justify their continued existence in Washington. There were about fourteen of them who used to meet each day, and after conference, someone usually succeeded in digging out a story worthy of transmission.

One day there was nothing, absolutely nothing. They sat disconsolate, fearing an immediate recall owing to the dearth of news in the Capital.

"Can't we send a society item?" suggested one.

"Yes, if you've got one; there isn't a line in sight now," replied a second.

"Then let's manufacture one," said the first. There they sat solemnly trying to think of something that would do.

"I've got it!" said the originator of the idea. "Let's say that Mrs. Cleveland has decided to abolish the bustle."

"Brilliant!"

They sat and scribbled, and in an hour the message was being broadcast—a message that was to revolutionize the fashion of the day.

Mrs. Cleveland was young and beautiful then, and the nation looked to her as a guide in such matters. It was a trivial thing, of course, and she didn't consider it worth a contradiction. Yet if she appeared in the old-fashioned bustle after this, despite statement to the contrary, it would mean so much explanation. So she did the simple, courteous thing and immediately ordered a gown without a bustle.

Terror

We may remember how much Mrs. Reagan was criticized for her spending on clothes while the country was in deep recession during the early years of her husband's administration. Mary Todd Lincoln was a compulsive shopper more on the scale of Imelda Marcos. She was hounded by the press on her shopping trips to New York, when she would order enormous quantities of clothes which she never wore. Her closets were filled with unused merchandise. While Abraham Lincoln was busy prosecuting the War Between the States, Mrs. Lincoln bought three hundred pairs of gloves in a four-month period. She spent small fortunes on shawls and evening dresses, until her debts reached

$27,000—this in an age when a working man's salary was less than ten dollars a week.

Mary lived in terror of her extravagance being discovered by her husband. During Lincoln's reelection campaign she told her friend Elizabeth Keckley:

"I do not know what would become of us all. If he is reelected I can keep him in ignorance of my affairs; but if he is defeated, then the bills will be sent in and he will know all."

Watchdog

Lillian Rogers Parks was for thirty years seamstress at the White House. She witnessed the unceasing battle between the closely knit Trumans about the question of clothes:

The First Lady I felt sorriest for, in the clothing department, was Mrs. Truman. The most conservative dresser herself, she was shocked at the wild clothes the President loved to deck himself out in.

She had to be a kind of watchdog. The funniest moment was when she was getting ready for a trip to Florida with the President, and caught Prettyman, Mr. Truman's valet, packing a pair of red trousers into the President's suitcase. They had been a gift and she lived in mortal fear that he would someday wear them.

If he wanted to bring the bow tie back into style—which he succeeded in doing—she could stand that; and if he wanted to wear hibiscus-flowered sport shirts among his buddies in and out of the press, she could grit her teeth and bear that too; but the bright red slacks—no, never!

Every few weeks the President would go over his wardrobe and throw out a lot of his clothing, including the dozens of neckties and shirts he would receive, and Mrs. "T" always hoped he'd include the wild red pants. He would put out the clothes he was discarding for the ushers, Secret Service men, butlers, and housemen to take.

When Mrs. "T" saw Prettyman packing those pants, she said

that the red trousers were not going on any trip *she* was going on. So the pants stayed at the White House that time. But the very next time that the President made a trip to Florida without his wife, he wore those pants.

Mrs. Truman was also Margaret's watchdog on clothes; I suppose she hoped that her daughter would be as conservative as she. But Margaret was theatrical like her father, and wanted something with dash. There was one dress that Mrs. "T" could not stand on her daughter. It was black with bright red flowers, and was cut on Oriental lines with a Chinese neckline. Margaret tried to plan a way to please her mother and still save the dress.

She came to me with her problem. "Will you take off the Chinese collar?" she asked. "I think Mother will like it then." Mrs. Truman happened to come into the room when I had the collar off and was fitting the dress. She looked very displeased.

"What are you going to do with that dress?" she asked Margaret.

Margaret said, "Oh, Mother, when Lillian gets through, you won't know this dress."

Mrs. "T" gave the dress a look of disdain and said, "Well, when she gets through fixing it, tell her to dye it." And out she went.

As for her own clothes, Mrs. Truman was always simple and dignified. She went in for suits—even silk suits for teas. Her favorite color was black, and she used to tell me, "You can't go wrong with black."

Once I tried to argue with her, because she looked so well in blue, which matched her eyes, that I wanted her to wear it more often. I ventured to say, "Well, fashion claims that when you get older, you shouldn't wear too much black, because black makes one look tired." Mrs. "T" pondered that a moment.

"Well, Lillian," she repeated, "you can't go wrong with black."

Battle of the Underwear

One of the most widely read stories during the 1960 campaign was about fashion—who spent more on her clothes, Jacqueline

Kennedy or Pat Nixon? Jackie said she couldn't spend as much on clothes as Pat Nixon did "unless I wore sable underwear."

Nan Robertson of *The New York Times* got the story about Jackie's clothes while doing a running interview with her which started in the bedroom of a Waldorf Towers suite (while Nan helped Jackie try on maternity clothes by "buttoning her up") and ended at the Commodore Hotel, where Jack Kennedy was making a campaign speech. "The male reporters were simply furious when I followed Jackie into the ladies' room and they had to stand outside," said Nan. "But not as furious as Jack Kennedy was when he read the story. One of his aides said he hit his forehead and cried, "Good Christ!" That was the last interview they let Jackie do until after the election."

Recurring Nightmare

Unlike the practice of her predecessor, Rosalynn Carter, who emulated Martha Washington in making her own clothes out of fabric bought at a remnant house, Nancy Reagan's love of designer clothes led to the malicious joke that she was a Christian of the Dior persuasion.

Parade magazine printed a letter from a reader in Glendale, California, who wrote, presumably tongue in cheek: "Is it true that Nancy Reagan has a recurring nightmare where she is abducted from the White House, taken to a Sears store, and forced to buy a dress off the rack?"

Ill Will

When the embattled First Lady's office announced that Nancy Reagan would be donating one of her gowns to the well-known collection at the Smithsonian, Goodwill Industries offered to replace it by giving Mrs. Reagan a purple floral dress which cost about three dollars. However, the offer was withdrawn after a flood of calls to Goodwill showed that people disapproved of the First Lady being made fun of.

BELIEFS

Churchgoing

Rachel Jackson visited Washington with her husband in December 1824. The pious lady confided her impressions of the capital in a letter to her friend, Mrs. Kingsley:

To tell you of this city, I would not do justice to the subject. The extravagance is in dressing and running to parties; but I must say they regard the Sabbath, and attend preaching, for there are churches of every denomination and able ministers of the gospel. We have been here two Sabbaths. The General and myself were both days at church. Mr. Baker is the pastor of the church we go to. He is a fine man, a plain, good preacher. We were waited on by two of Mr. Balche's elders, inviting us to take a pew in his church in Georgetown, but previous to that I had an invitation to the other. General Cole, Mary, Emily, and Andrew went to the Episcopal church.

Oh, my dear friend, how shall I get through this bustle. There are not less than from fifty to one hundred persons calling in a day. My dear husband was unwell nearly the whole of our journey, but, thanks to our Heavenly Father, his health is improving. Still, his appetite is delicate, and company and business are oppressive; but I look unto the Lord, from whence come all my comforts. I have the precious promise, and I know that my Redeemer liveth.

Don't be afraid of my giving way to those vain things. The apostle says, I can do all things in Christ, who strengtheneth me. The play-actors sent me a letter, requesting my countenance to them. No. A ticket to balls and parties. No, not one. Two dinings; several times to drink tea. Indeed, Mr. Jackson encourages me in my course. He recommends it to me to be steadfast. I am going today to hear Mr. Summerfield. He preaches in the Methodist church; a very highly spoken of minister. Glory to God for the privilege. Not a day or night but there is the church opened for prayer.

Gentle Request

Mrs. Franklin Pierce, although an invalid, bore up bravely under the fatigues of her position. She was very pious, and her scruples in regard to keeping the Sabbath had an influence upon public life. Her biographer wrote that "each Sunday morning of her four years' stay in the White House, she would request, in her gentle, conciliatory way, all the attachés of the mansion to go to church."

Female Suffrage

Although she had a mind very much of her own, Mrs. Lincoln expressed her opposition to giving women the vote in a letter to Mrs. John Dahlgren, author of Thoughts on Female Suffrage. *Returning from Europe in the spring of 1871, the widow of the Great Emancipator wrote to her:*

Dear Madame:

I have read with great pleasure your *spirituelle brochure*, and can assure you of my entire sympathy in your eloquent opposition to what are falsely called woman rights. As if we women in America were not in the fullest possession of every right—even of that one which I think the French call "le droit d'insolence." I would recommend our strong-minded sisters to take a trip to Savoy or Saxony, where I have seen women hitched to the plough or harnessed with dogs drawing little carts through the streets.

The movement seems to me, however, one of those which should be treated with wholesome neglect, since should Congress give them the privilege of voting—those who would avail themselves of it are sure to behave in so inconsequent a manner as to reduce the whole matter to an absurdity. I know not whether it is indolence or because I am so thoroughly anti-protestant but I never signed a protest against any thing in my life; however, out of respect for your talents and opinions, I shall avail myself of the first opportunity to lay this pamphlet & petition before my friend Mrs. Peters to get her signature at the head, and then try to obtain others—as also subscribers for the *True Women*.

Accept, dear lady, the sincere sympathy and admiration of
Yours truly,

Mary T. Lincoln.

Fund-raiser

When Johns Hopkins was starting its now famous medical school in 1890, Caroline Harrison was asked to help with the fund-raising. She only agreed once assurances were given that women would be admitted on an equal basis. And that is how one of the First Ladies most associated with domesticity helped to provide equal opportunities for women.

A Woman's Place

One of the features of the 1893 World's Fair at Chicago was the Woman's Building, which was to represent the many talents and activities of the world's women. Several promising female sculptors were hired for the project, including the twenty-two-year-old Enid Yandell. When Julia Grant, General Grant's widow, visited Chicago in October 1891 for the unveiling of an equestrian statue of her husband at Lincoln Park, Mrs. Bertha Palmer, President of the Board of Lady Managers for the Exposition, gave a reception for the former First Lady at which she was anxious to show off her young artists:

"I want to introduce you to Mrs. Grant," she said, taking Enid's hand. "Let me present you to Miss Yandell, the young sculptor; she is at work on the Woman's Building and we are very proud of her and think we have conferred on her an honor." Mrs. Grant, a woman of few words, said: "A sculptor! You cut marble?" Miss Yandell replied that she indeed cut marble. "I met one before," Mrs. Grant said, fixing Enid with a steely eye. "She was a great deal about the General, but I don't approve of women sculptors as a rule."

Mrs. Grant was evidently referring to Vinnie Ream Hoxie, who had created a storm of controversy when she was commissioned to execute a statue of Lincoln for the capital; she was only fifteen at the time. Evidently she had spent a lot of time with General Grant.

Mrs. Grant's response cast a damper over the conversation.

Mrs. Palmer tactfully introduced another guest. But a little while later, Miss Yandell spotted Mrs. Grant sitting alone. Undaunted, she took up the subject once more. "So you do not approve of me, Mrs. Grant?" Mrs. Grant said that it was nothing personal. "I don't disapprove of *you*, Miss Yandell, but I think every woman is better off at home taking care of husband and children. The battle with the world hardens a woman and makes her unwomanly." "And if one has no husband?" Miss Yandell asked. Mrs. Grant had an answer to that. "Get one," she said. Miss Yandell refused to give up. "But if every woman were to choose a husband the men would not go round; there are more women than men in the world." Mrs. Grant could handle that one too. "Then let them take care of brothers and fathers." She then waxed eloquent. "I don't approve of these women who play on the piano and let the children roll about on the floor, or who paint and write and embroider in a soiled gown and are all cross and tired when the men come home and don't attend to the house or table. Can you make any better housewife for your cutting marble?" "Yes," Miss Yandell said energetically. "I am developing muscle to beat biscuit when I keep house."

This slowed down Mrs. Grant considerably. Miss Yandell was not content to quit when she was ahead. "But, Mrs. Grant," she said, "are there no circumstances under which a woman may go to work?" Mrs. Grant thought it over. "I may be old-fashioned," she said. "I don't like this modern movement. But I don't think so. And yet, there are certain sorts of work a woman may well do: teaching, being governess, or any taking care of children." Miss Yandell forged ahead. "But suppose a case: a young brother and two strong sisters. The young man makes a good salary but can't get ahead because all his earnings are consumed in taking care of the girls. Hadn't they better go to work and give him a chance to get ahead and have a house of his own, they being as able to work as he? Are they being unwomanly in so doing? Or, the case of a father with a large family of girls and a small income—are they less gentlewomen for helping earn a living, lessening the providing of food for care of so many mouths by adding to the family funds?"

Mrs. Grant stared out the window at the lake. "You may be right. In that case," she said slowly, "they ought to go to work."

Split Persona

When Grace Coolidge found herself suddenly, upon the death of President Harding, mistress of the White House, she felt a strange sense of detachment about her new role:

"This was I, and yet not I—this was the wife of the President of the United States and she took precedence over me; my personal likes and dislikes must be subordinated to the consideration of those things which were required of her."

She Was Never Promised a Rose Garden

Jacqueline Kennedy had many plans to transform the famous White House Rose Garden. She had only had time to achieve a small part of her projects before the assassin's bullet intervened. Her successor wanted to pay tribute to her efforts but found that Mrs. Kennedy had unexpected views of her own importance. As Lady Bird Johnson wrote in her diary:

I asked Lyndon what he thought about the project of naming the East Garden the Jacqueline Kennedy Garden. He thought it was fine. I then tried out the idea on Clark Clifford, legal adviser-without-portfolio to the White House since the Truman days and gratefully continued by us. He thought it was an excellent idea but suggested that it might be well to mention it to two other people. I could readily see why.

First was George Hartzog, head of the National Park Service, whose job it is to oversee the White House grounds. I tracked him down and he was very much in agreement, although I asked him to make sure there wasn't any fine print lurking in the legislation anywhere that might make it difficult. He called me back and said that there wasn't anything and it would be fine. And then I called Bill Walton of the Fine Arts Commission. Bill Walton, too, was very much in favor of the idea. It only remained to call Mrs. Kennedy herself. When I did, she said no. She said she didn't think First Ladies deserved any recognition, that it was really just her husband and his job that had accomplished anything.

Ribbing

During her vociferous campaign to help ratify the Equal Rights Amendment, Betty Ford was asked by journalist Myra Mac-Pherson if she pushed her point of view with her husband. "If he doesn't get it in the office in the day," laughed Mrs. Ford, "he gets it in the ribs at night."

Seen and Heard

In January 1975 President Ford signed an executive order proclaiming a National Commission in connection with International Women's Year. At a ceremony held in the Cabinet Room, he turned to his wife and said, "Before I sign this, Betty, if you have any words of wisdom or encouragement, you are welcome to speak." Mrs. Ford congratulated her husband and added, "I am glad to see that you have come a long, long way." "I don't know how to take that," the President replied, shaking his head.

Reproach

During the 1976 presidential campaign, Jimmy Carter once made the mistake of speaking for his wife. Someone asked about her attitude to the women's liberation movement, and Carter said that Rosalynn was opposed to it. Rosalynn read about his comment in the newspaper and called reporters to state that her husband was quite mistaken about that.

Two hundred years before, Abigail Adams made herself even more clear in her humorous threat to her husband. Writing in May 1776 about the proposed Declaration of Independence, she noted an important omission:

I cannot say that I think you very generous to the Ladies, for whilst you are proclaiming peace and goodwill to men, Emancipating all Nations, you insist upon retaining an absolute power over Wives. But you must remember that Arbitrary power is like most other things which are very hard, very liable to be broken— and notwithstanding all your wise Laws and Maxims we have it in our power not only to free ourselves but to subdue our Masters, and without violence throw both your natural and legal authority at our feet—

> Charm by accepting, by submitting sway
> Yet have our Humour most when we obey.

FOIBLES

First Ladies Are Human, Too

Most of the First Ladies have been genuinely kind people, and all of them have tried to show their best side to the public. They did not always succeed:

When a bill came up in Congress providing for the purchase of a fine residence as a permanent home for the Vice President, Mrs. Harding with some effort managed to prevent its passage. She had never liked the reticent Vice President, Vermonter Calvin Coolidge, or his wife, and privately admitted killing the bill for that reason: "I just couldn't have people like those Coolidges living in that beautiful house."

Who Likes Whom

Florence Harding kept a little red book of her enemies. When her husband died suddenly, some of those enemies circulated gossip that she had killed him. At any rate, "those Coolidges" did not have to wait for their new residence; they moved into Mrs. Harding's place sooner than she expected.

Alice Roosevelt Longworth described the change in atmosphere at the White House "as different as a New England front parlor is from a back room in a speakeasy." Elizabeth Jaffray was housekeeper at the White House through five administrations, having been hired originally by Helen Taft in 1908. At each change of administration she had to start afresh with the new occupants of the Executive Mansion. In her book, Secrets of the White House, *she describes the last changeover, between two First Ladies who barely managed to hide their true feelings:*

Mrs. Harding was with Mrs. Coolidge in one of the upstairs rooms and sent the footman to my room to ask if I would come to her. I hurried down in answer to the summons.

"Mrs. Coolidge, this is Mrs. Jaffray," she introduced us, and turning directly to Mrs. Coolidge said, without realizing how it sounded, "I hope Mrs. Jaffray will like you." I was very much embarrassed and at once said, "My dear Mrs. Harding, it isn't a question of whether I like Mrs. Coolidge but of whether Mrs. Coolidge likes me."

Mrs. Coolidge reached out and gripped my hand in an understanding gesture, dismissing with her quick smile the whole uncomfortable episode.

"I would like, Mrs. Jaffray, for everything to go on just as it has in the past," she said a few moments later.

The Green-Eyed Monster

As if Abraham Lincoln did not have enough problems with waging the Civil War, Mrs. Lincoln continued to add to his burdens. Toward the end of the war, the President and Mrs. Lincoln had sailed down the Potomac toward the lower end of Chesapeake Bay, from which Lincoln and General Grant went on horseback to inspect the Army of the Potomac twelve miles away, while their wives were driven in a carriage by Grant's aide-de-camp, General Adam Badeau, who left this vivid account:

In the course of conversation, I chanced to mention that all the wives of officers at the army front had been ordered to the rear—a sure sign that active operations were in contemplation. I said not a lady had been allowed to remain, except Mrs. Griffin, the wife of General Charles Griffin, who had obtained a special permit from the President. At this Mrs. Lincoln was up in arms.

"What do you mean by that, sir?" she exclaimed. "Do you mean to say that she saw the President alone? Do you know that I never allow the President to see any woman alone?"

She was absolutely jealous of poor, ugly Abraham Lincoln.

I tried to pacify her and to palliate my remark, but she was fairly boiling over with rage.

"That's a very equivocal smile, sir," she exclaimed. "Let me out of this carriage at once. I will ask the President if he saw the woman alone."

Mrs. Griffin, afterward the Countess Esterhazy, was one of the best-known and most elegant women in Washington, a Carroll, and a personal acquaintance of Mrs. Grant's, who strove to mollify the excited spouse, but all in vain. Mrs. Lincoln again bade me stop the driver, and when I hesitated to obey, she thrust her arms past me to the front of the carriage and held the driver fast. But Mrs. Grant finally prevailed upon her to wait till the whole party alighted.

The same party went in the morning to visit the Army of the James on the north side of the river, commanded by General Ord. The arrangements were somewhat similar to those of the day before. We went up the river in a steamer, and then the men again took horses and Mrs. Lincoln and Mrs. Grant proceeded in an ambulance. I was detailed as before to act as escort, but I asked for a companion in the duty; for after my experience, I did not wish to be the only officer in the carriage. So Colonel Horace Porter was ordered to join the party. Mrs. Ord accompanied her husband; as she was the wife of the commander of an army she was not subject to the order for return; though before that day was over she wished herself in Washington or anywhere else away from the army, I am sure. She was mounted, and as the ambulance was full, she remained on her horse and rode for a while by the side of the President, and thus preceded Mrs. Lincoln.

As soon as Mrs. Lincoln discovered this her rage was beyond all bounds.

"What does the woman mean," she exclaimed, "by riding by the side of the President? and ahead of me? Does she suppose that he wants her by the side of him?"

She was in a frenzy of excitement and language and action both became more extravagant every moment.

Mrs. Grant again endeavored to pacify her, but then Mrs. Lincoln got angry with Mrs. Grant, and all that Porter and I could do was to see that nothing worse than words occurred. We feared she might jump out of the vehicle and shout to the cavalcade.

Once she said to Mrs. Grant in her transports, "I suppose you think you'll get to the White House yourself, don't you?" Mrs. Grant was very calm and dignified and merely replied that she was quite satisfied with her present position; it was far greater than she had ever expected to attain. But Mrs. Lincoln exclaimed:

"Oh! you had better take it if you can get it. 'Tis very nice." Then she reverted to Mrs. Ord, while Mrs. Grant defended her friend at the risk of arousing greater vehemence.

When there was a halt, Major Seward, a nephew of the Secretary of State and an officer of General Ord's staff, rode up and tried to say something jocular.

"The President's horse is very gallant, Mrs. Lincoln," he remarked. "He insists on riding by the side of Mrs. Ord."

This, of course, added fuel to the flame.

"What do you mean by that, sir?" she cried.

Seward discovered that he had made a huge mistake, and his horse at once developed a peculiarity that compelled him to ride behind, to get out of the way of the storm.

Finally the party arrived at its destination, and Mrs. Ord came up to the ambulance. Then Mrs. Lincoln positively insulted her, called her vile names in the presence of a crowd of officers, and asked what she meant by following up the President. The poor woman burst into tears and inquired what she had done, but Mrs. Lincoln refused to be appeased and stormed till she was tired. Mrs. Grant still tried to stand by her friend, and everybody was shocked and horrified. But all things come to an end, and after a while we returned to City Point.

That night the President and Mrs. Lincoln entertained General and Mrs. Grant and the General's staff at dinner on the steamer, and before us all Mrs. Lincoln berated General Ord to the President and urged that he should be removed. He was unfit for his place, she said, to say nothing of his wife. General Grant sat next and defended his officer bravely. Of course, General Ord was not removed.

No Love Lost

Nancy Reagan is said never to forget a slight or a misdeed, especially when done against her husband's interests. Washington columnist Diana McLellan listed some of her targets:

Nancy's foes are not legion. They are chosen with care, for specific offenses against her art.

She will never, ever forgive writer Judy Bachrach for describing her legs as "piano."

She will never forgive Lyn Nofziger, her husband's former aide, for leaking a little something about her way back in the beginning of their campaign, or for looking slobby in Daffy Duck ties and then dribbling Bombay gin all over them.

She will never forgive Betty Ford for her cavalier treatment throughout their joint history as fellow Republicans and fellow wives in pursuit of the same niche.

Her treatment at the 1976 convention still rankles in the early eighties. Nancy tells her friends that she never had a decent box at the Republican Convention until they *had* to get one.

"They have always tucked us away in the back," she claims, stuck beyond the view of the cameras in a box on the very highest tier. Blocking them was a glass shield that would reflect the lights, blind the cameras, and conceal her art.

At the time, Nancy told old friends, she believed that Betty Ford was on drugs. She "wasn't responding" to the people around her in the Ford box.

Nancy, who wished to respond, could barely snatch a glimpse of what was happening on the convention floor at all from her aerie. She had to "change badges with alternates in a delegation so the children and I could sit in the delegate section"; and when Reagan was nominated and the shouting and flag-waving began, the only way she could acknowledge the cheers was to stand up and lean dangerously over the glass.

Nancy believed that Betty tried to hog the limelight, at her expense, at the 1980 convention, too.

In return, Betty likes to get a poke in whenever she can, to please the apposing army in Nancy's looking-glass war. She likes to say she is "disappointed" in Nancy's ERA stand, abortion stand, or whatever. There are many excuses given at various Republican fund-raising events where it would be logical to see the two women together. I have not seen them.

Equal Time

Referring to that 1976 convention, Betty Ford wrote in her auto-biography:

A good deal has been written about Nancy Reagan and me, and how our boosters cheered our appearances as though she and I, and not our husbands, were the contestants.

The night most people remember, I was already on the floor of the arena when the band started playing "Tie a Yellow Ribbon Round the Old Oak Tree." Tony Orlando was there with me and Susan, and Susan said, "That's your song, Tony. Come on, you and Mom get up and dance." Susan had learned a few tricks on the campaign trail. She was wearing a blue denim shirt that had FORD spelled out between her shoulder blades, and she kept turning her back to the cameras. (We were never out of camera range.) Anyhow, she egged me and Tony on, we got up and danced for the sheer silliness of it, and I had no idea that Nancy Reagan was making her entrance into the hall at the very same time. I've been accused of trying to take the play away from her. What play? My feeling was that Nancy didn't want to play. She sat in a glassed-in box, separated from the hurly-burly, throughout the whole convention, except for the time she went upstairs to the television booth to be interviewed. I sat right in the front row of the gallery. "If they want me, they can come down here," I said.

Mom the Klutz

It is refreshing to read that Eleanor Roosevelt, one of the most competent and admired women in world history, was not perfect, at least in the eyes of her children. James, the eldest, recounted one of his mother's few failings:

Mother's adventures at the wheel occasionally were rather disastrous, as I'm afraid Mother was one of the world's least adept drivers. She had tried to learn to handle a car in 1918, but more or less gave it up after an occurrence which Anna, in a letter to Father from Hyde Park, described as follows: "Mother drove the Stearns the day after she came and nearly took off Grandmama's back doorstep because she ran into it." Her reemergence as a chauffeur provided us with numerous incidents about which to tease her, such as her knocking over one of the big stone pillars flanking the Hyde Park driveway, or letting the station wagon roll backward into a ditch. In fairness, I cannot blame Mother too much for the last mishap, for all—or most—of the kids were in the station wagon, each yelling instructions at her.

In one of my Groton letters to Mother from this period, I find the following needle: "I saw by the paper that you and your party were arrested for speeding. So did everybody else in school. It's rather a good way to get advertised don't you think?" I used this against Mother for years when she lectured me about my fast driving.

Pandamania

One of the benefits of President Nixon's reopening of relations with China was the gift of a pair of rare pandas to the Washington Zoo. The handling of the press announcement for the pandas' arrival was typical of the Nixon White House but, as columnist Judith Martin told it tongue in cheek, also showed a rare bit of assertiveness on the part of Mrs. Nixon:

Early preparations were handled by the zoo and the Smithsonian Institution, which administers it, and at that point you couldn't have asked for more frankness, clarity, or thoroughness. Several reporters, in fact, asked for less. The director of the zoo gave a press conference in which he not only answered a great many more questions than had been asked but passed out a Suggested Reading List, and rumors spread that there would be an hour exam the next time we showed up. Such information as what color pandas are and where they are to be found was not put on a "for background only" basis, as it would have been at a State Department briefing, and the superexpert, whose specialized information included the statement that it has been deemed unwise to separate pandas while they are getting ready to mate, allowed himself to be identified, as Henry Kissinger never would have permitted.

Then, two days before the big arrival, the White House took over. The sweet people at the Smithsonian and the zoo, good citizens who actually feel guilty when they lie to the press, were suddenly silenced. "Please don't ask me anything," pleaded one, who had been receiving threatening telephone calls from White House staff members in Canada, where the President and Mrs. Nixon were on a state visit. "We've been told by the White House to shut up. Mrs. Nixon wants to announce everything. They're her pandas."

BACKGROUND

PARENTAGE

Genes and Genealogy

The Todds boasted of a genealogical chart back to the sixteenth century. Mary Todd's grandfathers and great-grandfathers and great-uncles had been generals and governors, and one had been Secretary of the Navy. She herself had been educated in a snobbish French school in Lexington, Kentucky, conducted by Madame Victoire Charlotte Le Clere Mentelle and her husband—two French aristocrats who had fled from Paris during the Revolution in order to save their necks from the guillotine. They had drilled Mary to speak French with a Parisian accent and had taught her to dance the cotillion and the Circassian Circle as the silken courtiers had danced them at Versailles.

Somebody asked Lincoln once why the Todds spelled their names as they did, and he replied that he reckoned that one "d" was good enough for God, but that the Todds had to have two.

St. Patrick's Babe

Pat Ryan, the future Mrs. Nixon, was born on March 16, 1912, but she always celebrated her birthday the next day. She was officially christened Thelma Catherine and got her nickname

33

from her father. He had arrived from work after midnight in the early hours of March 17 and, first learning of the birth of his daughter, called her in a forgivable moment of Irish effusion "St. Patrick's babe in the morn."

Early Bloomer

"I always wanted to be called Elizabeth," wrote Betty Ford in her autobiography, "but it didn't happen. Once in a while my parents, hoping to make an impression on me, delivered both barrels: 'Elizabeth Ann, you stop that!' and my husband, when he's trying to hurry me along, because I'm late, will occasionally say, 'Ee-liz-a-beth, come on now,' but mostly I've been Betty or Bet or Bets."

Betty Ford drew much of her security, idea of marriage, and sense of humor from her parents:

My mother's name was Hortense Nehr Bloomer, my father's name was William Stephenson Bloomer. He worked for the Royal Rubber Company, and he traveled, selling conveyor belts to factories. My mother wrote him every single night. I can remember coming downstairs after my homework was done, and my mother would be at the desk writing to my father. Jerry and I are the same way: we've always communicated daily; the only difference is we've used the telephone.

One of my father's favorite pastimes was fiddling with an old crystal set. I can see him sitting hunched over that crystal set, earphones on, and all of a sudden crying, "Wow! I got Chicago, I got Chicago, come listen to it," and we'd run and take his earphones and listen to WKMG or whatever that famous old station was in Chicago.

Mother, who was thirty-five or thirty-six when I came along, always said I'd popped out of a bottle of champagne. I liked that idea.

Nancy Davis's Eyes

The future Mrs. Reagan was originally named Anne Frances, after one of her father's New England ancestors, Sister Anne Ayres, the first American Episcopal nun. Her mother, Edith Luckett, a struggling actress, had already become estranged from her husband, Kenneth Robbins, and immediately renamed her baby Nancy, which stuck. But the famous wide eyes were in doubt at the very beginning:

The birth had not been easy. It was almost as if the child did not want to leave her mother's womb. The doctor stood over Edith, complaining about the heat, saying that he wanted to finish up and head out to the golf course. To deliver the baby, he used forceps. When Edith first saw her daughter, the child's right eye was closed, and the doctor said that she might be blind in that eye. Edith told him she had heard what he said about wanting to hurry to play golf. "If my daughter's eye doesn't open, I'll kill you," she said.

The eye opened up finally, and the infant's eyes were as big as her mother's.

The Ugly Princess

Eleanor Roosevelt was born into a classic situation where she felt unloved by her mother, Anna, but formed a mutual admiration society with her father, the rather dissolute and ineffectual Elliott, younger brother of the formidable Teddy Roosevelt. Eleanor's friend and biographer Joseph Lash wrote:

From her mother Eleanor received the indelible impression that she was plain to the point of ugliness. As a young woman Anna had been captivatingly beautiful, her face and head so classic in outline that artists had begged to paint her. Anna had been, a friend of the family said, "a little gentlewoman." Eleanor, in her anxiety for people to do right, was more the little schoolmistress, saved from primness only by her grave blue eyes and the sweetness with which she admonished the grown-ups.

Eleanor, who sensed her mother's disappointment in her, considered this a reproach, but behind the reproach was a mother's bafflement over her little girl's precocious sense of right and wrong and the sadness in her appraising eyes. But these same traits amused and charmed her father, who called her his "little golden hair."

The Black Prince

Much of Jacqueline Kennedy's tastes and fascination can be traced to her father, Jack Bouvier, portrayed here by novelist Pearl Buck:

I can imagine the effect, the influence, of a father like Jack Bouvier on a sensitive, always lovely little girl. Her father was a true Bouvier in many ways. He had gone to Yale, had graduated in 1914 without significance, had found a job in a Wall Street brokerage firm through the help of a brother-in-law, and with his quick mind and charming manners, he had done well. Then came World War I.

With his upbringing he did not relish the idea of military service, but he joined the navy and then, with help, transferred to the army, where he found life more tolerable. He became engaged, then broke the engagement, a pattern that was to continue during the years. He went through the war, was honorably discharged in the spring of 1919, and returned to his job on Wall Street, where he was given a seat on the exchange. With financial aid from an adoring aunt, he planned soon to be very rich.

In the meantime he rented a fine apartment on Park Avenue and gave stupendous parties, and enjoyed attractive women and pretty girls. His striking good looks, his equally striking tailor-made clothes, his dashing sense of style made him a fascinating character. His French ancestry rather than the British accounted for his dark complexion, which he made darker by tan. So dark indeed was he that he was called "Black Jack," or "the Black Prince." He was dramatic and self-absorbed, in company preferring to create and stay in the limelight rather than take the trouble to learn to know other people. This, of course, made him always basically lonely, although he was sought after and spectacular in New York society. Of course money, much money, was necessary in order for him to live with the style in which he was determined to live.

Clash of Wills

Florence Kling Harding's father was the leading banker and wealthiest man in the small town of Marion, Ohio:

When Florence was born, Amos Kling was bitterly disappointed, because he had wanted a son. He was an obstinate, vigorous, quick-minded man whose forceful personality made him a virtual dictator over his family. He sent his daughter to the best school in Marion, and later to the Cincinnati Conservatory of Music to study piano. But while Florence was still in her teens, her mother died, and she returned home to teach piano and live with her father.

Florence had inherited her father's toughness, and her years away had given her a heady taste of independence. Kling demanded blind obedience; Florence defied him; and the two locked in a lifelong battle of bitterness. Kling set down rigid rules of conduct. If Florence dated a boy of whom he did not approve, or stayed out beyond his 11:00 P.M. deadline, he would simply lock her out and let her fend for herself overnight. As the town's richest man, Kling felt that no man was good enough for his daughter. Florence suffered while her father rudely drove away beau after beau. She was rather ordinary-looking, and never very popular because of her overbearing ways; her father didn't seem to understand that she had a hard enough time attracting eligible young men without his interference.

When she was nineteen, Florence Kling met Henry DeWolfe, a neighbor who came from an old and wealthy Ohio family. DeWolfe was the first man who was not intimidated by her spiteful father—he was probably hardened to disapproval, for his own family deplored his excessive drinking, his instability, his spendthrift ways, his predilection for lower-class ladies and shady men. Florence, however, was inexperienced enough to consider him dashing and bold and her best chance to escape from her father's tyranny. They eloped. In the next year they had a son, Marshall Eugene DeWolfe, and moved to Galion, Ohio, where DeWolfe accepted a job managing a roller-skating palace. On Christmas Eve, however, two days before the Ice Palace was to open, DeWolfe vanished. He left behind him a bewildered young wife barely out of her teens, with an infant son, no money, no food, and no friends in a strange town.

Florence was learning, the hard way, how to fend for herself; the harsh, aggressive shell to protect her from further pain was forming. Carrying her baby, she went to the train station, where she persuaded the conductor to let her ride free to Marion on a promise that she would pay the fare later. Cold, hungry, and lonely, she arrived at Marion in the middle of the night. But then she lost her courage: she could not face her wrathful father. She was not even sure that he would forgive her enough to take her back, for he had not spoken to her since the marriage. So Florence crept into a vacant house near the train station, where she huddled, nearly frozen, with her son until dawn.

She made her way to the home of old friends, still afraid to approach her father. She had good reason to be worried, for when the friends told Kling he coldly refused to see his deserted daughter and grandchild. So others helped Florence find a place to live, and she persuaded Simon DeWolfe, her father-in-law, to provide her with food and other necessities. She boarded little Marshall temporarily with another couple. She borrowed a piano and began giving piano lessons again and eventually earned enough to support herself and her son.

Once she had shown she could manage without him, Amos Kling relented. Florence got a divorce. Kling let her return to live in the biggest house in town, and he adopted her little Marshall.

Whatever Nancy Wants

When Nancy Reagan was eight years old, her mother married a brilliant and controversial Chicago neurosurgeon, Dr. Loyal Davis. After years of vicariously living her mother's life as an actress and being supervised by an aunt in a Washington suburb, Nancy seized upon her chance for a regular family life:

Edith and Loyal invited Nancy into their happiness. One evening little Nancy let herself out of the apartment and knocked on the door of a neighbor, a retired judge. The judge answered the door to find a very serious young lady standing there.

"Judge, I've come to see you on business."

"What is it, Nancy?" the jurist asked, peering down at her.

"I'd like to know how to adopt Dr. Davis."

"That's a little difficult," the judge said, nodding his head gently. "But I think it can be arranged."

When Nancy left, he called Dr. Davis and told him what she had said. "I've always wanted that," the doctor said. "But I didn't know how to approach Nancy or her mother."

At the age of fourteen, when she had the legal right, Nancy took adoption papers with her on a trip to Verona to visit her father. Ken Robbins had come to visit his daughter in Chicago, and he still loved her and wanted her as his daughter. But when Nancy asked him to sign her away, he didn't let on how terrible he felt. Nancy's grandmother, gray-haired old Nanee, the one Robbins whom Nancy loved with pure and certain affection, could not hide how hurt she was. But Nancy left for Chicago with the papers all neatly signed and proudly told her classmates at Girls Latin that they could call her Nancy Davis.

Her stepfather was always "Dr. Loyal" to Nancy. Sometimes she went to the hospital to see him. When she was old enough, Dr. Davis allowed Nancy to watch him operate and accompany him on house calls.

Nancy loved Dr. Davis in part because they were kindred souls. She, too, believed in order and neatness. She, too, sometimes couldn't make people understand her motives. As she grew older she became so much like Dr. Davis that she did indeed seem to be his natural daughter.

CHILDHOOD

Perilous Voyage

Rachel Jackson underwent many adventures in childhood when in 1779–80 her father, Colonel John Donelson, a brave and wealthy old Virginian surveyor, made a perilous voyage "in the good boat Adventure, *from Fort Patrick Henry on Holston river, to the French Salt Springs on Cumberland river":*

They were four months on the journey, the sufferings and privations of which can scarcely be appreciated. They started in the depths of winter and were obliged to encounter excessive cold and frosts. But worse than all, the Indians were ever on the watch to entrap them. Donelson's journal says, "We still perceived them, marching down the river in considerable bodies, keeping pace with us." The wildest, most romantic and lonely spot on this continent is the "Whirl," in the Tennessee river, where the river is compressed within less than half its usual width by the Cumberland mountain which juts in on both sides. Its beauty is equaled only by its danger. In passing through this place, a large canoe, containing all the property of one of the emigrants, was overturned, and the little cargo was lost. The family had gone into a larger boat for safety.

"The company," wrote Colonel Donelson, "pitying their distress, concluded to halt and assist in recovering the property. We had landed on the northern shore, and were going up to the place, when the Indians, to our astonishment, appeared immediately over us on the opposite cliffs and commenced firing down upon us, which occasioned a precipitate retreat to the boats. We immediately moved off."

One of this intrepid little band of emigrants, sharing in its hardships and dangers, was Rachel Donelson, the daughter of Col. John Donelson. She was then a bright-eyed, black-haired, sprightly, pretty child of about twelve years. On the 24th April, 1780, they reached the little settlement of log cabins that Captain Robertson and his band had made ready for them.

Trauma

Eleanor Roosevelt was two and half when her parents decided to take the whole family to Europe. After one day's sailing, their boat, the Britannic, *collided with the* Celtic.

Several passengers were killed, a child beheaded, and many injured. Grown-ups panicked. Stokers and boiler men emerging from the depths of the *Britannic* made a wild rush for the lifeboats until the captain forced them back at the point of his revolver. The air was filled with "cries of terror," Eleanor's among them. She clung frantically to the men who were trying to drop her over the steep side of the ship into the outstretched arms of her father, who stood in a lifeboat below. Although the sea was calm, the lifeboats were pitching, and the distance seemed vast to Eleanor. The transfer was finally completed, despite Eleanor's struggles, and they were rowed to the *Celtic*, which took them back to New York.

Anna and Elliott decided to go through with their plans, because Elliott's health depended on it. But Eleanor, in terror, refused to go and remained unmoved even by her father's endearments and pleas.

This violent experience made an indelible impression on Eleanor. She never lost her fear of the sea. Throughout her life she felt the need to prove that she could overcome her physical timidity by feats of special courage. Desertion of the young and defenseless remained an ever-present theme—in her reading and her compositions for school; the mere suspicion that someone she loved might have turned away from her always caused the same taut, hopeless bewilderment.

Phobias

One hateful aspect of Nancy Reagan's young life were the visits with her natural father. On one occasion, when little Nancy took exception to a remark he made about her mother, he locked her in a bathroom. Nancy still cannot bear locked doors.

Five formative years were spent in Bethesda, with occasional trips to New York to see her mother.

"She used to live in residential hotels or in brownstone apartments," Nancy has said. "To this day, I can't pass this type of building without getting a terrible sinking feeling in my stomach."

Fat Kid

My mother was an attractive woman (writes Betty Ford), my father was a good-looking man, and I was a fat little kid. We had a cottage up at Whitefish Lake, where we went out every summer, chugging off in an old Cole Eight touring car.

We left for the lake the day school let out, and we didn't come home until school started again, so we had dozens of friends up there.

There was a hotel near the cottage, Hart's Hotel, which featured picnic grounds. Being a baby who liked to wander, I'd find my way to the picnic grounds—there's a snapshot of me out there in my rompers, with the Dutch-boy bob many children sported in those days—and I'd stagger from table to table, and everybody had a cookie or a piece of cake or some ice cream for me. I just got fatter and fatter until finally my mother hung a sign on my back. It said, PLEASE DO NOT FEED THIS CHILD.

Generosity

During the earliest years of Harriet Lane's residence with her uncle (President Buchanan) in Lancaster, she attended a day school there, and though she evinced much more than the usual aptitude for study, she was chiefly distinguished as a fun-loving, trick-playing romp and a willful domestic outlaw.

There was one anecdote her uncle liked to tell of her. When she was about eleven years old, she was well grown and, indeed, mature-looking for her age. Unlike most young ladies at that ambitious period of life, she was entirely unconscious of her budding charms, never dreaming that men must pause to wonder at and admire her, and that her actions were no longer unimportant as those of a child. One day Mr. Buchanan was shocked upon beholding from his window Miss Harriet, with flushed cheek and hat awry, trundling along, in great haste, a wheelbarrow full of wood. Upon his rushing out to inquire into the cause of such an unseemly and undignified proceeding, she answered in some confusion that she was just on her way to her mammy, old black Tabitha, with a load of wood, because it was so cold. In administering the reproof that followed, Mr. Buchanan took good care that she should not see the amused and gratified smile with which he turned away from the generous culprit.

Sophomore

When she was eleven, Frances Folsom lost her father, who was thrown from his carriage and killed almost instantly. His partner, Grover Cleveland, became her legal guardian.

Her childhood was passed in much the same way as that of the average American girl. Her primary education was carefully conducted and, after her father's death, was continued in the high schools of Medina and Buffalo. She was admitted to the sophomore class at Wells College, Aurora, New York, graduating in June 1885 with the approbation and affection of teachers and pupils alike.

Meanwhile Mr. Cleveland had risen from Governor of New York to be President of the United States. His strong interest in the young girl was well known. During the second year of her college life, flowers came regularly from the conservatories of the gubernatorial mansion in Albany, and on the day of her valedictory a superb floral gift of white flowers was sent by the President from the White House.

Amour Propre

Jacqueline Kennedy was born in July 1929, just a few months before the crash that ruined her father and her parents' marriage. Yet Jack Bouvier, as novelist Pearl Buck observed, remained the crucial influence on his daughters, Jacqueline and her sister, Lee:

I do not doubt that Jacqueline Kennedy's love of beauty, her sense of drama and style, came from her father. He was careful about his own appearance and he pointed out to her what he liked or disliked in the appearance of women they saw. He taught her how to wear clothes with distinction, as he himself did. So the girls learned that, though they might wear clothes not different from those of other girls, there must always be the illusion of difference.

And he taught his daughters that this difference must be expressed not only in clothes. It must be expressed even more explicitly in behavior. A woman, he taught them, must be a mystery. She must be withdrawn, reserved, slow to yield to a man's advances. As he pursued, she must retreat, she must withhold, she must charm by her silence, by her reticence rather than by her revelations.

As Jacqueline developed into her teens, he praised her to her face, in the presence of others, openly and frequently. She was the prettiest girl in the world. If she was all this now, what would she be at twenty? She was the best equestrienne in the world already. If a cousin teased or troubled her, Jack threatened the most violent punishment. Of course, Jacqueline blossomed under the father's praise and protection. She learned to admire herself in the shelter of his adulation and protection.

Rosalynn Carter's Social Debut

The first time I went to the White House, Herbert Hoover was in office. I was six years old and I went with my family—mother, father, older sister, and brother. All of us were invited to luncheon.

We took the overnight train from New York to Washington and I still remember every detail of the musty drawing room with its scratchy upholstery that I shared with Mother. I don't believe I slept at all.

In the morning we stopped at the Hay-Adams Hotel and later walked across Lafayette Park to the White House. We entered by the big door, with its porte cochere fronting on Pennsylvania Avenue.

An enormous golden bas-relief eagle was set in the floor of the front hall as you walked in. As the eagle was just in front of me, I stepped gingerly in my black patent-leather party slippers. It didn't seem right to step on that eagle.

Years later Harry Truman apparently agreed and along with other renovations he had the golden eagle taken up and installed over a doorway instead.

Our luncheon with the Hoovers took place in the interim period after Roosevelt had won the election but had not yet been inaugurated. Inevitably there was a certain gloom in the air. We were all dedicated Republicans in my family then and more than sympathetic to my father's old friend (beginning with the Commission for Relief in Belgium days of World War I) "the Chief," as Pa called him, and to the Chief's disappointment at losing his bid for reelection.

There were just the President and Mrs. Hoover and the Galpin family at lunch. To fill a silence at the table, I took it upon myself to repeat a story I'd heard at home about how "they were going to take the brains out of the White House and put in a donkey." I suppose I imagined there was literally to be a donkey in the White House—an intriguing idea. This sally was met with frozen silence. My first effort at social repartee was a distinct failure.

But later Mr. Hoover kindly wrote a letter to my ten-year-old brother, whose school friends were insisting that no one could possibly have had spinach for lunch at the White House. "We indeed had spinach at the White House," the letter read. "And I don't like it either. Mrs. Hoover makes me eat it."

ACCOMPLISHMENTS

But What Is It in English?

Martha Washington was not an educated woman and her letters of form, which required better orthography than she was mistress of, Washington drafted for her, pen-weary though he was. One can see why: in 1758, the year often given as the meeting with George, she wrote in her own hand to her London agents:

"I have sent a night gound to be dide of an fashonob Corler fitt for me to ware and beg you would have it dide better that I sent Las year that was very badly don this gound is of a good Lenght for me."

Danger of Meddling

To learning, in the ordinary sense of that term, Abigail Adams could make no claim. She did not enjoy an opportunity to acquire even such as there might have been, for the delicate state of her health forbade the idea of sending her away from home. In speaking of her deficiencies, the year before her death, she wrote:

"My early education did not partake of the abundant opportunity which the present day offers, and which even our common country schools now afford. I never was sent to any school, I was always sick."

Although Massachusetts ranked then first in point of educational facilities, it is certainly remarkable that its women received such entire neglect.

"It is not impossible," says Mr. Adams, "that the early example of Mrs. [Anne] Hutchison, and the difficulties in which the public exercise of her gifts involved the colony, had established in the public mind a conviction of the danger that may attend the meddling of women with abstruse points of doctrine; and these, however they might confound the strongest intellects, were nevertheless the favorite topics of thought and discussion in that generation."

Philosophy

Louisa Catherine Adams, wife of John Quincy Adams, wrote to her father-in-law, ex-President John Adams, in 1819:

The woman selected for your wife [Abigail Adams] was so highly gifted in mind, with powers so vast, and such quick and clear perception, altogether so superior to the general run of females, you have perhaps formed a too-enlarged opinion of the capacities of our sex, and having never witnessed their frailties, are not aware of the dangers to which they are exposed, by acquirements above their strength.

The systems of the ancients have been quite out of my reach, excepting the Dialogues of Plato, which Mr. A. recommended to me last year, and which I read attentively. I cannot say that I am entirely unacquainted with their different theories, but that acquaintance has been too superficial to make them well understood, and I have been too much inclined to view them as difficult of practice and not tending much to the real benefit of mankind. With the modern philosophers I have become more intimate, if I may make use of such a word, speaking of works which I have read, but which I could not understand or digest. Locke has puzzled me, Berkeley amused me, Reid astonished me, Hume disgusted me, and Tucker either diverted me or set me to sleep. This is a very limited sort of reading, and you will laugh at my catalogue of names which have at best, I believe, but little title to the rank of philosophers, or at least must come in at the fag end. I have dipped into others and thrown them aside, but I have never seen anything that would satisfy my mind, or that would compare with the chaste and exquisitely simple doctrines of Christianity.

A Writer

Charles Francis Adams, son of Louisa, was less modest about his mother's accomplishments:

She wrote much and read a great deal, both of French and English literature, and translated from the former for the amusement of her friends. She also wrote verses frequently in the same way. Although she lived to quite an advanced age, her health was always delicate and variable, so as to interrupt the even tenor of her life and disincline her to the efforts required for general society, especially during her twelve years spent at different courts in Europe.

An Exception

M. de Baucourt, a French diplomat in Washington during the Van Buren administration, described the ladies of Washington society as "badly dressed, badly trained, and badly combed, in fact like third-rate English people," while, if possible, their dinners and suppers were more execrable than themselves. The critical Frenchman excepted only Mrs. Abraham Van Buren in his sweeping and adverse criticism of the belles and beauties of the capital. "The daughter-in-law of President Van Buren would," he said, "in any country pass for any amiable woman of graceful and distinguished manners and appearance."

Teacher

As a boy, Andrew Johnson was a ragged urchin, a street Arab, until he was ten years old, supported by the manual labor of his mother, who belonged to that most unfortunate class known in the South as "poor whites." He could not even read; indeed he did not learn the alphabet until some time after. At eighteen, the village schoolteacher, Eliza McCartle, a girl of superior intelligence and considerable education, became his instructor and taught him to write. He married her, and she continued to teach him while he worked at the humble trade of a tailor. She read to him while he worked and taught him in the evening arithmetic, geography, and history.

An Intellectual

Mrs. Abigail Fillmore, the daughter of a Baptist clergyman, grew up in western New York, when it was a frontier and a wilderness. Yearning for intellectual culture, with all the drawbacks of poverty and scanty opportunity, she obtained sufficient knowledge to become a schoolteacher. It was while following this avocation that she first met her future husband, then a clothier's apprentice. They were married in 1826 and began life in a small house built by her husband's hands. She bore full half of the burden of life, and her husband, with the weight of care lifted from him by willing and loving hands, rose rapidly in the profession of law and in less than two years was chosen a member of the State Legislature.

Strong in intellect and will, her delights were all feminine. Her tasks accomplished, she lived in books and music, flowers and children.

It was Mrs. Fillmore who turned the famous Oval Room at the White House into a library:

Mrs. Fillmore, with her scholarly tastes and pursuits, felt the need of books at the White House, and at the President's suggestion Congress was induced to supply them as part of the furniture of the Executive Mansion. As the appropriation granted was for books solely, and as there was no fund for refurnishing, Mrs. Fillmore used her own ingenuity in making the room habitable. Being a good housekeeper, like most intellectual women, she soon discovered that the new carpet in the Blue Room had been put down over the old one. Both were taken up and cleaned, and the old carpet put down in the Library. A few pieces of furniture were borrowed from other rooms at the White House, which with addition of some comfortable chairs, favorite books, and Miss Fillmore's piano and harp, made the room homelike and attractive. In this pleasant Library, with its cheerful wood fire, the President and his family spent their evenings and received intimate friends.

Training

The maternal grandfather of Lucy Webb Hayes was one of the first settlers of Chillicothe and belonged to the best Puritan stock of New England. Her mother, Mrs. Webb, was a lady of unusual strength of character and of deep religious convictions. After the death of her husband she removed to Delaware in order to be near Wesleyan University, where her sons were educated. Lucy studied with her brothers and recited to the college instructors, and had the advantages of a training which prepared her for the Wesleyan Female College at Cincinnati.

She was a clever student, as one of her companions in school described her in a letter: "Lucy Webb was a first-class student in botany and other studies, and I have reason to recall my feeling of mingled annoyance and admiration as our teacher, Miss De Forrest, would turn from us older girls to Miss Webb, who sat at the head of the class, and get from her a clear analysis of the flower under discussion, or the correct transposition of some involved line of poetry. Somewhat of this accuracy was doubtless due to the fact that she had been trained in the severe drill of the Ohio Wesleyan University."

A Linguist

The Hoovers met as geology students at Stanford, and they continued their intellectual partnership as young newlyweds. Lou was an excellent linguist. She mastered Latin, spoke four modern languages, including Chinese, and had a reading knowledge of another two.

While staying in London, Herbert and Lou began to translate from Latin the first great treatise on mining, Georgius Agricola's *De Re Metallica*. This work, published in 1556, had defeated previous scholars because the geologists did not know enough Latin, while the Latinists lacked expertise in geology. The Hoovers were good at both, and after five years' work their translation appeared in 1912. Visiting London in 1938 almost thirty years later, Herbert Hoover waxed sentimental in writing to his wife about the Red House where they had collaborated:

"I imagined again manuscripts and reference books of Agricola piled between us as we worked over the translation of *De Re Metallica*. Again I saw 'Pete' at the little table in the corner making marks and announcing that he was writing a book, too; and 'Bub' clambering into his mother's lap and demanding to know what the book said."

Wit

Jacqueline Bouvier Kennedy also knows Latin and is fluent in French and Spanish. As a sophomore at Vassar, she managed to get into a Smith College program that enabled her to study a year in Grenoble and at the Sorbonne. In her school graduation yearbook it is stated that Jacqueline was "Most Known For" her "Wit," and as if to prove it, under "Ambition" she wrote: "Not to be a housewife."

She was accomplished at drawing and painting, and Mrs. Kennedy sometimes used her skills for satirical ends. She once did a watercolor sketch of the whole Kennedy clan dotting the beach. In the sky above, a small plane was trailing a banner with the words: "YOU CAN'T TAKE IT WITH YOU—DAD'S GOT IT ALL."

Old Joe Kennedy was so pleased that he hung it in his Palm Beach mansion, where he would proudly show off his daughter-in-law's wit.

MANNERS

Up to Snuff

"An old citizen has informed me," wrote Mr. Gobright in his *Men and Things at Washington*, "that the levee of Mr. Madison, in February 1816, was remembered for years as the most brilliant ever held up to that date in the Executive Mansion. The most notable feature of the evening was the magnificent display of the Diplomatic Corps, prominent in which was Sir Charles Bagot, special ambassador from our late enemy, Great Britain. It was on this occasion that Mr. [sic!] Bagot made the remark that Mrs. Madison looked 'every inch a queen.'

"Mrs. Madison, like Mr. Clay, was very fond of snuff. The lady offered him a pinch from her splendid box, which the gentleman accepted with the grace with which he was distinguished. Mrs. Madison put her hand into her pocket, and pulling out a bandanna handkerchief, said, 'Mr. Clay, this is for rough work,' at the same time applying it at the proper place; 'and this,' producing a fine lace handkerchief from another pocket, 'is my polisher.' She suited the actions to the words, removing from her nose the remaining grains of snuff."

Mrs. John Logan, writing during Theodore Roosevelt's administration, commented on the change in manners:

If the wife of the President today were to perpetrate such an act at one of her receptions, not even the fact that it stands recorded against the graceful, gracious, and glorious Dolley Madison would save her from the taunt of being "underbred" and suggestive of the land of "snuff dippers."

Mob Scene

In 1817, James Monroe became President and removed his family to the White House, where they continued to reside during both terms of his administration. A leading paper of the day worried whether the elegant and fragile Mrs. Monroe could adjust to the rough-and-tumble of Washington society:

Mrs. Monroe is an elegant, accomplished woman. She possesses a charming mind and dignity of manners, which peculiarly fit her for her elevated station. Her retired domestic habits will be much annoyed by what is here called society, if she does not change the etiquette (if it may be called so) established by Mrs. Washington, Adams, and Madison, a routine which her feeble constitution will not permit her to encounter. To go through it, she must become a perfect slave to the sacrifice of her health. The secretaries, senators, foreign ministers, consuls, auditors, accountants, officers of the navy and army of every grade, farmers, merchants, parsons, priests, lawyers, judges, auctioneers, and nothingarians—all with their wives and some with their gawky offspring—crowd to the President's house every Wednesday evening; some in shoes, most in boots, and many in spurs; some snuffing, others chewing, and many longing for their cigars and whiskey-punch left at home. Some with powdered heads, others frizzled and oiled, with some whose heads a comb never touched, half-hid by dirty collars, reaching far above their ears, as stiff as pasteboard.

Graceful Gesture

Among the many graceful acts of Louisa Adams during her official life in Washington, none appeared more gracious and diplomatic in retrospect than the ball given by her to General Jackson in January 1824, when he was already a formidable rival of her husband. This ball was given while Mr. Adams was Secretary of State and living in the house on F Street, near Fourteenth, later known as the Adams Building. In this large double house the ballroom was on the second floor, and, according to various chroniclers, two young relatives who were staying with Mrs. Adams spent a week in preparing its elaborate decorations of tissue paper and evergreens. In their pleasant task the two pretty girls were doubtless assisted by the two sons of the house, George and John Adams, both of whom were said to be in love with one of the girls.

The floor of the ballroom was chalked with spread eagles, flags, and the motto "Welcome to the hero of New Orleans." The pillars were festooned with laurel and wintergreen, while wreathings of evergreens and roses, interspersed with small, variegated lamps, with a luster in the center, gave what Miss Abigail Adams considered a beautiful effect. She further recorded that there were eight pieces of music, and that General Jackson, who stood beside Mrs. Adams to receive with her in the passage between the two houses, looked remarkably well. A semicircle of distinguished persons gathered around Mrs. Adams and the General, and into this choice group the guests entered two by two and made their bows, there being no handshakings in those days.

Fancy That

Mrs. Robert Tyler, a clever and charming young matron, presided over many of the White House entertainments. (Her mother-in-law, the first Mrs. John Tyler, was an invalid.) Once, when receiving Mr. Joseph Nourse, an old friend of her father's, whom she had not seen since her childhood, she exclaimed, "Ah, Mr. Nourse, truth *is* stranger than fiction, which is exemplified by my receiving you here in the White House."

The Second Mrs. Tyler

Julia Gardiner, of New York, was many years younger than the President and was handsome and youthful in appearance. Although, as Mrs. Frémont says, the new mistress of the White House was somewhat commented upon by old-fashioned people "because she drove four horses (finer than those of the Russian minister) and because she received seated, her armchair on a slightly raised platform, in a velvet gown with three feathers in her hair," young Mrs. Tyler made numerous friends during her eight months of official life and left the Executive Mansion regretted by many. It is said that even political enemies of the President had only words of praise for his charming young wife.

Hoops

President Buchanan's niece Miss Harriet Lane, although universally admired, was not a popular woman. She lacked magnetism. She followed a prescribed rule of manner from which she never deviated, no matter with whom she was thrown. Always courteous, always in place, silent whenever it was possible to be silent, watchful, and careful, she made no enemies, was betrayed into no entangling alliances, and was involved in no contretemps of any kind.

She was very handsome, a fair, blue-eyed, self-contained young woman. She was dignified—as indeed all women had to be, in gesture at least, when they wore great hoops! The "curtsy" was a perilous duty. "How does she do it? She never makes a cheese of herself," said one, looking on at a morning reception.

No Gossip

One of Lucy Hayes's former schoolmates, writing of her in 1880, while she was yet in the White House, referred to her great likeness to her mother in mental and moral qualities:

"There is one trait in the character of Mrs. Hayes which I should like to emphasize. She absolutely will not talk gossip. Even in the intimate confidences of daily intercourse she is as guarded as in the presence of a multitude. The Executive Mansion has for its mistress one who is a living exemplification of Christ's Golden Rule. Except in very rare instances, when some act of oppression to the poor or the defenseless outrages her sense of right, she is always thoroughly kind in expression. I think this trait of carefulness for the feelings of others a gift from her mother, who had a nature exceedingly genial and kind. It is indeed a blessed thing for our country that such a woman had the training of our President's wife."

But Can One Major in It?

Speaking of Jackie Kennedy's upbringing, one relative remarked that "she was really prepared for one eventuality in life—to be exquisite."

Bedtime with Bonzo, or, While Reagan Slept

Even Mrs. Reagan's wifely consideration for her husband's rest elicited this acerbic comment from columnist Diana McLellan:

Nancy Reagan is a woman of exquisite manners. Who else, craving a cookie at night, would instead sit up in bed and silently peel and eat a banana, so as not to disturb the slumbering President?

ROMANCE

ATTRACTION

Mars and Venus

It was in 1758 that an officer, attired in a military undress, attended by a body servant, crossed the ferry over the Pamunkey, a branch of the York River. On the boat's touching the southern or New Kent side, the soldier's progress was arrested by one of those personages who give the beau-ideal of the Virginia gentleman of the old regime: the very soul of kindliness and hospitality.

It was in vain the soldier urged his business at Williamsburg—important communications to the Governor. Mr. Chamberlayne, on whose domain the officer had just landed, would hear no excuse. Colonel Washington was a name and character so dear to all Virginians that his passing by one of the old estates of Virginia without calling and partaking of the hospitalities of the host was entirely out of the question. The Colonel, however, did not surrender at discretion, but stoutly maintained his ground, till Chamberlayne brought up his reserve in the intimation that he would introduce his friend to a young and charming widow then beneath his roof. The soldier capitulated on condition that he should dine, only dine, and then, by pressing his charger, and borrowing of the night, he would reach Williamsburg before His Excellency could shake off his morning slumbers.

The Colonel now proceeded to the mansion and was introduced to various guests, above all, to the charming widow. Tradition relates that they were mutually pleased on this their first interview. The lady was fair to behold, of fascinating manners, and splendidly endowed with worldly benefits; the hero, fresh from his early fields redolent of fame, and with a form on which "every god did seem to set his seal, to give the world assurance of a man."

While the Colonel was so agreeably employed in the parlor, the day passed pleasantly away and evening came. Proclaiming that no guest ever left his house after sunset, Mr. Chamberlayne persuaded his military visitor to put up the horses for the night.

The sun rode high in the heavens the ensuing day when the enamored soldier pressed with his spur his charger's sides and sped on his way to the seat of government, when, having dispatched his public business, he retraced his steps, and at her country seat, the White House, after which the home of the Presidents was called, the engagement took place, with arrangements for the marriage.

Charms

Young Dolley Madison became so famous because of her charms that, as one of her girlfriends declared, "gentlemen would station themselves where they could see her pass." "Really, Dolley," remonstrated the same young lady laughingly, "thou must hide thy face, there are so many staring at thee."

Thy Neighbor's Wife

Rachel Donelson (the future Mrs. Andrew Jackson) was first married, while living in Kentucky, to Lewis Robards, a man of good family. Judge John Overton, then a young lawyer in the fall of 1787, went to Mercer County, Kentucky, and became a boarder in the family of Mrs. Robards, where Lewis Robards and his wife were living. Judge Overton was not long in discovering that they lived very unhappily, because Captain Robards was jealous of a gentleman named Short. His disposition was extremely unfortunate and kept the whole family in uneasiness and distress. This unpleasant state of affairs continued to increase until Captain Robards wrote to his mother-in-law, requesting that she would take her daughter home, as he did not intend to live with her any longer. Sometime in the latter part of 1788, Samuel Donelson came and started away with his sister.

Judge Overton, in his account of Jackson's marriage written in 1827, says that when he decided to settle in what was then West Tennessee he solicited Mrs. Donelson, the mother of Mrs. Lewis Robards, to give him board in her house, good accommodations being rare in that part of the country. About the same time Andrew Jackson entered the family, of which Captain and Mrs. Robards (who had reached a reconciliation in 1789 and were now reunited) were also inmates.

"Here," says Judge Overton, "we lived in the same cabin room and slept in the same bed as young men of the same pursuits and profession, and with few others in the country with whom to associate, besides sharing, as we frequently did, common dangers, such an intimacy ensued as might reasonably be expected. Not many months elapsed before Robards became jealous of Jackson, which I feel confident was without the least ground. Some of his irritating conversation on this subject with his wife I heard amidst the tears of herself and her mother."

According to Judge Overton, Jackson was very much disturbed by the thought that he had caused trouble between Robards and his wife, who is described as a gentle, sensitive woman, while of Jackson his friend wrote, "in his singularly delicate sense of honor, and in what I thought his chivalrous conception of the female sex, it occurred to me that he was distinguishable from every other person with whom I was acquainted."

Instead of leaving Mrs. Donelson's home, as Jackson was advised to do by Judge Overton, he, with lamentable want of tact and understanding of human nature, undertook to remonstrate with Lewis Robards upon his treatment of his wife. It is said that Jackson's chivalrous feeling toward the persecuted wife so far overcame his judgment that he exclaimed, "If I had such a wife, I would not willingly bring a tear to her beautiful eyes!" To which Robards wrathfully retorted, "Well, perhaps it is a mistake, but she is not *your* wife." From this beginning the domestic infelicities of the Robards family rapidly passed from bad to worse. Lewis Robards seemed to have been possessed of a moody and revengeful disposition. He continued to foster his jealous wrath against his wife and young Jackson until it gained the mastery over his common sense and led him to apply to the Legislature of Virginia for a divorce.

Searching for Mr. Right

Mary Todd was possessed of a high and haughty manner, an exalted opinion of her own superiority, and an abiding conviction that she would one day marry a man who would become President of the United States. Incredible as it seems, she not only believed that, but she openly boasted of it. It sounded silly, and people laughed and said things; but nothing could shake her conviction and nothing could stop her boasting.

Her own sister, speaking of Mary, said she "loved glitter, show, pomp, and power," and was "the most ambitious woman I ever knew."

Unfortunately, Mary had a temper that was frequently out of control; so one day in 1839, she quarreled with her stepmother, slammed the front door, and walked out of her father's home in a rage and came to live with her married sister in Springfield.

If she was determined to marry a future President, she had certainly chosen the right place, for there wasn't another spot where her prospects would have been brighter than there in Springfield, Illinois. At that time it was a dirty little frontier village, sprawling out over the treeless prairie, with no pavements, no lights, no sidewalks, no sewers. Cattle roamed about the town at will, hogs wallowed in the mudholes of the principal streets, and piles of rotten manure filled the air with a stench. The total population of the town was only fifteen hundred; but two young men who were destined to be candidates for the presidency in 1860 lived there in Springfield in 1839—Stephen A. Douglas, candidate for the Northern wing of the Democratic party, and Abraham Lincoln for the Republicans. Both of them met Mary Todd, both courted her at the same time, both held her in their arms, and she once stated that both of them had proposed.

When asked which suitor she intended to marry, Mary always answered, according to her sister's report, "Him who has the best prospect of being President."

Dancin'

Because of his height and personal diffidence, Abraham Lincoln moved awkwardly. Mary Todd used to describe their first meeting at a social event, when Abe introduced himself to her saying, "I want to dance with you in the worst way." Afterward, she remarked that he must have meant "in the very worst way."

Her Ideal Beau

The young Woodrow Wilson, first an indigent lawyer and then a struggling professor, was agonized about asking Ellen Axson to marry him: soon after she accepted, he sent her an engagement ring. She wrote back:

The ring also came this afternoon. It is a perfect beauty in every respect. I can't tell you, my darling, how much I prize it. You are very, very good—but are you not also very extravagant? Please excuse my impertinence, but really I was startled and amazed at the unexpected apparition of a diamond. You know it is not absolutely necessary to wear that particular sort of ring in order to "feel engaged."

Yes, perhaps I do feel more engaged with this outward symbol of it on my hand. I seem already to look back at my former self, the girl who had never loved, as at a stranger, and I recall with wonder and amusement some of the thoughts and opinions she entertained. Yet my "theories" have been by no means overturned. I was writing to [my friend] Beth the other night—about you. I could honestly say that I had found my—yes, I must say it—my "ideal," though I am a little out of humor with that much abused word. Now I know you will laugh at me, but it is so! Why even those lines which Beth and I selected together, years ago, as best expressing our ideal were written for you! I never saw so perfect a description of anyone. A "jersey" jacket couldn't fit more closely! You may remember the words, for with calm audacity I once quoted them to you myself, knowing that you could not read my thoughts as I did so.

> A mouth for mastery and manful work,
> A certain brooding sweetness in the eyes,
> A brow the harbour of grave thought.

Hot Pursuit

A few months after the death of his first wife, Woodrow Wilson fell in love with an attractive widow, Edith Bolling Galt. The courtship excited the Washington gossips, including the following anonymous speculation:

"What on earth attracted him to Edith Galt?" I heard a woman remark when the engagement was announced. One authority states that he was first attracted to her by the simple statement that she had never been to the White House until invited there to lunch by Margaret Wilson [Woodrow Wilson's daughter]. Some say that Margaret Wilson planned the match, and that she is now devoted to her stepmother.

There is another version, a more authentic one, I believe. Dr. Grayson, who so often accompanied the President on his drives, had noticed a very attractive woman driving alone in an electric machine. "I like the look of her. I wonder who she is?" he said to the President. When the lady turned right, so did the presidential car.

One night Dr. Grayson met her—no, it wasn't Mrs. Galt, it was Miss Gordon, her intimate friend. I believe the way the Doctor convinced the lady that his gracious greeting was really the outcome of a sincere desire to have met her was to recite from memory the registration number of her car.

Soon afterward he met Mrs. Galt. He liked her, and he had a hunch that the President would also like her. And it was in this way that the invitation to lunch issued by Margaret Wilson came about, via Dr. Grayson. But Mrs. Galt didn't say yes the first time of asking.

Amazing Grace

Grace Goodhue was in her second year of teaching at the Clarke Institute for the Deaf in Northampton when she looked up from watering some flowers and saw a man shaving through an open window. He was wearing a hat and a union suit so much at odds with his preoccupation that she burst out into a loud peal of laughter. Calvin Coolidge, a young lawyer who was boarding with Robert Weir, the school steward, looked up, saw, and was conquered—if somewhat gradually. It might have been a difficult courtship, since the Vermonter was notorious for his reserve and taciturnity. They called him Silent Cal, and one of the many stories told about him later has a pushy woman at a reception betting him that she could get more than two words out of him: "You lose," Coolidge replied.

Only three years before meeting Grace, he wrote to his father: "If I ever get a woman, someone will have to support her, but I see no need of a wife so long as I have my health." Given this temperament, it was an awkward courtship, though Grace had no doubt of his sincerity. Still she sought advice and approval, and at one point she persuaded her close friend Ivah Gale to go on a long buggy ride with Calvin. When they returned, she asked her whether he had said anything. Miss Gale said that she liked him and did not tell Grace that in fact Coolidge did not open his mouth once during the entire three hours. Then Grace showed her friend the first love letter Calvin wrote her—a five-line, businesslike note which made no mention of any of his feelings. She later confessed that if she hadn't been told it was a love letter, she would never have guessed.

After several months, he suddenly showed up one day at the Goodhue home in Burlington, where Grace had gone to spend a summer vacation. He sat silently, stiff as a ramrod, in the parlor, while Grace's father, Captain Goodhue, was searching for an opening.

"Up here on law business, Mr. Coolidge?" he tried.

"No. Up here to ask your permission to marry Grace."

"Does she know it?" asked the Captain, somewhat startled.

"No, but she soon will."

Coolidge had a good sense of humor about himself, and his comment about his marriage that "having taught the deaf to hear, Miss Goodhue might perhaps cause the mute to speak" was often quoted by Grace herself.

Rocks

Lou Henry was training to be a teacher at the San Jose Normal School when she heard a geology lecture by Professor John Casper Branner on "The Bones of the Earth." It inspired the nineteen-year-old Lou to enroll in his program at the newly established Leland Stanford University nearby. She was the only woman in the class and the first ever to major in geology.

One afternoon the freshman and the professor were looking at a piece of rock in the laboratory and discussing its origin. A senior by the name of Herbert Hoover happened to walk in and the professor asked him whether he agreed with Miss Henry that the rock was precarboniferous. The shy young man, who was widely considered a shining star in the program, became tongue-tied; instead of looking at the rock his eyes were trying to steal glances at Miss Henry.

They soon went on a field trip together in search of rocks. They came to a fence with no gate. Just as Bert was trying to figure out how to get Miss Henry in her long Victorian skirt over it, Lou took a running jump and cleared the fence. That was the moment she won the young geologist's mind. In the months that followed, their mutual interest in rocks and each other grew. At the end of the year Bert graduated and went off to various exotic parts of the world. He was working in the Australian desert in 1898 when the Kuang Hsü, the emperor of China, asked him to become his mining consultant. Bert knew that Lou was about to graduate, and he sent her a telegram asking her to marry him and accompany him to China. She wired back a single word, the only one that mattered: YES.

The Real Tinsel

In the fall of 1949 Ronald Reagan was an important man in Hollywood, the president of the Screen Actors Guild. On the other hand, his acting career since the war seemed to have been put on hold, his marriage to actress Jane Wyman was on the rocks, and he had broken his leg in six places while playing football for a charity event. Just when things seemed to be near the bottom, his union position brought him together with someone who changed his life. In his autobiography Reagan describes the turning point:

One day I received a phone call from Mervyn Le Roy, the director. As soon as I got over my disappointment that he wasn't paging me for one of the many fine pictures he did so well, I gathered that he was calling on behalf of a young lady under contract to MGM, who was working on his picture. (It should happen to me.) It seems that this young hopeful, Nancy Davis by name, was very much distressed because her name kept showing up on rosters of Communist front organizations, affixed to petitions of the same coloration, and her mail frequently included notices of meetings she had no desire to attend, and accounts of these meetings as covered by the *Daily Worker*.

Mervyn wanted me to call the young lady and have a talk with her about this problem. He guaranteed that she was more than disinterested in Leftist causes: she was violently opposed to such shenanigans. I told Mervyn that I'd take care of it—having made the switch from Ronald Reagan, actor, regretfully to Ronald Reagan, SAG president.

Stopping at the Guild office, I reported the call to Jack Dales. We did a little quick checking and could discover nothing detrimental to her. We were satisfied that Nancy Davis was in the clear, and we were in a position to defend her in the event of any unpleasantness. I called Mervyn and told him what we had learned and to assure the young lady she had nothing to worry about.

It seems the young lady was not satisfied with the secondhand report: please, wouldn't I call her and take her to lunch or dinner and quiet her fears? I don't know why it took all of this to get me to call an unknown girl. She surely couldn't be repulsive and on the contract list at MGM. Mervyn finally made his point and I called.

I introduced myself on the phone, hastily explained that I had a very early call in the morning, so if she didn't mind a short dinner date, I'd be very happy to talk to her about her problem. She very pleasantly informed me that she too had an early call and couldn't consider anything other than an early dinner date—so on that pleasant California evening, there I was, propped up between two canes before that door in Westwood (this was back in my just-out-of-the-hospital days).

The door opened—not on the expected fan magazine version of a starlet, but on a small, slender young lady with dark hair and a wide-spaced pair of hazel eyes that looked right at you and made you look back.

Don't get ahead of me: bells didn't ring or skyrockets explode, although I think perhaps they did. It was just that I had buried the part of where such things happened so deep I couldn't hear them.

They quickly discussed Nancy's political problems over dinner at La Rue's, a fashionable dining establishment on the Sunset Strip. Then they talked about themselves, and as he learned about her show-business background, Ronald Reagan fell more and more under Nancy Davis's spell:

I had discovered her laugh and spent most of my time trying to say something funny. A lot of George Burns and Georgie Jessel material got an airing that night, and not always with credit given to them. We hastily finished our early dinner—after all, we had those sunrise calls in the morning and, besides, she had never seen Sophie Tucker, who was opening that night at Ciro's. I figured Sophie could help me make her laugh some more. She did, so much so that we decided to stay for the second show and then—since she had never before heard Sophie and because her mother had been a star on Broadway—Sophie came to the table and joined us for a late snack. We got home about 3:30 A.M., but it was all right because neither of us really had an early call at all.

Cross Purposes

Julia Dent Grant wanted to try a newly developed surgical procedure to correct her eyes, which were somewhat crossed. Her husband, Ulysses, talked her out of it. "I like you with crosseyes," the President revealed to his lady.

COURTSHIP

If Music Be the Food of Love

Martha Skelton was a young widow of twenty-three when Thomas Jefferson was courting her.

Two of Mr. Jefferson's rivals happened to meet on Mrs. Skelton's doorstone. They were shown into a room from which they heard her harpsichord and voice, accompanied by Mr. Jefferson's violin and voice, in the passages of a touching song. They listened for a stanza or two. Whether something in the words or in the tones of the singers appeared suggestive to them, tradition does not say, but it does aver that they took their hats and retired to return no more on the same errand!

Tragedy and Romance

President Tyler's first wife, long an invalid, died in the third year of her residence at the White House. His romance with a girl thirty-five years his junior attracted a great deal of comment. At the age of twenty Julia Gardiner was already a famous belle of New York society and was called the "Rose of Long Island." During the 1842 social season her parents introduced her to Washington, where she attracted the attention of a number of eminent men, including the recently widowed President. The acquaintanceship matured into a romance under tragic circumstances. In early 1844, the Gardiners were invited by a Captain Stockton to accompany a party of the President's friends to Alexandria on a vessel of war. When they were opposite the fort, returning home, it was proposed to fire a gun called "the peacemaker" as a salute. The Secretary of War pretended to be nervous, and saying, "I don't like this—I believe I shall run," walked to the other end of the boat and thus narrowly saved his life, for the gun exploded, killing the Secretary of the Navy and the Secretary of State and Mr. Gardiner and two other gentlemen. The President himself was below with the ladies and, according to a contemporary account, "witnessed the fortitude and dignity with which Miss Gardiner bore the news of her overwhelming sorrow. Admiration for her self-control at that hour grew to a warmer attachment," which ended in their wedding on June 26, 1844.

Age of Consent

Grover Cleveland was only one of three Presidents to get married while in office. It was an unusual marriage: he called his bride "Frank." Her real name was Frances, and she was the daughter of Cleveland's law partner; and after his death, Cleveland became her legal guardian. When the wedding took place, the President was forty-nine, his ward twenty-one. Asked why he had postponed marrying so long, Grover Cleveland replied: "I was waiting for my wife to grow up."

The Time of Her Life

Colonel Starling had the problem of guarding Woodrow Wilson during his whirlwind romance with Edith Galt:

When Mrs. Galt returned to Washington in September my role in the romance became more personal. In order to be alone—or as much alone as was possible—with her, the President changed the routine of his afternoon automobile ride to include a walk in Rock Creek Park. It was my job to follow them on this daily stroll and to keep my eyes on the President every moment. I wanted to look away; I wanted to let a tree get between me and the two of them. But I couldn't. Something might happen.

He was an ardent lover, and a gay one. He talked, gesticulated, laughed, boldly held her hand. It was hard to believe he was fifty-eight years old. He had a natural lightness of foot, and walking along the woodland paths he leapt over the smallest obstacles, or skipped around them.

Every now and then they would glance back at me, as if my name had been mentioned—he with the embarrassed half smile of a man who wishes you would go away and leave him alone; she with the frank laughter of a woman who is enjoying the predicament of both men. She was having a wonderful time.

The Course of True Love

Florence Kling had lived almost a decade as a single mother in her father's large house, under his tyranny, when she met the handsome publisher of the Marion Star, *which Warren Harding had recently purchased for three hundred dollars:*

Harding was the son of a poor doctor and a domineering, doting, overpossessive mother who had well conditioned him for a woman who would tell him he was wonderful at the same time she told him what to do. The accounts of their courtship vary, but there is little disagreement on the question of who was the aggressor. Florence was thirty, a lonely divorcée with a child, and she was determined to marry Harding. With his kindly attitude toward life, his devil-may-care air, his easy popularity, his gift of gab and charm, Harding was everything that Florence would have liked to be but was not.

Amos Kling, of course, flew into a rage when he heard the

gossip about Florence and Harding, whom he considered an irresponsible scalawag, and a penniless one at that. Kling trapped Harding one day on the courthouse steps and threatened to shoot him if he set foot on his premises. He stomped around town charging that Harding came of "mixed blood." It was thought at the time that Kling was the instigator of a full-page article in the *Mirror*, Marion's other paper, alleging that Harding's family had always been regarded as Negroes, and treated as such, in their former hometown of Blooming Grove.

Meanwhile, at home, Amos Kling issued his daughter an ultimatum: "You must make your choice—your father or Warren Harding. Which is it to be?" There wasn't any hesitation. Her father goaded Florence into her second elopement. She secretly married the twenty-five-year-old publisher on July 8, 1891.

It was seven years before her father would pass her on the street with any sign of recognition, and fifteen years before he visited their home, although it was only a few blocks from the Kling edifice. The Hardings never seemed very affectionate, but Florence had gotten away from her father, into a home of her own, and Harding—well, he was a nice chap who could never say no to anybody. Somebody who had known Harding nearly all his life once commented that "if Warren had been a woman, he would have been pregnant all the time."

Bread

Mrs. Goodhue was not keen on the idea of her daughter marrying the silent young lawyer, Calvin Coolidge. She advised Grace to leave her job at the Clarke Institute for the Deaf and spend a year with her improving her homemaking skills. She deplored to Calvin the fact that Grace did not even know how to bake bread. "I can buy bread" was Coolidge's riposte. Grace was a grandmother and her husband had been dead for a decade when she finally got around to adopting her mother's advice and learned to make bread at home during the Second World War. She confided to one of her former college friends: "I have always turned pale at the mere mention of a cake of yeast."

All in the Family

Eleanor Roosevelt's parents were godparents to Franklin Delano Roosevelt, so she met her fifth cousin (once removed) at their future home in Hyde Park at the age of two. "I am told," she wrote in later life, "that Franklin, probably under protest, crawled around the nursery (which has since been our children's), bearing me on his back."

Love at First Sight

In 1890, when Harry was six years old, his mother, Martha Ellen Young Truman, persuaded her husband to move to Independence, because she wanted her children (a second son, Vivian, and a daughter, Mary, had followed Harry) to get a better education than the rural schools could give them.

Not long after they came to town, Martha Ellen Truman met the local Presbyterian minister on the street. He invited her to send her children to his Sunday school. Although she was a Baptist by birth, she accepted the invitation. Thus, six-year-old Harry Truman walked into the classroom of the First Presbyterian Church and saw "a little blue-eyed golden-haired girl" named Bess Wallace. To the end of his life, he insisted that he fell in love with five-year-old Bess on the spot and never stopped loving her throughout his boyhood years. "She sat behind me in the sixth, seventh, and high school grades," Harry Truman later recalled, "and I thought she was the most beautiful and the sweetest person on earth."

Occasionally, Bess would allow Harry Truman to carry her books home from school. He would be dazed with happiness for the rest of the day. More moments of near ecstasy occurred when Bess joined Harry and several other classmates at the home of his first cousin, Ethel Noland, to be tutored in the intricacies of

Latin verbs by her older sister, Nellie. Both Nolands soon noted Harry's adoration of Bess, and he did not try to conceal it from them.

One day he appeared in their house with a broad smile on his face and announced that he wanted to play his first musical composition for them. The Nolands seated themselves in their parlor, expecting something very solemn and high-toned. Cousin Harry had been taking piano lessons for years and was playing Bach, Beethoven, Liszt, and other European masters. He reeled off a swarm of arpeggios and then played a series of lilting notes that they instantly recognized. "It's Bessie's ice cream whistle!" Ethel exclaimed.

Unfortunately, Bess Wallace did not have the slightest interest in Harry Truman, or the least idea that he was in love with her. He was never part of the Delaware Street gang. Never was he invited to a ball at the Swope mansion. Nor did he participate in those moonlit hayrides. The Trumans were far beneath the social world inhabited by the Wallaces and the Gates, the Waggoners and the Swopes. They were country folk and newcomers in the bargain. John Anderson Truman's profession, horse trading, was considered less than genteel by most people, and his income was erratic. During high school, Harry had to work at odd jobs to improve the family's finances.

After high school, Harry Truman went back to help his father with farming and did not see Bess Wallace for nine years. Her family in the meanwhile had seen a string of tragedies, including bankruptcy and her father's suicide. As a result Bess developed a pessimism and a need for security which she did not think Harry, despite his vast optimism, could provide. In the remarkable courtship that followed for the next nine years, she turned him down several times. One turning point in Bess's attitude came when they were both in their late twenties, as recounted by Margaret Truman's recent biography of her mother:

So it went through the fall of 1913 until the first Sunday in November. On that day, three years and five months after they had renewed their friendship on the porch of 219 North Delaware

Street, Bess confided to Harry Truman news that he did not believe at first. She told him that in the two and a half years since she had rejected his proposal, her feelings for him had undergone a profound change. She had begun to think that if she married anyone, he would be the man.

Harry was literally speechless. He could only sit and look at this golden-haired young woman. Once more, Bess did not know what to make of him. She found herself wondering again what there was about this odd mixture of farmer and thinker and humorist and roughneck who was tempting her to leave the sanctuary of 219 North Delaware Street to risk disappointment and perhaps worse in an uncaring world. "Harry Truman," she cried, "you're an enigma!"

They got married six years later.

Kids

Jimmy Carter and Rosalynn Smith knew each other as children in tiny Plains, Georgia. Jimmy's sister, Ruth, and Rosalynn were the closest of friends, so the future lovers often ran into each other. But being three years older, he looked on her as just a kid. Then one day the young cadet was on a visit back home from the Naval Academy at Annapolis, and, according to his mother, Miss Lillian:

"Jimmy and some of his friends decided to give a dance over here at the pond house. We had a sort of jukebox there, and they could make all the noise they wanted to, because we have no close neighbors, as you can see. It just happened that Ruth and Rosalynn were spending that weekend here with us. I don't know what it was that gave them the idea—maybe there was a temporary shortage of girls, or something—but the boys saw Ruth and Rosalynn here at the house and they said, in a sort of offhand way: 'Why don't you girls get somebody to bring you, and come and join the party.' Now you can imagine that no high school girl is going to pass up an invitation to go to a college boy's party.

So that's what they did. They got dates—I don't remember who—and they went to the dance."

Miss Lillian got the rest of the story in confidence in a kitchen-table talk with Rosalynn later. "Jimmy danced first with Ruth and then with her—Rosalynn. And while he was dancing with her, Jimmy said to Rosalynn: 'Don't you think the date I brought is pretty?' And Rosalynn said she snapped right back at Jimmy: 'She's not half as pretty as I am!'

"Well, I think Jimmy must have taken a closer look at Rosalynn at that point, because it was only a few days later that he came into the kitchen and said: 'Mother, do you know who I have a date with tonight?' And I said: 'Who?' And he said: 'Rosalynn.' And they began to date just about every night after that, when he came home from Annapolis. And I don't think he ever again dated anyone else."

Back at Annapolis, Jimmy wrote to Rosalynn every other day, and she wrote to him about as often. And when he came home at Christmas he proposed to her and she turned him down. He says she told him she didn't know for sure yet what she wanted in life.

Labor Negotiation

After that first enchanted evening, Ronnie and Nancy went out with increasing frequency. But still, the Hollywood actor and union activist resisted following the Hollywood script:

This story, I know, will be a disappointment to those who want romance neatly packaged. The truth is, I did everything wrong, dating her off and on, continuing to volunteer for every Guild trip to New York—in short, doing everything which could have lost her if Someone up there hadn't been looking after me. In spite of my determination to remain footloose, in spite of my belief that the pattern of my life was all set and would continue without change, nature was trying to tell me something very important.

In the months that followed, it didn't even frighten me to

discover our friends were taking us for granted and automatically inviting us to dinner parties as a twosome. We went to the premiere of her picture, *The Next Voice You Hear*, and for the first time I found myself remembering that she was an actress and at the same time discovered that she was a damn good one. Before we left the theater, remembering the first time I had ever seen myself, I told her she could go home and unpack—she'd be around for quite a while.

We had deserted the nightclubs to a great extent and many of our dates were spent at the home of Bill and Ardis Holden. Someplace along here I know there should be a scene of sudden realization, the kind we'd write if we were putting this on film. It just didn't happen that way. To tell the truth, I'm glad—although I get scared thinking I could have lost her. Gradually I came out of the deep-freeze and discovered a wonderful world of warmth and deep contentment. My friends had been extremely patient, as I discovered one night at a meeting of the Motion Picture Industry Council. Bill and I, as Guild representatives, were seated at the huge round table in the Producers Association meeting room. For the first time I was strangely indifferent to all that was going on. Suddenly I picked up one of the scratch pads always available and wrote a note to Bill: "To hell with this, how would you like to be best man when I marry Nancy?"

Right out loud he blurted, "It's about time," and that ended the meeting for us. To everyone's surprise we got up without a word and walked out, not caring that the producers would probably have a sleepless night, thinking that some new Guild crisis was about to hit the picture business.

Theatre

Thelma "Pat" Ryan graduated from the University of Southern California magna cum laude *and was intent on pursuing a career in merchandising. Instead she accepted a teaching job in the Los Angeles suburb of Whittier, hometown of Richard Nixon, who had recently moved back to start practicing law. They met in a community theatre production, which is the only fact that sources agree upon. According to Pat Nixon's biographer, Lester David:*

Casting had just begun for the opening performance of the 1938 season of the Whittier Community Players, an amateur little theatre group which put on five or six plays each year. The first production was to be *The Dark Tower* by Alexander Woollcott and George S. Kaufman, a dreadful mystery melodrama which survived only fifty-seven performances on Broadway. (Woollcott was so ashamed of it that he omitted the play from his list of published works in *Who's Who*.) Its only claim to fame now may be the fact that it brought together Richard Nixon and Pat Ryan.

The story of how the romance began has by now been layered over by sentiment and apocrypha. According to the version in most biographies, Nixon heard of a "smashing" new teacher in town and went down to the little theatre group to look her over. Not true, Hortense Behrens and Elizabeth Cloes, who were in the cast, told me. Nixon had been invited to join the players, had consented, and had already been chosen for the part of Barry Jones in *The Dark Tower* when Pat came to read.

Another and more romantic part of the legend is that Nixon blurted out a proposal on their first date. The story has not escaped the psychohistorians, who have seized upon the "impulsive" act as a key to the labyrinths of Nixon's mind. Pat's recollection, as related by Earl Mazo in the first full-scale biography of Richard Nixon, is that Nixon asked her to marry him the first night he met her. "I thought he was nuts or something," he reports her as saying. "I guess I just looked at him. I couldn't imagine anyone ever saying anything like that so suddenly. Now that I know Dick much better, I can't imagine that he would ever say that, because he's very much the opposite; he's more reserved."

It may be that, over the years, Pat has sentimentalized what was actually said, or that she took too literally a "line" that a young man, reserved or not, might hand a very pretty girl. The "proposal," such as it was, came on the third evening after they met and, since it was made in the presence of Miss Cloes and in a somewhat jocular mood, may hardly have been intended quite so seriously as Nixon's biographers seem to believe.

Miss Cloes says that Nixon hovered around Pat all that first evening and, when the rehearsal ended, offered to drive the two girls home. They accepted. He drove them home a second time and a third.

"We got into his Model A Ford," Miss Cloes recalls. "I sat in the middle, Pat sat on the outside. And he said to her, 'I'd like to have a date with you.' She said, 'Oh, I'm too busy.' So he laughed and drove us home. As we were coming out to go home from the third rehearsal, I said, 'Pat, you sit next to him. He doesn't want to sit next to me.' She said, 'I don't want to sit next to him!' So I was again in the middle and he leaned across me and said to her, 'When are you going to give me that date?' She laughed. He said, 'Don't laugh. Someday I'm going to marry you.' He pointed his finger at her and she laughed again."

A few nights later, she consented to go out with him.

WEDDINGS

The Minister's Daughter

On the 26th of October, 1764, Abigail Smith was married to John Adams. She was at the time twenty years old. Mrs. Adams was the second of three daughters, whose characters were alike strong and remarkable for their intellectual force.

When Abigail's eldest sister, Mary, was married, her father preached to his people from the text, "And Mary hath chosen that good part, which shall not be taken away from her." The disapprobation to his second daughter's choice was due to the prejudice entertained against the profession of the law. Mr. Adams, besides being a lawyer, was the son of a small farmer of the middle class in Braintree and was thought scarcely good enough to match with the minister's daughter, descended from a line of ministers in the colony. Mr. Smith's parishioners were outspoken in the opposition, and he replied to them immediately after the marriage took place, in a sermon, in which he made pointed allusion to the objection against lawyers. His text on this occasion was, "For John came neither eating bread nor drinking wine, and ye say, *He hath a devil.*"

Royal Sanction

All of Dolley's friends were delighted when it was whispered about that she was to marry Mr. Madison. Mrs. Washington sent word for her to come to the presidential mansion. When Dolley arrived, the Mistress President took her by both hands and looked anxiously into her eyes, as if trying to decide whether Dolley was coquettish or in earnest.

"Dolley," she inquired, "is it true you are engaged to James Madison?"

Dolley's eyes went into mourning under her dark lashes and she grew rosier than ever as she faltered:

"I—think—not."

In spite of this negative response, Mrs. Washington seemed satisfied. The young widow's manner told her more than the words.

"Do not be ashamed to confess it, my dear," she said affectionately. "James Madison will make you a good husband. The President and I are much pleased with your choice."

Thus it was that Dolley obtained the "royal" sanction. Having that, she allowed her engagement to James Madison to be formally announced, and arrangements were made for a speedy marriage. Mr. Madison, so deliberate in all things else, was impatient to claim his bride.

Just Married

After wooing her with music, Thomas Jefferson married Mrs. Martha Skelton on New Year's Day in 1772 at her father's estate, called the Forest, in Charles City County, Virginia. After the bridal festivities Mr.

and Mrs. Jefferson set out for Monticello. The journey was not without adventures, as preserved in an account by their eldest daughter, Mrs. Randolph:

They left the Forest after a fall of snow, light then, but increasing in depth as they advanced up the country. They were finally obliged to quit the carriage and proceed on horseback. Having stopped for a short time at Blenheim (the residence of Colonel Carter) where an overseer only resided, they left it at sunset to pursue their way through a mountain track rather than a road, in which the snow lay from eighteen inches to two feet deep, having eight miles to go before reaching Monticello.

They arrived late at night, the fires all out and the servants retired to their own houses for the night. The horrible dreariness of such a house, at the end of such a journey, I have often heard them both relate.

Part of a bottle of wine, found on a shelf behind some books, had to serve the new-married couple both for fire and supper. Tempers too sunny to be ruffled by many ten times as serious annoyances in after life now found but sources of diversion in these ludicrous contretemps, and the horrible dreariness was lit up with songs, and merriment and laughter.

White House Wedding

President Cleveland was married at the White House at seven o'clock on the 2nd of June, 1886, to Miss Frances Folsom, the daughter of his former law partner. Since the historic mansion had been occupied there had been eight marriages within its walls, but for the first time a President of the United States was the bridegroom. Only a few relatives of the bride and high officials were invited, but a large crowd assembled around the door of the White House, where they could only hear the music of the Marine Band when the ceremony was commenced. At the same time a presidential salute was fired from the Arsenal, and the church bells chimed merry peals.

Precisely at seven o'clock the Marine Band struck up Mendelssohn's Wedding March, and the President came slowly down the staircase with his bride leaning on his arm. They were unaccompanied—even the bride's mother awaiting her coming. The bride wore a train four yards in length. Attached to the lower side of the train on the left was a scarf of soft, white India silk, looped high, and forming an overskirt, which was bordered on the edge with orange blossoms. Across the bodice were full folds of muslin, edged with orange blossoms. Long gloves were worn with short sleeves. The bridal veil was of white silk tulle, five yards in length, fastened on the head with orange blossoms, and falling to the end of the beautiful train, which, as the bride stood with bowed head beside the President, lay far behind her on the floor. Her only jewelry was a superb diamond necklace, the President's wedding present, and an engagement ring containing a sapphire and two diamonds.

President Cleveland wore an evening dress of black, with a small, turned-down collar and a white lawn necktie; a white rose was fastened to the lapel of his coat. The bridal couple turned to the right as they entered the Blue Parlor from the long hall, and faced the officiating clergyman, Rev. Dr. Sutherland, who immediately commenced the ceremony in accordance with the usages of the Presbyterian Church.

At the conclusion of the ceremony the bride's mother, Mrs. Folsom, was the first to tender her congratulations. She was followed by other relatives and friends in turn. Then the band struck up the march from *Lohengrin*, and the President and his wife led the way through the East Room to the family dining room, where the wedding supper was served. The decorations were of an elaborate character. A mirror in the center of the table represented a lake, on which was a full-rigged ship, made of pinks, roses, and pansies. The national colors floated over the mainmast, and small white flags, with the monogram "C.F." in golden letters, hung from the other masts. The guests were not seated, but stood up and enjoyed the croquettes, game, salads, ices, and creams. The health of the bride and bridegroom was pledged in iced champagne. Each guest received a box of cardboard, containing a white satin box filled with wedding cake five inches long by two broad and two deep. On the cover the date was hand painted in colors, and a card affixed bore the autograph signature of Grover Cleveland and Frances Folsom, which they had written the previous afternoon.

At a quarter past eight the President and his wife left the supper room and soon reappeared in traveling dress. He wore his usual black frock business suit and she a traveling dress of deep gray silk, with a large gray hat lined with velvet and crowned with ostrich feathers. They left the back door of the White House amid a shower of rice and old slippers and were driven to the Baltimore and Ohio Railroad, where they took a special train to Deer Park in the Allegheny Mountains.

Silver Wedding

On the 31st of December, 1877, President and Mrs. Hayes stood together in the Blue Room of the White House to celebrate the twenty-fifth anniversary of their marriage. This silver wedding, the first ever celebrated in the White House, was a social event which proved of genuine interest to the people of the country. The anniversary was celebrated on the afternoon of the 30th, when the Rev. Dr. McCabe, who married them, renewed his pastoral blessing in the same words and heard the same pledges given that were uttered a quarter of a century before. Mrs. Hayes wore the same satin dress and slippers which she wore on her wedding day, and they were surrounded by their five children. The next evening the formal ceremonies were held, and one hundred guests were present. The Executive Mansion was brilliantly illuminated, and the parlors and the East Room were elegantly decorated with flowers. Mrs. Hayes wore a reception dress of white striped silk, trimmed with point lace. Her wedding dress of white satin was exhibited to her lady friends, but the idea at first entertained of wearing it [for this formal ceremony] was abandoned because of its size, it being too small.

The Empty Nest

One of the memorable White House weddings was the occasion on which Nellie Grant married Algernon Sartoris on May 21,

1874. Sartoris came from a rich English family, with an income of $60,000 a year, which was a fortune in those days. The dashing young man fell in love with the President's daughter when they met on a steamer bound from England to New York. He was nearly twenty-two years old, while Nellie Grant was barely seventeen. It took eighteen months before she could secure her father's approval. During the ceremony, the bride and groom stood under a huge floral bell, with a background of flowers filling a window behind them. There were six bridesmaids, and General Grant gave away his daughter with ill-concealed emotion.

The East Room was decked for the wedding with real orange blossoms from the South. The window shades were closely drawn so as to render more effective the hundreds of lights which glistened from the crystal chandeliers. The lace alone on the bride's dress cost $1,500. The young couple advanced to the embrace of the great eastern window, where hung an enormous floral bell, along an aisle formed by army and navy officers in glittering uniforms.

According to Thomas Pendel, the White House doorkeeper who lived to witness Alice Roosevelt's wedding more than thirty years later: "After the ceremony was all over the invited guests repaired to the Red Parlor; that is the ladies did, and I had the pleasure of presenting to them the wedding cake—put up in little white boxes about six inches long and three inches wide—for them to dream on, that those who were single might dream of their future husbands. After Miss Nellie had sailed for Europe, one night after dinner the President took a walk downtown, and everybody had left the house with the exception of Mrs. Grant, Jerry Smith, the old colored duster, and myself. When the President had been gone probably fifteen minutes, Mrs. Grant, who was sitting in the Blue Parlor, seemed very lonesome. She called me away from the front door to come in near the Blue Parlor door and be seated, as the house was perfectly deserted, except for us three. While I was there the conversation turned to Miss Nellie. I said to her, 'I am very sorry, Mrs. Grant, that Miss Nellie has gone away. We all miss her very much.' Mrs. Grant spoke up and said, 'Yes, but we will have her back home again.' I chatted with her until the President returned and then took my post again at the front door."

Slashing the Cake

The marriage of Theodore Roosevelt's eldest daughter, Alice, to Congressman Nicholas Longworth was the social event of 1906. According to an eyewitness:

The decorations at the wedding were alone of a value sufficient for a king's ransom. The ceremony took place in the East Room, in front of one of the windows, which was draped with cloth of gold rimmed with curtains, the whole being ornamented with ropes of smilax and Easter lilies. The bride and bridegroom stood on a raised platform, or dais, where all present could see the happy pair. On the platform under their feet were priceless Oriental rugs. And at the rear of the platform was a little improvised altar, just large enough for Bishop Satterlee to conduct the service.

When the bride entered the East Room on the arm of her father, the President, to proceed to the improvised altar, she advanced down an aisle formed by means of two ropes of white ribbon. The East Room was otherwise divided into two compartments, as it were, the one for the Cabinet, members of the Diplomatic Corps, their families, and the intimate friends of the Roosevelt family, and the other for the hundreds of other invited guests.

After the ceremony came the cutting of the wedding cake. Alongside the cake was a knife, and at first Mrs. Longworth thought to cut the cake with this, but the glazing either offered more resistance than she expected or the knife was dull. Anyway, the cutting proceeded much too slowly for a young woman of her impulsive disposition, and gaily turning to Major McCawley, she called out, "Oh, Major, let me have your sword to cut the cake with."

The Major promptly drew his sword and, gallantly taking it

by the blade, extended the hilt to her. The saber was admirably adapted to the purpose, and when Mrs. Longworth brandished it aloft and began slashing the cake with it the slices fell right and left, and great was the scramble among her friends for it. It melted away like snow under a hot sun, and within marvelously few minutes after the first stroke of Major McCawley's saber not a crumb of it was to be had.

The Shadow of Presidents

Eleanor Roosevelt's wedding to Franklin took place the year before Alice's to Nicholas Longworth. The two girls had been close friends while growing up. Later, the President's daughter became very competitive, which intimidated Eleanor. When Alice heard of her cousin's engagement, she wrote her: "It is simply too nice to be true—you old fox, not to tell me before." Eleanor asked her to be a bridesmaid. "It will be too much fun," Alice replied. Her view of the groom was somewhat contemptuous: "Franklin was the sort of boy you invited to the dance, but not to the dinner."

Ironically, Eleanor and Franklin were upstaged at their own wedding. As their eldest son, James, wrote in a book about his parents:

Many people left the parade to gather around the Ludlow place in hopes of catching a glimpse of the President and his daughter. Inside, once the vows were said, the newly wedded couple found themselves alone while the guests gathered around Teddy and Alice in another room. I was told this story by my parents when, after I was married for the first time, my bride and I found ourselves alone while the guests gathered around another President, my father. I suppose when one follows in the footsteps of Presidents, one must expect to be overshadowed, even on what should be one's day in the sun.

Get Me to the Church on Time

Lady Bird Taylor was in a state of complete indecision about spending the rest of her life with a young man whom she had only met two months before. She sought the advice of her aunt Effie, who advised caution; of her father, who urged her on; and then she still wanted to consult her friend Gene Lassater in Austin.

Lyndon went with her [to Austin], and as they started he issued his ultimatum: "We either get married now or we never will. And if you say good-bye to me, it just proves to me that you just don't love me enough to dare to. And I just can't bear to go on and keep wondering if it will ever happen."

Lady Bird wondered if every prospective bride had to go through such indecisions. She was torn in two directions more deeply than ever. She did not want to let him go, but she also realized the hazards of the future. Only two days earlier she had read the marriage ceremony in her prayer book. "Do you realize what we are agreeing to?" she asked Lyndon. "I don't think he had ever read the marriage vows," she said later. But he persuaded her that then was time for them to get married. At seven-thirty that morning he telephoned his friend Dan Quill, the postmaster in San Antonio, to make arrangements for the wedding to be held there that evening. So instead of going to Austin they headed for San Antonio, nearly four hundred miles away.

The ceremony was performed by the Rev. Arthur K. McKinstry, rector of St. Mark's Episcopal Church in San Antonio. At first he rebelled at performing the ceremony. He told Dan Quill: "You are asking me to perform a justice-of-the-peace ceremony. I don't marry people that fast. I want to get to know them, meet with them two or three days, talk with them and explain the seriousness of marriage."

But Postmaster Quill explained that Johnson had only one day in Texas, and the minister relented. Lyndon Johnson used to say that he was still persuading Lady Bird to marry him as they walked up the church steps. It was to be a simple, quiet ceremony with no music and only two or three witnesses. In the church Lady Bird turned to her intended—the man who was to become known as the master of great detail—and asked, "You did bring a wedding ring, didn't you?"

The nervous bridegroom snapped his fingers. "I forgot!" While the rector waited, Dan Quill dashed across the street to the nearest store, a Sears Roebuck, to get one. The clerk asked him what size. Quill, a bachelor, had not thought of that. So he took the whole tray of inexpensive rings back to church for the bride to select one that fit her finger. Quill paid $2.50 for the ring, his wedding gift to the bride and her husband, and it was used in the ceremony as they were pronounced man and wife.

Promised in the Rose Garden

Helen Thomas recalled the wedding of the Nixons' older daughter, Patricia, to Edward Cox:

Tricia chose the Rose Garden of the White House as the setting for her June 1971 wedding, the first outdoor wedding at the White House in the 171-year history of the mansion.

The guest list was limited to four hundred select friends and government officials. I was one of the small pool of reporters who attended the wedding ceremony. Martha Mitchell arrived wearing an orange-sherbet flouncy garden party dress with matching parasol. "Everyone else checked their umbrellas," grumped Defense Secretary Melvin Laird as he sat behind Martha and her husband, John.

Rain delayed the nuptials a few hours before the ceremony. Nixon dropped by the huge tent on the South Lawn where the press was ensconced, sheltered from the downpour. He revealed that Tricia had been advised to move the wedding to the East Room, but had decided to gamble on the weather clearing. Reverend Billy Graham told reporters he would pray for the rain to stop.

The site of the wedding was now touch and go. At 12:30 P.M. Connie Stuart, Mrs. Nixon's staff director, who had been bringing weather bulletins, announced to cheers, "Tricia has decided the ceremony will be in the Rose Garden."

The seats were still damp when the guests sat down for the brief ceremony. Washington's dowager, "Princess Alice" Roosevelt Longworth, said that she felt as if she had been "sitting on a wet sponge during the ceremony." Someone asked her if she was reminded of her own White House wedding in 1906, and she replied, "Good God, not a bit. I was married twenty years before Hollywood. This wedding was quite a production."

Tricia was petite and exquisite in white lace as she came down the aisle on her father's arm. Nixon, who wore a cutaway, told her that she looked "beautiful" as they started down the path to the altar.

The wedding was traditional in all respects, except for passages from *The Prophet* by Kahlil Gibran, requested by the bride and groom: "Stand together, but not too near together, just as the pillars of a temple stand apart yet stand together."

Dr. Edward Latch, the Chaplain of the House of Representatives, who performed the services, addressed the couple with "Love gives and forgives, accepts and adjusts . . ."

President and Mrs. Nixon looked happier than I have ever seen them before.

When Nixon danced with his wife, lovely in a pastel lace short party dress, she threw her arms impulsively around him. Guests applauded.

In fact, this was the first time the President danced publicly. "My parents were Quakers. They didn't believe in this sort of thing," he said, setting off with Tricia to the tune of "Thank Heaven for Little Girls."

Lynda Bird Robb, who also two-stepped with Nixon, told him that her father, who loved to dance, was a "backsliding Baptist."

Later, when Nixon was asked if he would ever dance again at a White House party, quipped, "Never again."

The following day, on June 13, 1971, next to the wedding story in *The New York Times*, was the sensational revelation about the "Pentagon Papers," a story that would lead eventually to the White House plumbers and, in the end, to Watergate and disaster.

4

RELATIONSHIPS

MARRIED LIFE

Newlyweds

Colonel Starling, worn out with his late-night stakeouts of President Wilson at Edith Bolling Galt's home, wrote to his mother: "I will be glad when he gets married, for he certainly has us on the go." Woodrow Wilson and Mrs. Galt finally did get married on December 18, 1915. But the Chief Executive seemed as stricken as ever, and played golf every morning with his wife:

Neither of them really cared about the game. Walking along the fairway between shots, the President regaled her with dialect stories and gave impromptu impersonations, one of his best being an interpretation of serious little Dr. Grayson addressing a ball. One day, tired of carrying her niblick, Mrs. Wilson laid it across her husband's shoulders and bent him forward so that it would not slip off. Immediately he changed his stride to imitate the lumbering gait of an ape. When he tired of the jest he bent forward, let the niblick roll over the top of his head, and caught it as it fell. They both laughed—they laughed at anything and everything in those days. They were completely happy, and the increasing burden of his job rested lightly on the President's shoulders.

They played until ten o'clock, then returned to the White House. The President was due at his office in the Executive Building at eleven. A few minutes before that hour he would

appear in the Rose Garden, walking slowly and talking animat-
edly to Mrs. Wilson, who clung to his arm. At the office building
he would look at his watch, kiss her, then stand gazing after her
as she walked back along the path. When she reached the other
end she would turn and wave at him. He would look at his watch
again. There was still a minute. Quickly he would walk to meet
her. Again they would embrace, again part. Finally, at the stroke
of eleven, with a final reluctant look at her retreating figure, he
would enter the building. He was never late, but after the marriage he was never early.

After the Honeymoon

Calvin Coolidge had traditional ideas of marriage and of a wife's
place in the scheme of things. Just how traditional, Grace Coolidge found out a few weeks after the honeymoon. They were
still living in a hotel when the future President arrived one day
with a leather bag. Like a magician, he produced no fewer than
fifty-two socks which needed darning. "There'll be more," he
promised. The bride was expert at darning and took it in good
humor. She asked half in jest whether he married her in order
to get his socks mended. "No, but I find it mighty handy," he
replied truthfully.

His Dear Patsy

When Colonel Washington married Mrs. Custis, the ceremony
was performed under the roof of her own home [the White
House], and the broad lands about it were but part of her large
estate. Her share of the Custis property equaled "15,000 acres
of land, a good part of it adjoining the city of Williamsburg;
several lots in the said city; between 200 and 300 Negroes; and
about eight or ten thousand pounds upon bond, estimated at the
time about twenty thousand pounds in all, which was further
increased on the death of 'Patsy' Custis in 1773 by a half of her
fortune, which added ten thousand pounds to the sum."

Immediately after their wedding, which has been described

repeatedly as a most joyous and happy affair in which every belle and beau for miles around took part, they repaired at once to Mount Vernon. This property, a gift to Colonel Washington from his elder brother, Lawrence, was situated on the southern side of the Potomac, about fifteen miles from Washington City, and remarkable for the magnificent view of the river in front, as well as the cultivation and adornment of the vast estate. Here for seventeen years they enjoyed the society of relatives and friends and the constant companionship of each other.

When absent from Mount Vernon, Washington wrote many and long letters to his wife, which were full of ardent affection, but "Lady" Washington destroyed them before she died, no doubt because they were so largely devoted to a free discussion of public affairs. Only one letter escaped—the one in which he announced his appointment as commander in chief of the colonial army. He begins the letter "My Dearest" and closes it with the statement that he is "with unfeigned regard" her "very affectionate George Washington." He uses several times in the letter his pet name for his wife, which was "my dear Patsy," and says he has made a will with which he doubts not she will be pleased. During the forty years of his married life he wore (according to his adopted son, George Washington Parke Custis) "suspended from his neck by a gold chain and resting on his bosom, the miniature portrait of his wife."

So Much for History

Martha Washington was not the last wife of a President to burn his letters:

Harry Truman called Bess "the boss"—and in many ways she was, though she never pretended to be more than a displaced housewife. Once Truman found her burning some of the letters he had written to her. "Bess, you oughtn't to do that," protested Harry. "Why not? I've read them several times," said Bess. "But think of history!" pleaded the President. "I have," murmured Bess as she tossed the last bundle into the fire.

She Liked Ike

As soon as Mamie Eisenhower moved into the White House, Chief Usher J. B. West got a quick orientation about his new employers' bed habits:

There'd be no separate bedrooms for the Eisenhowers. Marie Geneva Doud Eisenhower made that perfectly clear her first morning in the White House, after she'd spent the night in Bess Truman's narrow single bed in the little room known as the First Lady's dressing room.

That morning, January 21, 1953, she called for Mr. Crim and me.

We adjusted our neckties, picked up our notebooks, and hot-footed it upstairs for our first conference. As we stepped off the elevator, we looked down the hall to where Rose Woods, Mrs. Eisenhower's personal maid, stood beckoning to us from the First Lady's bedroom door.

Mr. Crim and I walked into the room and stopped in our tracks, both assuming our deadest deadpans to hide our surprise. For Mrs. Eisenhower was still in bed!

Standing awkwardly at the foot of the narrow bed, we managed to say good morning as Mamie Eisenhower pushed away her breakfast tray. She was wearing a dainty pink-ruffled bed jacket and had a pink satin bow in her hair.

"I'd like to make some changes right away," she said, lighting a cigarette and surveying her new quarters.

"First of all, I'm not going to sleep in this little room. This is a dressing room, and I want it made into *my* dressing room. The big room"—she indicated with a sweep of her arm the mauve-and-gray chamber next door, where Mrs. Truman [the President's mother] had sat listening to baseball games—"will be *our* bedroom!"

"Prior to the Roosevelts, it had been used that way," Mr. Crim ventured.

"Good!" Mrs. Eisenhower went on. "We need a 'king-size' bed—with a mattress twice as wide as a single bed—and we'd like it as soon as possible, please." Taking a pencil from her bedside table, she quickly designed a double headboard for the bed, to be upholstered and tufted in the same pink fabric as the easy chair in Margaret Truman's sitting room, and a dust ruffle to match.

The bed must have been an immediate success. The morning after it arrived in a White House truck from New York, Mr. Crim and I accompanied the butler bringing Mrs. Eisenhower's breakfast tray.

"Come in, come in," the First Lady sang out as Rose Woods opened the door to the new bedroom.

She was nestled in the big bed, propped up against half a dozen pillows, deep in conversation on the white bedside telephone. Waving gaily at Mr. Crim and me to take a seat, she said, still talking to her friend, "And I've just had the first good night's sleep I've had since we've been in the White House. Our new bed finally got here, and now I can reach over and pat Ike on his old bald head any time I want to!"

I Am Glad You Asked

A year after Betty Ford moved into the White House she still astonished journalist Myra MacPherson by her frankness:

Betty Ford freely admits to smoking, being divorced, seeing a psychiatrist, taking tranquilizers, drinking with her husband, and—heaven forfend—sleeping with him. One afternoon after her cancer operation she talked with me on the telephone and giggled at how practically all the world had seen the Fords' king-size bed being moved into the White House. Declining to follow the White House tradition of separate bedrooms, Mrs. Ford had said with amusement that she could do only so much for politics.

Before her mastectomy, Mrs. Ford had said with a sigh, after countless interviews: "They've asked me everything but how often I sleep with my husband, and if they'd asked me that, I would have told them." When I asked her what she would have said, she shot back, "As often as possible!"

Some Enchanted Evening

Because her husband spent so much time traveling throughout their marriage, Betty Ford was unaccustomed to have him around so much when they moved into the White House. "I wake up in the middle of the night," she confessed to *Vogue* magazine, "and say to him: 'What are *you* doing here?' "

Chief Executive

Jack Kennedy believed in dividing the responsibilities within his marriage. His wife did not always agree. She told Joan Braden: "When I start to ask him silly little insignificant questions, though, about whether Caroline should appear at some reception, or whether I should wear a short or long dress, he just snaps his fingers and says, 'That's your province.' And I say, 'Yes, but you're the great decision maker. Why should everyone but me get the benefit of your decisions?' "

Differences

Although the Carters' marriage is an unusually balanced partnership, they don't paper over their differences. In the White House, Jimmy Carter usually took time off at 4:30 and invited Rosalynn to join him. "He drives me crazy until I quit working and watch a movie or bowl with him," she told *Newsweek*, while he expressed exasperation that she never lets up: "I stop myself to look at a movie, but Rosalynn will plow through a stack of thank-you notes instead."

There are other small bones of contention: she thinks he has lost too much weight (thirteen pounds) from jogging, and she sometimes gets annoyed at his habit of playing country singer Willie Nelson near the stereophonic threshold of pain. They are at impasse on both. "He's told me enough on the jogging," Mrs. Carter has confided to aides, and though she turns down the volume of Willie Nelson, the President turns it back up.

The Cat Out of the Bag

Jimmy Carter is an early riser; his wife sacrificed her beauty sleep for twenty-five years in the belief that her husband would like a cooked breakfast. Year after year Rosalynn got up at dawn to prepare a full meal, only to find out that he did not care for anything more than orange juice. The devastating revelation came just after Jimmy Carter's election to the governorship of Georgia, when finally Rosalynn could look forward to giving up this tiresome chore. As she was organizing the staff duties at the Governor's Mansion, she remarked that she would ask one person to come to work at dawn in order to prepare breakfast for her husband. According to Rosalynn, it was at that point that Jimmy Carter decided to confess. He looked her straight in the eyes and said: "The best thing about campaigning for Governor was that I didn't have to eat breakfast. You made me eat breakfast for twenty-five years, and I don't like breakfast!"

Magic

Despite their Hollywood background Nancy and Ronald Reagan have enjoyed an old-fashioned marriage that has endured intact despite many trials and sorrows, as journalist Bernard Weinraub depicted it in McCall's *magazine in late 1985:*

When they moved into the White House, cynics said that their relationship was almost too good to be true. But, after nearly five years in the public glare of Washington, Nancy and Ronald Reagan still seem, without doubt, a couple in unabashed, unapologetic love.

After his cancer surgery last July, she placed a Cabbage Patch doll in a nurse's outfit, labeled *Nancy*, beside his bed to remind him to heed her demand that he take it easy. She frequently buys him surprise presents for the ranch—a pickup truck, electric saw, lawnmower, and what the President has called the pièce de résistance, a manure spreader.

White House insiders say that, when she leaves her husband

for several days at a time, Nancy cries all the way from the White House to Andrews Air Force Base. "There's magic to that marriage," David Fisher, the President's personal aide, told *The Washington Post* some time ago. "It's kind of like that magic that's in everybody's courtship has never left the Reagans. Once we were on a plane, coming back to Andrews, and she was coming in on another flight. And they hugged and kissed each other as if they'd been away for days. They hug and kiss all the time. They're really in love with each other."

Before Mr. Reagan left Bethesda Naval Hospital after his surgery, he delivered a nationwide radio speech with his wife beside him in the bedroom. The President said quietly, "I'd like to indulge myself for a moment here. There's something I want to say, and I wanted to say it with Nancy at my side, as she is right now, as she always has been. First Ladies aren't elected, and they don't receive a salary. They have mostly been private persons forced to live public lives, and in my book they've all been heroes. Abigail Adams helped invent America. Dolley Madison helped protect it. Eleanor Roosevelt was FDR's eyes and ears. Nancy Reagan is my everything." At that point Nancy broke down and cried.

DIFFICULTIES

Sensitive Monomaniac

It was Rachel Donelson's misfortune to be married to two jealous husbands—to one of them twice:

Andrew Jackson, or "Andy" as he was commonly called, was twenty-four when he married Mrs. Robards. She and her first husband were boarding with her mother, Mrs. Donelson, then a widow, when Jackson became a boarder under the same roof. Mrs. Robards's husband, suspicious and morose, was needlessly jealous of her and made her very unhappy. Jackson was fond of her society, though he in no manner passed the boundaries of the most conventional decorum. Her husband believed, or pretended to believe, that Jackson was his wife's lover, and applied to the legislature for an act preliminary to divorce. Jackson and Mrs. Robards supposed the act itself a divorce, and they were married two years before the divorce was allowed.

This innocent mistake (they were married again as soon as it was discovered) was the source of endless annoyance and sorrow to them both. To the day of Jackson's death he was so sensitive and fiery on the subject that if any man hinted at any impropriety in their relations, he at once called the slanderer to account. Indeed, he was little less than a monomaniac in regard to his wife. Several of his most savage conflicts grew directly or indirectly out of what he believed to be reflections on her fair fame. He fancied his wife to be a goddess, an angel, a saint, and he wanted to kill anybody who dared express any other opinion. His resentful disposition kept him alert for the slightest insinuation against her.

One of the most tragical of his experiences was his duel with Charles Dickinson, who had committed the unpardonable sin of commenting freely on Mrs. Jackson. They had several disagreements, and Jackson finally spoke of Dickinson in so violent a manner that his language was repeated, as the General wished it should be, to the man himself. Thereupon Dickinson wrote Jackson a letter, denouncing him as a liar and a coward. Jackson challenged him, and they met on the banks of the Red River in Logan County, Kentucky, early in the morning of May 30, 1806. Dickinson got first fire, breaking a rib and making a serious wound in the breast of his opponent, who showed no sign of having been hit. He had felt sure of killing his antagonist, and exclaimed, "Great God! have I missed him?"

Jackson, then taking deliberate aim, pulled the trigger, but the weapon did not explode. It stopped at half cock. He cocked it fully, and again calmly and carefully leveling it, fired. The bullet passed through Dickinson's body, just above the hips; he fell and died that night after suffering terrible agony. Jackson never recovered from the hurt and never expressed the least remorse for what many persons pronounced a cold-blooded murder. Any man who had spoken discreditably of Mrs. Jackson had, in his opinion, forfeited the right to live.

Jealousy

Mrs. Lincoln's jealousy was evident from very early in her marriage. One of her husband's closest friends was Joshua Speed, whom Mary Lincoln blamed for influencing Abraham in backing out of their first engagement. Joshua was happily married, and Lincoln, in his letters, would always remember to ask that his love be conveyed to Fanny. After his own marriage, Lincoln was forced by Mary to send only his "regards to Mrs. Speed."

Little Wife

The marriage of Lucretia Rudolph and James Garfield did not start well. She was a teacher, making her own living and decisions, and just before the wedding she wrote to him about her apprehensions: "My heart is not yet schooled to an entire submission to that destiny which will make the wife of one who marries me." She considered their union based only "upon the cold, stern word duty," while he thought the marriage was a mistake and blamed it on her. Still she kept promising "to try harder than ever before to be the best little wife possible. You need not be a bit afraid of my introducing ever again one of those long talks that strike such a terror in you."

In Sickness

According to Thomas Pendel, doorkeeper at the White House:

President McKinley was very kind and gentle to Mrs. McKinley at all times. Often I would go in with cards after she had recovered from spells of sickness after dinner. They would be sitting in the grand corridor near the entrance to the dining room. She would have her knitting, which she was very fond of, and the President would be reading his paper or looking over some documents that required his attention. He seemed to do everything in his power to please her. They were a very happy man and wife.

And Mrs. John Logan wrote:

No matters of State could ever engross the President so as to make him forget his delicate wife for an hour. She deeply appreciates the thoughtfulness that prompts him to leave Cabinet meetings or other important councils, if they are at all protracted, to seek her and see that she is happy and has the companionship of some agreeable person. She enjoys everything the President does, traveling, driving, music, flowers, and the sight of people. She can never be induced to be separated from her husband even for a day, unless it is impossible for her to accompany him. I heard her rebuke a wife one day who announced her intention of going to Europe, leaving her husband and children at home; and I am not sure, after Mrs. McKinley's remarks, that the lady had the heart to carry out her plans.

Traphes Bryant, keeper of the White House kennels, recalls a different tradition:

Scratch almost any President and you will find a bit of a lady's man. Even McKinley, with his reputation as a stiff neck, had a fine eye for the ladies. When he was President, he supposedly taught a parrot to tell the difference between men and women. Every time a female approached the parrot would shriek: "Look at the pretty girl!" But McKinley didn't need a parrot to tell him.

Unmerry Christmas

The Hardings seemed to love a good time and gave many parties. Publicly they were gregarious. They surrounded themselves with other people and rarely dined alone. But the tensions began to build up after their first year in the White House. Florence Harding strove for perfection in everything she did, to make up for her husband's laxity. She worried about aging, since she was older than her husband, and had a specialist visit the White House every day to give her a facial. She drove herself to appear gay even when she did not feel well. She nagged Harding relentlessly, trying to get him to apply himself to business. They quarreled so much that it became a matter of common gossip throughout Washington. Mrs. Harding complained piteously to a White House maid that her husband was "ungrateful" for all she had done for him and acted as if he thought he didn't need her anymore. An observer noted that she was "at all times jealous and most times suspicious" of Harding.

One day the President accidentally met a friend taking a shortcut across the rear White House lawn. Harding, in a melancholy mood, confided that his life had been unhappy and empty. "And he cried," the dismayed friend recalled. Charles Forbes was invited to share the Hardings' first Christmas in the White House, but when he arrived he was greeted with a scowl. "This is a hell of a Christmas," Harding growled at him. "What is the matter?" asked the startled Forbes. "Everything's the matter," the President complained, stalking away. The White House doctor, Charles Sawyer, who had also been invited for Christmas dinner, signaled to Forbes behind the President's back. "They had a hell of a row this morning," Sawyer muttered under his breath, warning Forbes to be extra charming at dinner.

Mother-in-law

Eleanor Roosevelt's relationship with Franklin's mother was a lifelong trial and an uneven struggle. All her married life Eleanor had to take second place to the formidable Sara Delano Roosevelt, who ruled the family with her money and personality. She spoiled and bribed her grandchildren with expensive presents. Until she moved to Washington, Eleanor never had a home she could call her own. Finally, for a few years, at least, the White House would be her place. But Sara descended on Washington almost immediately to offer advice to her son about running the country. Then she began to criticize her daughter-in-law for the domestics she hired and for running her household differently from her own at Hyde Park. One of these arguments took place in front of a maid, who overheard Eleanor stating in a tense but firm voice something she must have long wanted to say:

"Mother, I have never told you this before, but I must tell you now. You run your house your way, and I'll run mine."

Let Them Eat Cake

People who were surprised by Jacqueline Kennedy's marriage to Aristotle Onassis were not aware of her dissatisfaction with her previous role. Journalist Fred Sparks commented in his book about the first year of her marriage to the Greek tycoon:

Her life with Ari is concocted of such pure, fairy-tale glamour that she must remember life in the White House, and her husband's eternal concern with social problems, as a big fat bore. One time one of Jackie's oldest friends said: "Jackie has the social consciousness of Louis XIV."

John Kennedy did not have Ari's ability to leave his troubles in the office. The talkative members of the White House domestic staff often whispered, in the corridors and employees' mess, that when Mr. and Mrs. Kennedy dined alone, the President would often complain and groan about his tremendous responsibilities and problems, from the first bite of food to the last sip of coffee. This really nettled Jackie, who never felt that she was married to the faceless electorate. In fact, she was more than somewhat jealous of the people of the United States. She simply could not regard national problems as her problems. One night, according to a gossipy White House butler, just when a succulent roast had been served, the President suddenly exclaimed, dead serious: "What in hell am I ever going to do about air pollution?"

Disgusted, Jackie said: "It's very simple, my dear. Get the Air Force to spray our industrial centers with Chanel Number Five."

OTHER WOMEN

Father of His Country

Gossip about the amorous proclivities and sexual peccadilloes of Presidents and of presidential candidates began, appropriately enough, with George Washington, who was said to have been father of the nation in more than just a metaphorical sense. In a recent book titled, Rumor!, *Hal Morgan and Kerry Tucker more or less clear the General's name:*

Four separate slanderous attacks were made on Washington during his illustrious career. The first concerned a letter he allegedly sent a friend, inviting him to Mount Vernon and mentioning the attractions of a certain slave girl as an inducement. The letter has never been brought to light, and the witnesses who claimed to have seen it always turned out to be of the third hand so common in rumors. A second rumor claimed that Washington had kept up an affair with a New Jersey woman named Mary Gibbons while he headquartered in New York during the Revolution. According to this rumor, Washington regularly rowed across the Hudson River at night to visit her. The stories sometimes went a step further to allege that Miss Gibbons had been a British spy and had received important information from Washington during their trysts. That the story was first promoted as a Tory pamphlet is indication enough of its falsity. Another rumor connected Washington with an illegitimate son who became a well-known officer in the Continental Army. According to this tale, Washington was only eighteen when he fathered the boy, and he made good his mistake by paying for the child's education. Washington did actually fund the education of several young men, but if he was the father of all of them he must have been a busy ladies' man. Another rumor about Washington's immoral relations with his slaves was started by an angry army officer, Major General Charles Lee, after his court-martial for unnecessary retreat in battle. In his humiliation, Lee managed to strike a real blow at General Washington, for the rumor stuck. With added embellishments—such as the assertion that numerous children survived to tell the story—the rumor persisted, and it is still in circulation after nearly two hundred years.

Friendship

There was, however, another woman who commanded Washington's affections throughout his life. Through his half brother, Lawrence, the sixteen-year-old George came to know Colonel William Fairfax, who managed almost five million acres of a Virginia land grant for his cousin, Lord Fairfax of Leeds. Young Washington often visited his house at Belvoir, which was conveniently close to Mount Vernon. There he fell under the spell of the Colonel's wife, Sally, a witty woman two years older and several decades more sophisticated than George. Sally taught the future President to dance, to dress properly, and they performed together the lead roles in Addison's turgid tragedy, *Cato*.

Little was known about this relationship until 1877, when two of Washington's letters to Mrs. Fairfax were published by the *New York Herald Tribune*. Both of them are dated following his engagement to Martha Dandrige, and yet reveal a romantic attachment to Sally. Another eighty-one of his letters to her were published in 1886, but none of hers survived to establish the exact nature of their relationship. What Washington did not burn himself, Martha destroyed after his death. Public curiosity reached another peak in the 1920s, when financier J. P. Morgan announced that he had bought some of George Washington's letters, but burned them after finding them "smutty."

During the Revolutionary War, Belvoir was burned down, the estate was lost, and the Fairfaxes moved back to England, where William died in 1787. His widow lived in genteel poverty at Bath until 1811. George and Sally Fairfax's friendship continued after he married Martha, and indeed to the end of his life. The year before he died, Washington wrote to her:

"So many important events have occurred, and such changes in men and things have taken place as the compass of a letter would give you but an inadequate idea of. None of which events, nor all of them together have been able to eradicate from my mind the recollection of those happy moments, the happiest of my life, which I have enjoyed in your company."

Disgust

The presidential campaign in 1800 was one of the most sordid in American history. Both Federalist candidates (John Adams and Charles Cotesworth Pinckney) and the two Republicans (Thomas Jefferson and Aaron Burr) were smeared and covered with mud from top to bottom. Abigail Adams declared that she had "heard so many lies and falsehoods propagated to answer electioneering purposes that I am disgusted with the world." Her husband, the sitting President, managed to keep his sense of humor. When he heard the slander that he had sent General Thomas Pinckney (brother of Charles) to procure four mistresses, two for each Federalist candidate, he commented: "I do declare if this be true, General Pinckney has kept them all for himself and cheated me out of my two."

Taboo

The attacks on Thomas Jefferson after his election grew even more vicious. His enemies began circulating stories about liaisons he had with two married women while he was Minister to France in the 1780s. James Thomson Callender, a Scottish-born muckraking journalist, published in the *Richmond Recorder* in 1802–1803 the most damaging accusations about Jefferson's secret relationships, which have been the staple of controversy among historians ever since. One claim, that Jefferson had incurred the enmity of Virginia Senator John Walker by repeated attempts to seduce his wife, was almost certainly libelous. More widely accepted is Callender's charge that Jefferson had sired five children by Sally Hemings, his slave. "The African Venus," he wrote, "is said to officiate as a housekeeper at Monticello." Later he wrote an editorial that was as long on racism as it was short on math:

"Put the case that every white man in Virginia has done as much as Thomas Jefferson has done toward the utter destruction of its happiness, that eight thousand whites had each of them been the father of mulatto children. Thus you have four hundred thousand mulattoes in addition to the present swarm. The country would no longer be habitable, till after a civil war, and a series of massacres. We all know with absolute certainty that the continent has as many white people as could eat the whole race before breakfast."

Other pro-Federalist papers took up the story with glee. Joseph Dennie, editor of *The Port Folio*, in Philadelphia, wrote a satirical version of "Yankee Doodle," "supposed to have been written by the Sage of Monticello," with an opening stanza:

> Of all the damsels on the green
> On mountain, or in valley,
> A lass so luscious ne'er was seen
> As Monticellian Sally—
>
> *Chorus*: Yankee Doodle, who's the noodle?
> What wife was half so handy?
> To breed a flock of slaves for stock.
> A black amour's the dandy. . . .

The legend that Jefferson's mistress and two of their daughters were sold at a New Orleans auction, fictionalized in *Clotel; or, The President's Daughter* by William Wells Brown in 1853, is accepted by some black historians as factual, while those for whom Jefferson embodies the whole system of American values reject the Sally Hemings story entirely as a libelous fabrication. In her controversial history of the third President, Fawn Brodie considers it unlikely that Jefferson remained a celibate widower from the age of thirty-nine, and traces a pattern in his attraction to women who were in some way forbidden or taboo. She defends his relationship with Sally Hemings not as the "scandalous debauchery with an innocent slave victim as the Federalists and later the abolitionists insisted, but rather a serious passion that brought Jefferson and the slave woman much private happiness over a period lasting thirty-eight years."

All in the Family

In 1873, Madison Hemings, claiming to be Jefferson's son by Sally Hemings, published a brief memoir in the Pike County (Ohio) Republican, *which describes how the Hemings family was already interrelated with Jefferson's in-laws:*

Thos. Jefferson was a visitor at the "great house" of John Wales, who had children about his own age. He formed the acquaintance of his daughter Martha (I believe that was her name, though I am not positively sure), an intimacy sprang up between them which ripened into love, and they were married. They afterwards went to live at his country seat Monticello, and in course of time had born to them a daughter whom they named Martha. About the same time she was born my mother, the second daughter of John Wales and Elizabeth Hemings, was born. On the death of John Wales, my grandmother, his concubine, and her children by him fell to Martha, Thomas Jefferson's wife, and consequently became the property of Thomas Jefferson, who in the course of time became famous, and was appointed Minister to France during our revolutionary troubles, or soon after independence was gained. About the time of the appointment and before he was ready to leave the country his wife died, and as soon after her interment as he could attend to and arrange his domestic affairs in accordance with the changed circumstances of his family in consequence with this misfortune (I think not more than three weeks thereafter), he left for France, taking his eldest daughter with him. He had had sons born to him, but they died in early infancy, so he then had but two children—Martha and Maria. The latter was left at home, but was afterwards ordered to follow him to France. She was three years or so younger than Martha. My mother accompanied her as her body servant. When Mr. Jefferson went to France Martha was a young woman grown, my mother was about her age, and Maria was just budding into womanhood. Their stay (my mother's and Maria's) was about eighteen months. But during that time my mother became Mr. Jefferson's concubine, and when he was called back home she was *enceinte* by him. He desired to bring my mother back to Virginia with him but she demurred. She was just beginning to understand the French language well, and in France she was free, while if she returned to Virginia she would be re-enslaved. So she refused to return with him. To induce her to do so he promised her extraordinary privileges, and made a solemn pledge that her children should be freed at the age of twenty-one years. In consequence of his promises, on which she implicitly relied, she returned with him to Virginia. Soon after their arrival, she gave birth to a child, of whom Thomas Jefferson was the father. It lived but a short time. She gave birth to four others, and Jefferson was the father of all of them. Their names were Beverly, Harriet, Madison (myself), and Eston—three sons and one daughter. We all became free agreeably to the treaty entered into by our parents before we were born. We all married and have raised families.

Presidents and the Ladies

Chief Usher Ike Hoover, who served under nine Presidents, summed up the attitudes of eight of them to women as follows:

Harrison enjoyed the company of Mrs. Dimmick and often went walking with her.

Cleveland had no interest in any lady other than Mrs. Cleveland. He idolized her, thought of her as a child, was tender and considerate with her.

McKinley acted the part of a martyr. He gave thought to no one but his invalid wife.

Roosevelt was a man's man, through and through. Ladies had no place in his mind.

Taft was a ladies' man, pure and simple.

Wilson was a great admirer of the ladies, but very discriminating. He liked their company better than that of men.

Harding was a sporting ladies' man.

Coolidge had nothing to do with the ladies.

Campaign Issue

Ike Hoover's comment on Grover Cleveland ignores the terrible scandal of the 1884 presidential campaign which threatened to bury the second bachelor to run for the White House:

On July 21, the *Buffalo Evening Telegraph* came out with a big headline: A TERRIBLE TALE: A DARK CHAPTER IN A PUBLIC MAN'S HISTORY. The *Telegraph* subtitled its tale "The Pitiful Story of Maria Halpin and Governor Cleveland's Son," and went on to reveal that as a young man Grover the Good had taken up with a thirty-six-year-old Buffalo widow, had a son by her, and had since provided financial support for the two of them. The *Telegraph* even knew the boy's name: Oscar Folsom Cleveland.

Cleveland's friends were stunned by the revelation. But when they approached him, Cleveland admitted the story was basically true (though the *Telegraph* had added a few embellishments); asked how to handle it in the campaign, he said stolidly: "Above all, tell the truth." The Democrats then took the line that the real issue of the campaign was public integrity, not private misconduct. But Cleveland's enemies didn't see it that way. "We do not believe," wrote Charles A. Dana solemnly in the *New York Sun*, "that the American people will knowingly elect to the presidency a coarse debauchee who would bring his harlots with him to Washington and hire lodgings for them convenient to the White House." The *New York Sun* and the *New York Tribune* could scarcely think of words strong enough to convey their contempt for Cleveland: "rake," "libertine," "father of a bastard," "a gross and licentious man," a "moral leper," "a man stained with disgusting infamy," "worse in moral quality than a pickpocket, a sneak thief, or a Cherry Street debauchee, a wretch unworthy of respect or confidence."

But Maria's Cleveland had his defenders. The *Nation*'s E. L. Godkin compared the Buffalonian to Benjamin Franklin and Alexander Hamilton—talented but wayward—and insisted Cleveland would make a far better President than a wheeler-dealer like Blaine. And one Mugwump, comparing the privately conventional but politically dishonest Blaine with the publicly trustworthy but privately wayward Cleveland, concluded: "We should therefore elect Mr. Cleveland to public office which he is so well qualified to fill and remand Mr. Blaine to the private station he is admirably fitted to adorn." The Republicans had fun chanting, "Ma! Ma! Where's my pa?" But after the election the Democrats retorted: "Gone to the White House. Ha! Ha! Ha!"

Halo

Warren Harding was known as the man who could not say no—whether to women or to his cronies. He was selected as Republican candidate in the proverbial smoke-filled room during the deadlocked 1920 convention in Chicago. One of his ardent supporters, Senator Boies Penrose, lying sick in Philadelphia, was told by phone about Harding's nomination. His informant relayed also the worry that some of the power brokers expressed about the candidate's weakness for women. "No worries about that," Penrose declared. "We'll just throw a halo around his handsome head and everything will be all right!"

Harding's Luck

Some of the political scandals that engulfed and eventually killed President Harding became known before his mysterious death in August 1923. Details of his affairs were much slower to come to light, partly because Mrs. Harding spent several weeks after his death burning his letters and files. But in 1927 a young woman called Nan Britton privately published a book, The President's Daughter, *about the illegitimate child she bore during a long-standing relationship with Warren Harding. In the early 1960s, biographer Francis Russell discovered that Harding had an even longer affair with another woman, married to an Ohio merchant. When Mrs. Harding lay ill with a serious kidney ailment, the Senator from Ohio brought one of his mistresses to Washington to console him. Writes Francis Russell in his* Shadow of Blooming Grove:

In the pride of having this desirable young woman on his own he seemed to forget caution, strolling with her down Pennsylvania Avenue as he chewed gum and pointed out the sights. She registered at various hotels—the New Ebbitt, the Raleigh—still as Miss Elizabeth N. Christian. Sometimes evenings he took her to his office in the Senate Office Building and made love to her there. It was in that somewhat statutory atmosphere, late in January 1919, that she conceived. Harding had long been convinced that he could never become a father. "No such luck!" he used to tell Nan, and had become increasingly careless about using contraceptives. "And of course," as Nan put it, "the Senate offices do not provide preventive facilities for use in such emergencies."

Monkey Business

Eleanor and Franklin Roosevelt formed one of the great partnerships in American politics. Yet their marriage was marred forever by Franklin's affair with Lucy Mercer, as described by James, the eldest of the Roosevelt children, in his book about his parents:

She was twenty-two, dark-haired, graceful, and attractive, a lovely young lady by all accounts, when she came to work for mother. When mother was away, Lucy stayed to help with mother's business, and father, as is apparent from his letters at the time, began to make excuses for not joining mother when he was expected. Evidently mother began to be suspicious, and her fears were fed by gossip of her relatives. As mischievous as ever, Alice Roosevelt Longworth encouraged the affair by having father and Lucy to dinner when mother was out of town. Alice later said, "It was good for Franklin. He deserved a good time. He was married to Eleanor."

In June of 1917, father commissioned a naval yacht, the *Sylph*, for a short pleasure cruise and included Lucy in the party. Arriving by small boat, mother later joined the cruise. Shortly after what must have been an awkward cruise, Lucy enlisted in the navy as a woman volunteer. However, father had her assigned to his office as a yeoman and she shortly joined him on another cruise, one that mother missed. Lucy's tour of service duty ended abruptly when she was discharged that fall by special order of the secretary of the navy as a "hardship case" because of the death of her father, although she was neither living with him nor responsible for him. In response to a pointed demand by mother, father had put in an appearance at Campobello that summer, and mother, playing up to Sara [Franklin's mother], apparently enlisted her help in seeking to put an end to father's affair with Lucy. But it was not that easily ended, it seems.

In the summer of 1918 father went to Europe for the Navy Department. On his return in September, he came down with pneumonia. Mother took care of him and in going through his papers discovered love letters from Lucy. Confronted with these, father could no longer deny the affair, as he apparently had up till then.

[My brother] Elliott and others speak of this as the only hard evidence mother had, but in fact—and it has been a rather well-kept secret—there came to light during this time a register from a motel in Virginia Beach showing that father and Lucy had checked in as man and wife and spent the night.

Crisis

Eleanor Roosevelt never mentions this crisis in her published autobiographies, but Joseph Lash, who was close to her, describes what must have gone on inside her:

Her world seemed to break into pieces. After her wedding there had been a period of total dependency and insecurity from which she had slowly begun to emancipate herself. But Franklin's love was the anchor to which her self-confidence and self-respect were secured, and now the anchor was cut. The thought tortured Eleanor that having borne him six children, she was now being discarded for a younger, prettier, gayer woman—that her husband's love belonged to someone else. The bottom, she wrote, dropped out of her world. She confronted her husband with Lucy's letters. She was prepared to give her husband his freedom, she told him, if after thinking over what the consequences might be for the children he still wanted to end their marriage.

He soon discovered that divorce might have disagreeable consequences in addition to the effect upon the children. Sara was said to have applied pressure with the threat to cut him off if he did not give up Lucy. If Franklin was in any doubt about what a divorce might do to his political career, Louis Howe was there to enlighten him. Lucy, a devout Catholic, drew back at the prospect of marriage to a divorced man with five children. Eleanor gave him a choice—if he did not break off with Lucy she would insist on a divorce. Franklin and Lucy agreed never to see each other again.

Solace

Lucy was with FDR when he died in 1945. Eleanor Roosevelt never got over the hurt that Franklin's infidelity caused her. One of the people she turned to for comfort and love was a reporter, Lorena Hickok, who remained her friend for thirty years. The closeness of their relationship went unsuspected until May 1, 1978. Exactly ten years after Miss Hickok's death, and in accordance with her wishes, the Franklin D. Roosevelt Library in Hyde Park made public all her papers, including more than two thousand letters from Eleanor Roosevelt. Doris Faber, who first realized the significance of those letters, wrote a sensitive biography of Lorena Hickok, whom Eleanor called Hick. She shows how the connection between the two women suddenly ripened in the three weeks between the attempt on Franklin's life, in Miami on February 15, and his inauguration on March 4, 1933:

Probably Eleanor Roosevelt confided to Hick then about his affair with Lucy Mercer, which, fifteen years later, still tortured her.

Furthermore, it appears that as Franklin reached ever closer to *his* goal of the presidency, his wife was increasingly distraught by the prospect of having to bear new constraints on *her* hard-won independence; she even seems to have contemplated leaving her husband. Thus Hick's sympathy, personally and patriotically, would have been overwhelming.

But despite many uncertainties that can never be resolved, one fact must now be recorded. Just a few weeks after returning from Ithaca on March 4, 1933, when the forty-eight-year-old Eleanor Roosevelt did become the First Lady, she was wearing the same sapphire ring with which an opera singer had rewarded an enthusiastic young reporter many years earlier. And from the White House three days afterward, on Lorena Hickok's fortieth birthday, E.R. wrote to her:

> Hick darling, All day I've thought of you & another birthday I will be with you. . . . Oh! I want to put my arms around you, I ache to hold you close. Your ring is a great comfort. I look at it & think she does love me or I wouldn't be wearing it!

Statue Therapy

Despite Eleanor Roosevelt's new responsibilities in the limelight, the two women managed to get away to spend time together. One morning, following Eleanor's instructions, Hick appeared in a taxi at a side entrance to the Mayflower Hotel at 7:45, and, as Doris Faber continues:

Mrs. Roosevelt slipped out without being observed. First she told the driver to take them along R Street so she could show Hick the house where she had been so unhappy fifteen years earlier, upon discovering her husband's infidelity. But as they approached it, she saw a large sign on the lawn identifying this property as the former residence of the new President. Shaking her head, she asked the driver to proceed to the Rock Creek Cemetery.

Hick sensed that her companion did not want to talk, and contained her own curiosity. When they reached the cemetery,

Mrs. R. directed the driver through a maze of winding roads until they came to a clump of bushes through which Hick spied a large bronze statue. They left the cab to walk around in front of the bronze figure. Then they sat down on a curved stone bench facing it, still without speaking.

It was the figure of a seated woman, considerably larger than life-size, her body enveloped in the folds of a robe extending up over her head, leaving only the face visible. To Hick, as to so many others before and since, the expression on the face of the Saint-Gaudens "Grief"—more usually called the Adams Memorial because Henry Adams had commissioned it in memory of his wife—was incredibly beautiful. As Hick looked at it, she felt that all the sorrow humanity had ever endured was expressed in that face. She could almost feel the hot, stinging unshed tears behind the lowered eyelids. Yet in that expression there was something almost triumphant. There was a woman who had experienced every kind of pain, every kind of suffering known to humankind, and had come out of it serene and compassionate. Hick found herself thinking that whatever bitter unhappiness, whatever agony of body and soul she herself was going through, that woman had also known and would understand.

Mrs. R. clearly felt some of this, too, and when she broke the silence it was to say that during her stormy period, when she had been much younger and not so very wise, sometimes she had been very unhappy and [felt] sorry for herself. "When I was feeling that way," she said, "if I could manage it, I'd come out here, alone, and sit and look at that woman. And I'd always come away somehow feeling better."

Ike Liked Her

During World War II, a romance developed between General Eisenhower and his attractive Irish driver, Kay Summersby. In her book-length account, published after both were dead, she described what was ultimately a frustrated relationship:

Ike was smoking one cigarette after another—lighting one from the tip of the last, then throwing the stub into the fire. "I thought about you a lot," he said. "You know what I like to think about nights before I go to sleep?"

I shook my head.

"The first time I ever set eyes on you. I saw you walking along Grosvenor Square. You looked very glamorous. Beautiful. And all of a sudden, you started running straight toward me. It was as if you had read my mind. Then you stopped. All out of breath. And asked if one of us was General Eisenhower. Well! I thought I was dreaming. You would never believe how disappointed I was to discover that Claridge's was so close to headquarters. I wanted that drive to last forever."

"You never told me that," I said.

"You know me," he protested. "There are so many times I look at you and want to tell you how beautiful you are and how much you mean to me, but something always stops me. I suppose it's this stolid German-Swiss heritage of mine that makes me feel a man should not talk about such things. For God's sake, there were months when I could not let myself face how I felt about you. I used to think that if I had a daughter I would want her to be just like you. It took a disaster to ram the truth home to me. I had to nearly lose you before I could admit to myself that my feelings were more than paternal."

I suspect over the years—long before Ike and I ever set foot in Telegraph Cottage—many couples had sat in front of its fire and whispered confidences to each other. There was something about the atmosphere of that little house that bred intimacy and trust. It was easy to talk about all the things that one had never spoken of before. Of secret fears. Of past mistakes. Of withering sorrows.

It was in that living room one sunny morning that Ike talked very seriously and at length about his relationship with his wife. There was deep hurt on both sides, hurt so deep that they were never able to recapture their earlier relationship—although it was not for want of trying. Ike had applied himself the wisdom he had shared with me that "activity helps"; had thrown himself so completely into his work that there was room for nothing else. It was hard for him to tell the story, even in the benign atmosphere of Telegraph Cottage. He would say a few words, then halt. His voice was low. Most of the time he was leaning forward in his chair looking down at the floor.

"Kay, I guess I'm telling you that I'm not the lover you should have. It killed something in me. Not all at once, but little by little. For years I never thought of making love. And then when I did . . . when it had been on my mind for weeks, I failed. I failed you, my dearest. Didn't I?"

I sat on the arm of his chair and cuddled his head against my breast. "It's all right. It's all right," I crooned to him the way my mother used to soothe me when I was a child. "I love you. It's all right."

He straightened up, took out his handkerchief, and honked into it. His eyes were red. "I'm sorry. I'm a damned fool. But you know that. God, I don't know what's the matter with me."

"Nothing. Nothing at all," I whispered.

"Somehow I just lost the way," he said, standing with his back to me looking out the window.

"Someday things will be different," I promised him. "I'm not Irish and stubborn for nothing."

Sorry, No Sex, We're British

John F. Kennedy amazed friends, aides, fellow politicians, and newspapermen with the seemingly offhanded way with which he did little to hide his inordinate appetite for women. Newspapermen covering a summit conference in 1962 in Nassau, the Bahamas, couldn't believe their ears as he chatted informally to two very proper Englishmen. The Englishmen were none other than Prime Minister Harold Macmillan and his even more proper Foreign Minister, R. A. B. Butler. The elder statesmen were at the end of a tiring official function and were clustered together having a whiskey as the affair broke up. Clusters of newsmen were around them. One agency reporter recalls:

"Jack was very good with the press on these outings. He always made sure we were looked after and he would always leave us with a couple of quotes at the end of a dull function so we would have something to file. Well, we were in a group around Jack and Mac and RAB. We were in a knot about three feet away, scared to break into their conversation lest old Mac give us the chill. Anyway there was this very attractive lady, a government official, or maybe she was a reporter, I can't remember. Jack gave her the eye and as Mac and RAB raised their eyebrows in amazement as if to say: 'What's the matter with you, my dear Mr. President, is there anything wrong with the lady?' Jack comes out and says: 'You know, it's funny, but if I go too long without a woman, I get a headache, quite bad ones, isn't that strange?'

"Well, old Mac and RAB looked like they had been hit by a baseball bat between the eyes. Mac pretended he didn't hear anything and RAB started to cough and went on to another subject.

"Jack wasn't to be sidetracked. He just stared more at the girl and said: 'Lord, isn't she gorgeous?' Mac and RAB quickly scuttled off. Jack turned to us, gave us a cheery few words, kept on giving the girl the eye. She by now was the color of her lipstick. He then gave us a knowing wink and swirled out of the hall, chuckling to himself. He was an irresistible guy, like that."

Take Two, and Call in the Morning

President Kennedy took precautions that he would not be caught with a headache on any of his trips. There were always numerous pools of secretaries to select from when he hit the campaign trail or had to travel on state business. Many old-time Kennedy aides remember with some humor that some of the secretaries in the various pools had to be among the world's worst typists, with shorthand that was virtually nonexistent.

British director Jonathan Miller, who was a White House favorite and familiar sight around the Capital during those heady Camelot years, remembers the secretary pools well: "They were all attractive but not the sex-siren types," he says, "scrubbed, charming, and very virtuous-looking. Like unused tennis balls—they still had the fuzz on them."

Two of those "unused tennis balls" were more frequently seen than the others. Once again Jack Kennedy seemed to take few steps to hide the fact that as secretaries they would have made better mechanics. So familiar in fact were the two that the Secret Service men had a code name for them. The bustier of the two girls, both in their early twenties, was nicknamed, according to reports, "Fiddle" and the other, a slim girl with short blond hair, was called "Faddle."

"Fiddle" and "Faddle" were with the President for about ten months during 1962. They were assigned separate sleeping quarters as close to the President as possible. Whether it was in Los Angeles, New York, Chicago, or even at the Kennedy compound in Palm Beach, "Fiddle" and "Faddle" were there. They never had any contact with the press apart from a curt, formal smile and maybe a few words of vacuous pleasantry. But if the President ever left a room, they scurried after him like little Yorkshire terriers.

"Fiddle" and "Faddle" will probably go down in history as the country's only walking headache cures.

The Prince and the Showgirl

One of John Kennedy's most famous affairs was a brief fling with Marilyn Monroe, who was much more seriously interested in his brother Bobby. Asked about her first encounter with the President, who was in almost constant pain because of his war wounds, the sex goddess told a friend: "I made his back feel a lot better."

Dirty Old Man

The most recent President with an eye for the ladies was Lyndon Johnson, though much of it was for show, as Lady Bird knew well. Socialite Barbara Howar left a telling portrait of them in her book, Laughing All the Way:

Regardless of his moods, I came to enjoy Johnson's electric personality, and if his amorous gestures toward me were disconcerting, they were also flattering. Mine became the dilemma of

122

befriending a First Lady and her daughters while simultaneously fending off the advances of the man most important in their lives.

It was actually Mrs. Johnson who averted any confrontation between me and her husband. She was a woman of keen insight coupled with years of experience with Johnson's roving eye. She knew precisely when and how to interfere in his flirtations, a practice for her that bordered upon a second calling. She had already been forced to deal politely with several female employees whom Johnson fancied, and she was alert to keep me off the White House statistics list. When the President detained me too long in another room, Mrs. Johnson would call out: "Lyndon, don't be a hog, we all want to talk to you and Barbara"; or on the dance floor, where the President would become most ardent, she would approach him firmly, as she did the night of Johnson's Inaugural Ball. He and I had been dancing for fifteen minutes, he draped around my neck like a fox fur, and I, not realizing protocol prohibited another partner from breaking in, was loving it but petrified that the President of the United States was "stuck" with me. "Now, Lyndon," she said, "I know a young girl who is very tired and a President who has a mighty big day tomorrow." With a steely grip, Lady Bird would lead Lyndon Johnson home, a tactic that may not always have been successful given Johnson's passion for women and having his own way. I only know it worked for me, and while I am not suggesting that the thirty-sixth President of the United States was a dirty old man, I would not bet the rent money that he was not.

Hypothetical Question

It was during the Truman administration, in the early days of celebrity quiz shows on television, that Margaret Chase Smith, the Senator from Maine, was asked: "It is well known that you don't want to be President, but just suppose you woke up one fine morning and found yourself in the White House—what would you do?" "Well," said Senator Smith without much hesitation, "I'd try to find Mrs. Truman to apologize and then I'd go straight home."

5

HOMELIFE

FAMILY

Children First

Maria Monroe was one day in her father's office, during his presidency, when William H. Crawford came in, urging something on Mr. Monroe which he wanted time to consider. Crawford insisted with vehemence on its being done at once; saying, at last, "I will not leave this room till my request is granted."

"You will not?" exclaimed the President, starting up and seizing the poker. "You will now leave the room, or you will be thrust out."

Crawford was not long in making his exit.

Nagging Father

In one of his letters, written to his daughter Martha when she was still a child, Thomas Jefferson expressed his desire to have her dance three days in the week from eleven until one. In another letter he begs her to be tidy in appearance, in the morning as well as in the evening, and never to allow herself to be seen carelessly attired by anyone, especially by gentlemen, who, as a class, generally despise slovenliness.

Her Father's Companion

Maria Jefferson, who was much more beautiful than her sister, was so shy and reticent that she failed to make friends readily, while Martha always produced a pleasing impression in every circle that she entered by the charm of her manners and conversation. In her own home Maria, or Polly, as her father usually called her, was most engaging. The Duc de la Rochefoucauld, who visited Monticello in 1796, when Mr. Jefferson's youngest daughter was his inseparable companion, shrewdly remarked: "Miss Maria constantly resides with her father; but as she is seventeen years old, and is remarkably handsome, she will doubtless soon find that there are duties which it is sweeter to perform than those of a daughter."

A Great Favorite

Benjamin Stoddert was a great favorite of the President, and Mrs. Stoddert came in for a share of friendliness from Mrs. Abigail Adams, the good lady even carrying her attentions so far as to offer her "some drops" at one of her drawing rooms, "taking it into her head from my pale looks," said Mrs. Stoddert, "that I was going to faint, which brought a little red to my cheeks."

Elizabeth, the Stodderts' daughter, writing in January 1800 to Miss Lowndes, gives a pleasant picture of Mrs. Adams ministering to the sweet tooth of the Stoddert family: "I must not omit to tell you that though mamma has not been as yet to wait on Mrs. Adams, that good and handsome old lady called to see her this afternoon, with her daughter, Mrs. Smith, and brought more plum-cake for the children than all of them could eat. You may be sure after this she is a great favorite of the whole family."

Prodigal Son

The only permanent cloud on Dolley Madison's crowded social horizon was her wastrel son from her first marriage. Neglected by his busy parents as a child, at the age of twenty-one he was sent to Europe on a diplomatic mission by his stepfather. There he quickly acquired the reputation of a playboy and was called the Prince of America. What made it more difficult for his mother, according to one of her nineteenth-century biographers, was the fact that they remained on ostensibly close terms while he heaped fresh disasters on her:

Payne Todd's life represents a melancholy picture of wasted opportunities, of grace and charm blurred and at last obliterated by gluttony and dissipation, of demonstrative affection transformed into filial indifference and ingratitude by long years of self-indulgence. Yet, while this undutiful son was doing all in his power to break his mother's heart, he persuaded himself that he loved her and intended to do much, but always in the future, to make her happy. When his debts had made necessary the sale of Montpelier and its slaves, he soothed his regrets by building on his estate nearby, known as Toddsbirth, a strange conglomeration of cottages, one of which he intended for his mother's occupancy, and so arranged that by one of its long windows she could enter a great tower wherein he had planned a ballroom and state dining apartment. Of course lack of funds prevented the completion of this eccentric home, as well as the carrying out of his scheme for a silk farm, for which, after his usual unbusinesslike fashion, he had brought over from France a number of silk manufacturers before even planting mulberry trees or hatching silkworms.

His appetite he gratified as freely as his whims; and while Mrs. Madison and her devoted niece were struggling to secure the bare necessities of life, or dependent upon the bounty of comparative strangers, Payne Todd was in the habit of sending to Europe for rare cheeses and other table luxuries. As a result of his free indulgence, his face became bloated, and his figure shapeless, and so completely did his aspect change that few would have recognized in his sodden features and heavy form the alert, graceful, laughing-eyed lad who had entered manhood as "the Prince" with brighter prospects than any youth in America.

Daredevil

Colonel Crook, who started his lifelong career on the White House staff as Lincoln's bodyguard, describes some of the antics of President Garfield's son:

One of the first evidences I had that President Garfield's family had taken up their homelife in the White House occurred a few days after the fourth of March, 1881, when the new President was inaugurated. I happened to go on an errand which took me along the great corridor running through the main floor of the Executive Mansion. I was walking rapidly, thinking hard about the errand, looking neither to the right nor to the left, when suddenly, just as I reached the foot of the grand staircase leading to the living rooms of the President's family on the floor above, I was startled by a shrill cry of warning shouted in a boyish voice:

"Hoop-la!! Get off the track or you'll be run down!"

Without an instant's hesitation I sprang to one side, and as I did so quickly glanced upward. And there, perched on one of the old-fashioned bicycles with a high wheel, was President Garfield's young son Irvin, coasting down that staircase like lightning. In an instant he had reached the foot of it, "zipped" across the broad corridor, and with skill little short of marvelous turned into the East Room, the flashing steel spokes of his wheel vanishing like the tail of a comet.

I stood still for a moment and gasped. I confess that I was paralyzed for that moment. That any small boy, even a son of the President of the United States, would dare to start at the head of that great staircase on a bicycle and coast down it was almost unbelievable; and that he would do so as successfully as a trained circus performer was beyond my comprehension. These thoughts flared their way across my astonished brain in the fraction of a minute, and the next second I sprang forward to the door of the East Room to pick up the dismembered remains of Irvin Garfield. But it was not necessary. That enterprising American youngster was still on his high wheel and was treading it around and around the great East Room with evident satisfaction to himself, wholly regardless of two or three attendants who stood with their backs as close as they could get them to the wall, their faces gray with horror and apprehension, as the young human comet flashed past them in his orbit around and around the most magnificent apartment of state in the Western Hemisphere.

Grandpa

President Benjamin Harrison's grandchildren were called the "Baby McKees" and the "darlings of his heart." Mrs. McKee, the President's daughter, was a constant guest at the mansion, and the celebrations of Christmas for the benefit of little Benjamin and Mary Lodge were "as elaborate as any child would wish." Baby McKee, especially, was inseparable from Grandpa, and as a newspaper reported, "no picture of the President seemed complete without the twining arms of this little cherub about his neck." One day the baby was naughty and, climbing upon his indulgent grandfather's desk, touched in succession all its electric bells, and in a few minutes all the White House attendants rushed into the room to see what was the matter.

Kid Gloves

The eldest daughter of Edith and Theodore Roosevelt, who was universally called Princess Alice, dominated the Washington social life for more than seven decades. She was an original, who even as a child managed to shock hard-bitten journalists, such as the anonymous author of the following passage:

I remember a dinner at the White House one night, the first time I had been a guest of President Roosevelt. Alice wore a dress of her namesake blue, and long white kid gloves. I fairly gasped when I saw her eat asparagus with her fingers without removing her gloves! It may have been a bet or a dare, but it was probably just a perverse impulse, or perhaps there was present someone especially correct whom she wanted to shock! She was never in awe of the great, and parental discipline did not impose too rigid a regulation upon personal conduct.

Eccentricities

The unusual child grew into an unusual adult:

Alice Roosevelt had many of the privileges of a princess, without any of the restrictions. One night Mrs. Leitner gave a party. It was a large and gorgeous affair, with diplomats and officials and titles there. Few women were smoking then, and those who did kept it dark. In the middle of Mrs. Leitner's ball, Alice Longworth took it into her head to give an exhibition of the new dance, the turkey trot. But to add zest to the performance, she lit a cigarette first, and smoked while she danced. She sailed down the middle of the room, puffing little jets of smoke at the ceiling, to the horror of the women. As one of them said: "Alice looked like a steam engine coming down a crimped track."

One day a woman sat miserably talking about her health. She detailed her symptoms and their reactions, her sufferings and the heroic martyrdom which never permitted her pain to dim the happiness of her home. "Have you ever tried standing on your head?" asked Alice, leaning forward and betraying a sudden interest. The woman looked at her for a moment, uncertain whether or not to take offense. But there was not a flicker of a smile on that Roosevelt face. "It acts like a charm," she said. "Here, lend me a safety pin." She secured the hem of her skirt between her knees and, taking a cushion, placed it on the floor. The hypochondriac watched with bewildered interest.

Alice Longworth put her head on the cushion and shot her legs aloft, where she remained poised perfectly. Standing on her head and kicking at the chandeliers was a sort of daily exercise with her. The woman gasped and looked at the faces of the other guests—there were quite a number present. They all knew Alice, and being deeply rooted in respectable orthodoxy, they envied the woman her daring, because she could do it and get away with it. No other woman in that room could have stood on her head and retained such perfect equilibrium of body or composure of mind. "There, you try that every day, and you won't have lumbago or heart trouble," and she stood erect, returned the safety pin, and resumed her seat with leisurely ease.

Where Mommies Come From

Eleanor Wilson remembers how she and her sisters liked to question their parents about the time they first met. Woodrow Wilson once told them how he came to select their mother, Ellen: "I asked all the girls in the world to stand in a row, looked at them all, and I chose your mother."

Ineligible

Margaret Truman received her first invitation to a White House ball at the age of eleven. Her mother, Bess Truman, was puzzled and found out that there was a protocol directory on which Margaret was listed as an "eligible daughter" of the junior Senator from Missouri. Mrs. Truman sat down and wrote a polite note to Mrs. Roosevelt pointing out that she did not think Margaret was eligible for anything yet.

Hail to the Little Chief

At the first reception of the Kennedy administration for the Washington Diplomatic Corps, little Caroline watched from the grand staircase her parents greeting exotic-looking foreigners. The First Lady thought that a child would prefer to watch a party than hear about it afterward. The child's presence did not go unnoticed: after the Marine Band had played "Hail to the Chief," it struck up "Old MacDonald Had a Farm."

Where's Daddy?

Helen Thomas, often described as the First Lady of the Washington Press Corps, was the first to upstage political news out of the White House with stories about the President's family:

I had a field day with Caroline stories and so did other reporters. She captured national attention during the President-elect days when she wandered out onto the patio of Kennedy's Palm Beach villa during a news conference, wearing her pajamas, a robe, and her mother's high heels. "Where's my Daddy?" she asked a television technician. "He's over there, honey," the technician told her, pointing at Kennedy, who joined in the laughter.

Caroline and her brother, John, Jr., were the joy of Kennedy's life. He would come out of the Oval Office, clap his hands, and they would come running along with all their little friends. Kennedy liked to show them off, and even had photographs taken when Jackie was not around.

Caroline's most quoted remark was made when she was three years old and wandering around the White House. "Where's your Daddy?" she was asked.

"He's upstairs with his shoes and socks off, doing nothing," she said.

And Give Them Ten Percent

When the Johnsons moved into the White House, their daughters, Luci and Lynda, were teenagers. Fussing over them as they went out on dates, Lady Bird would remind them of the usual items, such as remembering to take a sweater. But now that the First Family was surrounded with Secret Service protection, she too had to remember to add: "And Luci, Lynda—don't forget to take your agents along."

I Just Work Here

Betty Ford's comment on "60 Minutes" that she wouldn't be surprised if her daughter, Susan, had an affair caused almost as much controversy as her husband's pardon of Richard Nixon. Although the majority of women polled supported her position, Betty Ford drew savage criticism from the right wing of the Republican party and people like Phyllis Schlafly. During a press briefing, White House spokesman Ron Nessen was asked how

Gerald Ford had reacted to his wife's remarks. He responded on the record: "The President has long ceased to be perturbed or surprised by his wife's remarks."

Bored Grandma

Miss Lillian, as Jimmy Carter's mother was affectionately known, joined the Peace Corps when she was already a grandmother. During her son's presidency she became known for her outspoken, homespun wit. White House correspondent Helen Thomas likes to quote Miss Lillian saying: "Sometimes when I look at my children, I wish I'd remained a virgin." Once, on a visit at the White House, she was asked how she was enjoying her stay in the nation's capital. "It's so boring," replied Miss Lillian. "When I'm in Washington I just feel like I'm waiting for Amy to come home from school."

Public Life

Amy Carter grew up in the limelight. Rosalynn Carter related an incident of her husband, then Governor of Georgia, telling the three-year-old Amy that he was taking her to the zoo. She ran up to her mother's room to ask her for a pencil to take along. When Rosalynn asked why she needed one, Amy replied: "To sign autographs."

FUN

A Children's Party

The children of Mr. and Mrs. Robert Tyler were often with them in Washington, and a fancy ball, given by the President to his eldest granddaughter, Mary Fairlie Tyler, was still recalled at the turn of the century by men and women who were among the guests of the evening.

Little Mary Tyler, representing a fairy with gossamer wings, a diamond star on her forehead, and a silver wand in her tiny hand, stood at the door of the East Room to welcome into Queen Titania's realm her delighted young friends. At this beautiful ball there were the usual number of flower girls and gypsy fortune-tellers. Miss Adele Cutts appearing as one of the former, and Miss Rosa Mordecai in the latter role, while the Señorita Almonte, daughter of the Mexican minister, represented an Aztec princess, and young Master Schermerhorn, of New York, an Albanian boy.

Girls Will Be Boys

Edith Roosevelt always gowned her children with comfort and utility. Her second daughter, Ethel, had lived in the White House about a month when girls of her own age and presumably of her own station began to call. But these little misses were clad like fairies in a play—satin skirts, knee-high, with silk stockings and slippers, and hats that looked like flower baskets. One such maiden came one Saturday and sat up prim and immaculate in the lower corridor, waiting until the White House attendant called her hostess. Ethel arrived on the scene rather breathless and disheveled. She had been down to the White House stables and was trying a new pony. The little guest explained that she came to make a visit and asked Ethel if she could play with the horses. "Play," said the President's daughter with horror, "play dressed up like that, while everybody would laugh at me? Go home and get on your everyday clothes and then we'll play."

Ethel's entrance into the White House caused considerable commotion. She arrived with her parents about four o'clock in the afternoon, a tall, rather awkward girl with bobbed hair and somewhat hoydenish ways of conducting herself. With her two brothers, Kermit and Archibald, she inspected her new home from roof to cellar, and then the trio turned their attention to the grounds. It was just getting dark when the children went into the park which fronts Pennsylvania Avenue, and the lamplighter, with his little ladder, was scampering up and down the posts. Ethel watched the proceeding with deep interest, and then and there she devised a new game. When the lighter would turn into a different avenue, up the post she would climb and turn off the light. The man was completely mystified, no sooner would one side of the park be illuminated when the other would be in darkness. Finally the watchman discovered the trouble, and from that first evening Ethel knew no more revels with her brothers. She was placed in the charge of a governess and was permitted to join no sports in which boys were actors.

Skittish

Just before Eleanor Roosevelt moved to Washington, she went to a farewell party given by one of her favorite causes, the Women's Trade Union League. She watched and laughed at skits which showed her giving pink teas to ladies at the White House, while secretly being the power behind the throne. Without losing her sense of humor, Mrs. Roosevelt stood up after one of the skits and declared: "There's one thing I won't do: I won't meddle in politics."

You Do Know How to Whistle?

Margaret Truman described her mother's athletic activities in her younger days:

She loved games, was a crack tennis player, and distinguished herself in boarding school by winning the shot put in a track meet. Her only comment on this last is that it has certainly come in handy as training for shaking hands with a thousand people at a time! It has also been reported that Mother could whistle through her teeth, play baseball, and beat all comers at mumblety-peg, but she has not been able to find later uses for these accomplishments.

Harry Gives Them Hell

One of the presidential perks is Air Force One, always ready to take off at the Chief Executive's command. Harry Truman took special delight in using the Sacred Cow, *as his plane was called. It was flown by Colonel Hank Myers:*

Truman was addicted to practical jokes and Myers delighted in assisting him whenever the opportunity arose. A memorable occasion came on Sunday, May 19, 1946, a day the President, on the spur of the moment, decided to fly home to visit his elderly mother at Independence.

It also happened to be a festive day in Washington. America had just entered the age of jet aircraft. Thousands of people were in the parks and on the rooftops to watch a dazzling air show by new P-80 fighter planes in the skies over the city. Truman, having given the press the slip, boarded the *Sacred Cow* at Bolling Air Field, across the Potomac from National Airport. With him were only two Secret Service agents. Myers took off quickly.

Moments after lift-off, the President came into the cockpit and looked out admiringly at the jet fighters swooping around Washington. As Myers related later to writer Seth Kantor in *Male* magazine, Truman said, "You know, Hank, those boys are putting on a fine show. They've given me—an idea. Mrs. Truman and Margaret are over there on top of our [White] House, and do you suppose we could . . . could we dive on them? Like a jet fighter? I've always wanted to try something like that."

"Well, there's no harm in it," Myers said to the President. "But somebody's sure gonna catch hell for it and I'm gonna blame you."

"I've got broad shoulders," Truman said. "How about it?"

Myers turned the *Sacred Cow* toward Washington, leveled off at 3,000 feet, and nosed the plane over the Washington Monument—already a violation of air security regulations. He had entered the zone encompassing the Capitol and the White House, which is out of bounds for air traffic.

"They can ground you for flying over it; they can take away

138

your license; for all I know, they can send you to the electric chair for it," Myers observed. "But so what? Even the President has to live a little."

He throttled up to full power and turned to Truman, strapped securely in a seat behind himself and copilot Elmer F. "Smitty" Smith.

"Now?" Truman asked excitedly.

"Now," replied Myers.

He set the *Sacred Cow* on a dive straight for the White House, the four engines screaming like buzz saws.

"We shot past 2,000 feet and I could see the handful of people on the Trumans' roof watching us stiffly. Down at 1,500 feet our angle was still steep and our noise was deafening. Past 1,000 feet—the flat, white target looked big, filling our whole world.

"At 500 feet, I had the *Cow* leveled and we roared over the White House roof wide open. I caught a split-second glimpse. Everyone there was frozen with fear and wonder.

"No one, least of all the Truman ladies, saw the President. But his face was pressed against the window; he was waving and laughing. They must have recognized the plane, though. Since it had been built in wartime, it didn't have any special markings or a presidential seal, but its tail number was clear to them— 2107451.

"We climbed up to 3,000 feet again, swooped, circled, and fell into another dive. Everybody was watching us. But this time, Margaret and her mother were jumping and waving. We shot past them at little below 500 feet and roared back upstairs once more. Then we went on as fast as we could toward Missouri. We'd buzzed the White House."

Just One of the Girls

Bess Truman was frankly bored by Washington social life and longed for the Tuesday Bridge Club of Independence, to which she had belonged for some twenty years back in Missouri. She caused a minor sensation when she invited the entire bridge club to stay at the White House. The Girls, as the plump matrons were called, lived it up on the presidential yacht, eating in the state dining room, hearing concerts from the presidential box at Constitution Hall, and a couple of them even sleeping in Lincoln's bed.

Bess Truman, through the long years in Washington, continued to be homesick for Independence and her beloved bridge club. She seized every opportunity to go back to Missouri. At one of her visits, the Girls gathered in anticipation of a visit of their most famous member. As Mrs. Truman entered the house, they solemnly rose in a body on a prearranged signal, bowed stiffly from the waist, and intoned in unison: "Welcome home, Madam President!" According to *Life* magazine, the response to this formal greeting was exactly what the Girls expected. "Oh, sit down! Sit *down*! You all make me so mad!" said the First Lady.

Soap Opera

Presidential families do different things to relax. With the Reagans, coming from Hollywood, film screenings are as frequent as they were with the Kennedys and several earlier first families. But in the fifties, television became the main form of entertainment both for America and for the White House. Chief Usher West reports on an early case of addiction:

Although two television sets had been installed during the renovation, one in the West Sitting Hall and one in the President's study, the Trumans hadn't cared much for the electronic novelty. Now, however, the medium had begun to come of age, and it fascinated the Eisenhowers.

In the evenings, President and Mrs. Eisenhower, with Mrs. Doud, took dinner on their tray tables in the West Hall while watching the television news. Along with the rest of the country, they were that caught up in the new TV mania.

"As the World Turns" initiated the Television Era in the White House. Watching the daytime serial was a daily ritual for

Mrs. Eisenhower, as I found out early in the administration.

I'd been out to lunch, and when I returned there was a note to "see MDE upstairs." But when I knocked on her bedroom door, the First Lady pointed me toward the pink overstuffed chair, never taking her eyes off the television set.

"Let's just wait till this is over," she said. And I watched while one tragic dialogue after another unfolded on the twelve-inch screen. Not even during the commercials could I find out what she wanted from me.

Every afternoon, while the President napped in his dressing room, Mrs. Eisenhower avidly followed the adventures and perils of her soap-opera heroines.

Home Movies

Lyndon Johnson was an unabashed narcissist, and one of his favorite recreations was to watch himself on home movies. Barbara Howar describes a typical evening in the White House theatre, where the President would fall asleep:

After a brief nap, Johnson would wake up and demand to see the spliced reel of home movies from his younger days. The film was narrated by Lady Bird Johnson with background music by John Philip Sousa. There was footage of vanished Christmases and Halloweens, of Johnson at Lynda Bird's sixth birthday at their old house in suburban Washington, Johnson casually saluting the camera as Mrs. Johnson's voice pointed out: "Now here is a younger, slimmer Lyndon . . ." The President would fall asleep again, only to wake up and order the film rerolled to the parts showing his ranch on the Pedernales in the days before he had turned it into an opulent showplace.

It did not take me long to see that Johnson was devoted to the telephone; he kept one handy in unlikely places. There was one beneath the dining table in the family quarters, and it was not uncommon for him to bring someone's name into conversation, reach under the table, and either growl or purr for the

White House telephone operators to get that person on the line. At dinner one evening, he turned and asked what my husband thought of my being away from home so much: "He's either mighty nice or mighty henpecked." Not certain which answer he would believe, I just smiled and nodded. Johnson picked up the phone and asked to be connected with Ed Howar, who was waiting at home in something less than a cordial mood about my not being there too. I was horrified Ed might think the call a practical joke and cut the conversation short with an expletive, but Johnson and Lady Bird chatted amiably with my absent partner until the President abruptly ended the exchange by thanking Ed for "giving me your wife," confirming, I fear, Ed Howar's worst suspicions of my White House visits.

Being Herself

In front of a conference of dance companies Betty Ford ended a little speech with an impromptu pirouette that had her audience cheering. Leaving the Kennedy Center after her fifty-seventh-birthday outing to see Pearl Bailey perform, the First Lady and the entertainer suddenly broke into the University of Michigan fight song, reading from the sheet music. Only a few hangers-on at the Center caught the act. They yelled, "Bravo!" The two women bowed, hugged each other, and then parted.

One Sunday Mrs. Ford was reading an account of how the American photographer Dick Swanson, in a daring move, flew to Vietnam and got his Vietnamese wife's family out on one of the last planes. She called Swanson, who happened to be a little groggy from celebrating his birthday. Mrs. Ford told him the article was a beautiful love story and wished him happy birthday.

Swanson "thought for sure it was some old girlfriend pulling a joke. I said, 'Watcha doing?' and she said, 'Oh, just hanging around the West Wing.' I joked some more and said, 'Watcha doing in the West Wing?' Then she giggled and said, 'Well, that's where they keep us.' All of a sudden I realized it really was the First Lady, and it blew my mind."

Dirty Stories

The day after President Reagan was shot in March 1981, Frank Sinatra rushed to his bedside. As he told it around Georgetown that evening, Nancy Reagan greeted him with "Frank! Thank God you're here. There's finally someone I can tell my dirty stories to!"

The Nancified Joke

Washington columnist Diana McLellan describes how Nancy Reagan told "dirty jokes":

Older friends agree that Nancy Reagan is "fun and relaxed" under the right circumstances. They also enjoy some fun at her expense. One California tradition holds that her most endearing trait is what is called the Nancified joke.

A joke is told to Nancy.

"What is the definition of a nymphomaniac?" asks the jokester. The answer is, "A woman who gets screwed an hour after she gets her hair done."

Retold by Nancy later, the whole thing is Nancified. This means it gains a flavor both genteel and surreal: "What do you call a woman who makes love right after she'd had her hair done?"

"A hypochondriac."

AROUND THE HOUSE

Menagerie

No household is complete without pets:

General Washington was fond of dogs. Following the War of Independence, when he retired to enjoy Mount Vernon, he had a pack of five French hounds sent to him by his old friend Lafayette. The largest of these enormous beasts, called Vulcan, was constantly hungry and would sneak into Mrs. Washington's kitchen to steal food. One evening Vulcan managed to get his teeth into a large dinner ham that Martha was preparing. The servants chased and tried to tackle him, but Vulcan made it safely back to his kennel. When informed of this, the father of the nation roared with laughter, while his wife was understandably less amused.

Martha, on the other hand, was fond of birds. One of her earliest suitors almost won her heart when he presented her with a mockingbird that he had tamed for her. As First Lady, Mrs. Washington kept a parrot which caused a headache for the President as he prepared to leave his office. Trying to pack up his household in Philadelphia and move it back to his Virginia estate, the General wrote to his secretary, Tobias Lear: "On one side I am called upon to remember the parrot, and on the other to remember the dog. For my own part, I should not pine much if both were forgot."

Home Economics

When James Polk was in Congress, serving on the Ways and Means Committee, he supported Andrew Jackson and opposed the setting up of a national bank. Once when he was leaving home and needed some cash, he turned to his wife. Sarah Polk proceeded to search the house, looking in every box and trunk. "Don't you see," she remonstrated to him, "how troublesome it is to carry around gold and silver? This is enough to show you how useful banks are."

Undomesticated

Sarah Polk did not care too much about domesticity. When her husband was running against Henry Clay, someone threatened to switch his support because Mrs. Clay made good butter and was the better housekeeper. The independent-minded Mrs. Polk is reported to have fired back: "If I get to the White House, I expect to live on $25,000 a year and I will neither keep house nor make butter."

In 1844 political supporters came to congratulate the Polks on his election victory. A friend of Sarah's advised her not to let the crowd inside where they would leave footprints on the carpet. "The only marks they left," Mrs. Polk said later, "were those of respect."

A Poor Housekeeper

On one occasion, Mrs. Pryor sent President Buchanan a Virginia ham, with directions for cooking it. It was to be soaked, boiled gently three or four hours, suffered to get cold in its own juices, and then toasted.

This would seem simple enough (writes Mrs. Pryor), but the executive cook disdained it, perhaps for the reason that it was so simple. The dish, a shapeless, jellylike mass, was placed before the President. He took his knife and fork in hand to honor the dish by carving it himself, looked at it helplessly, and called out: "Take it away! Take it away! Oh, Miss Harriet! You are a poor housekeeper! Not even a Virginia lady can teach you."

Details

According to Colonel Crook, who became President Lincoln's bodyguard in the fateful year of 1865:

Mrs. Lincoln was not merely an excellent housekeeper but a practical one, and she busied herself about the White House (then called the Executive Mansion) much as any other housekeeper would busy herself about her private home. She would go from room to room, seeing that the work was satisfactorily done, looking after the innumerable small details, especially those which had to do with the comfort of her husband and her little son.

Then, as a general thing, Mrs. Lincoln would attend to her personal correspondence in her own boudoir, where she had a desk; afterward, likely as not, going down to the old conservatory, long since supplanted, which was a favorite resort for her. She loved flowers and understood them and knew their needs; and was able to give the gardener directions as to what she wanted done and also how to do it. Many times have I seen her looking at some favorite flower as if she were helping it to give forth its bloom and fragrance. Sometimes she would say to me with real enthusiasm: "Crook, look at this beautiful bud! Soon it will be in full bloom!"

Paging Theodore

Theodore Roosevelt was a sound sleeper but did not like to go to bed. The family usually retired at about 10:30, and the President would promise to follow Mrs. Roosevelt in a minute. But then he would get absorbed reading a magazine, and according to Usher Ike Hoover, "it was generally after much effort and much persuasion that he would finally turn in for the night. Mrs. Roosevelt would call and call. The sound of her voice calling, 'The-o-dore!' is well remembered by all the older employees. She often appealed to me to go to the President and 'see if you cannot persuade him to come to bed.' "

Mistress of All that She Surveys

In Europe, the Eisenhowers had already been feted by royalty, and Mamie seemed determined to bring to her Executive Mansion all the grandeur, all the autocracy of those palaces, as well as all the prestige, status, and deference she felt was due the First Lady of the land. Once behind the White House gates, though she appeared fragile and feminine, she ruled as if she were Queen.

She could be imperious.

"When I go out," she insisted, "I am to be escorted to the diplomatic entrance by an usher. And when I return, I am to be met at the door and escorted upstairs."

One day, dressed, hatted, and gloved to go outside, she started to get on the elevator, and to her amazement it shot up to the third floor. So she sailed right up, curious to see who was using her elevator. It was George Thompson, a wizened little houseman.

"Never use my elevator again!" she admonished George, and she called Mr. Crim immediately to make an order that *none* of the household staff must ever use the "family" elevator.

And So to Bed

On June 9, 1964, President and Mrs. Johnson gave a state dinner for the Prime Minister of Denmark, Jens Otto Krag, and his wife, Helle. It was memorable for Mrs. Johnson as her daughter Luci's first state dinner, and they all enjoyed the music and dancing afterward. However, the evening was not quite over, as Lady Bird confided to her diary that night:

And then late at night, after everybody was gone, occurred one of my funniest little moments in the White House. In my robe and slippers, ready for bed, I observed that all the lights in the second-floor hall were still on, and I went from one to the other, turning them off. When I got to the staircase that leads down to the State floor, I could hear a few clattering feet below disappearing in the distance, and I could see a great blaze of light going down the steps. If I could step out into the hall only a few feet I could turn off the main lights, but I was afraid the door would lock behind me.

Cautiously I pushed the door open, held it with my foot, reached as far as I could—it was quite obvious I couldn't get to the switch. Some giddy instinct of daring led me to just let the door close gently and to walk over and turn out the lights. Then I went back and turned the knob—sure enough the door was locked tight! I knocked, hoping maybe the guests in the Queen's Room would hear me. I called gently, I called a little louder, nobody heard me! There was no sound below now, but there were a few lights still on. I thought about all those funny ads— "I went to the Opera in my Maidenform Bra"—and I thought how awful it would be if I walked through the main entrance hall of the White House at about 1:30, in my dressing gown, and met a dozen or so of the departing guests. But there was nothing else to do, so with a very assured look (I hope!) I went walking down the stairs and through the hall where I met only two or three of the departing musicians and staff members. I smiled as if the whole thing were a matter of course, caught the elevator back up to my own floor, and so to bed, thinking this had been a remarkable day in many ways.

Oops!

Rosalynn Carter had a similar experience in Georgia:

I remember a friend of the Kennedys once saying that it was odd to be upstairs in the private family rooms and hear the shuffle of people's feet from the White House tours going on below. In the Governor's Mansion (in Georgia), well, there was no way for me to get out of that house except through the main halls. We lived on the second floor there, too, so it was the same situation as here. Except that here you can come and go privately.

One time here, though, I did get caught. I wanted to press a dress—just quickly. I had on my blue bathrobe and I went down with the dress over my arm and suddenly a group of sightseers came around the corner and there I was!

AT WORK

A WOMAN'S DAY IS NEVER DONE

Always Knitting

Martha Washington was remembered as always busy in her workroom at Mount Vernon:

It was a plain, good-sized apartment, arranged and furnished with a view to facilitating work. At one end there was a large table for cutting out clothes. At that time every garment worn by slaves had to be cut out and sewed, either by ladies of the mansion-house or under their superintendence. The greater part of General Washington's slaves worked on plantations several miles distant from his home and were provided for by their several overseers; but there were a great number of household servants at Mount Vernon, besides grooms, gardeners, fishermen, and others, for whom the lady of the house had to think and contrive. At the broad table sat a skillful Negro woman, somewhat advanced in years, with a pair of shears in her hand, cutting almost all day and every day the countless trousers, dresses, jackets, and shirts needed by a family of perhaps a hundred persons. Everything worn by the General or by herself, except their best outside garments, which were imported from London, was made in that room, under the eye of the lady of the house.

All the commoner fabrics, too, were homemade. On one side of the room sat a young colored woman spinning yarn; on another, her mother knitting; elsewhere, a woman doing some of the finer

151

ironing; here a woman winding; there a little colored girl learning to sew. In the midst of all this industry sat Mrs. Washington, ready to solve difficulties as they arose, and prompt to set right any operation that might be going wrong. She was always knitting. From morning till dinnertime—which was two o'clock—her knitting was seldom out of her hands. In this workroom she usually received the ladies of her familiar acquaintance when they called in the morning, but she never laid aside her knitting. The click of her needles was always heard in the pauses of conversation.

Housekeeping

It was the custom of Mrs. Martha Patterson [Andrew Johnson's eldest daughter] to rise early; and after a simple toilet to skim the milk and attend to the dairy before breakfast. In the hall connecting the conservatory to the main building, her clean pails might be seen ranged in regular order. When, on Saturday afternoons, the greenhouses were thrown open to the public, these evidences of her housekeeping propensities were removed. Fond of the delicacies of the table, she valued homemade articles, and the delicious food found always upon her table gave evidence of her personal oversight and thoughtfulness. Caring for real comforts to the exclusion of costly expenditures, she prided herself upon gratifying the wants and tastes of her household and rendering the domestic life of the White House a reality.

Working Duchess

When Warren Harding married Florence Kling, he was trying to make a go of a small weekly newspaper:

Warren Harding, easygoing and affable, allowed his wife to be the dominant force in their household and at the *Star* as well. At one point, with more malice than admiration, he referred to her as the "Duchess," and the name stuck. She called him "Wurr'n," in her flat, midwestern style, and made it sound like a command.

Life with the unfeminine, demanding Florence must have been trying for Harding; his health troubled him and he teetered more than once on the edge of a nervous breakdown. In 1894, Florence sent him to Battle Creek Sanitarium for a long rest. She herself was often tense and edgy, but she found a remedy for her nerves at the offices of the *Star*. She had long complained to "Wurr'n" that he was too lax; his newspaper lacked efficiency and system. While he was away at the sanitarium his circulation manager quit. Florence took over; her stay, she thought, would be a short one. She later said that she "went down there intending to help out for a few days," and she "stayed fourteen years."

She did bring system to the *Star*, with the brisk, tight-lipped autocracy she had learned from her father. She organized the newsboys into a well-drilled unit. She did not shrink from punishment, and at least once spanked one of the boys. She scrupulously counted the pennies, something Harding had never bothered with, and she herself scrubbed the floors.

One of her newsboys was Norman Thomas, the perennial Socialist candidate for President. He wrote this about her:

"Mrs. Harding in those days ran the show. She was a woman of very narrow mentality and range of interest or understanding, but of strong will and, within a certain area, of genuine kindliness. . . . Her husband was the front. He was, as you know, very affable; very much of a joiner. He was always personally more popular than his wife, [but] it was she who was the real driving power in the success that the Marion *Star* was unquestionably making in its community."

The *Paparazza*

Despite her well-publicized battles with the press, Jacqueline Bouvier was an aggressive newshound when she worked as a journalist. As a couple of admiring members of the Washington press corps wrote:

Having been an "Inquiring Photographer" herself for the Washington *Times-Herald* (later bought by the *Post*) not long after she left Vassar, she understood what the press was up to from its side of the fence. "Who will be Washington's number one hostess now that the Republicans are back in power?" photographer Jacqueline Bouvier asked Patricia Nixon, whose husband had just been sworn in as Vice President in 1953, just a month earlier. Mrs. Nixon answered:

"Why Mrs. Eisenhower, of course. I think her friendly manner and sparkling personality immediately captivate all who see or meet her. She is equally gracious in small groups or long receiving lines, where she has the knack of getting acquainted with each person, instead of merely shaking hands with the usual phrase, 'How do you do?' The people of America will always be proud of their First Lady."

The aggressive type of reporting she later viewed with horror was used by Jackie when she stalked Ellen Moore, the eleven-year-old niece of Mrs. Eisenhower, home from school and talked to her about her baby-sitting jobs. The precocious niece of the new First Family told Jackie that she was thinking of raising her rates: "I've been charging fifty cents an hour, but now that my uncle is President of the United States, don't you think I should get seventy-five?" Ellen's mother wasn't pleased about unsolicited publicity. She asked a newspaper friend, the late George Dixon, to "do something to make that brash camera girl, whoever she is, know her place."

Priorities

Among the people the Inquiring Girl Photographer interviewed was the freshman Senator from Massachusetts. They began dating quietly, while retaining a hectic working and social schedule. After their engagement in 1953, Jacqueline insisted on keeping it a secret at least until the *Saturday Evening Post* ran its story on Jack Kennedy as "The Senate's Gay Young Bachelor." Always a professional, she did not want to scoop the *Post*.

MISSIONS

Ambassadress

During the time that James Monroe was Ambassador of the United States to France, the Marquis de Lafayette had been taken prisoner by the Austrians (in August 1792). Meanwhile, as the French Revolution dissolved into the Reign of Terror, the Marquis's estate was confiscated, and his wife and children were also thrown into prison by his own countrymen.

The Marquis de Lafayette was adored by Americans, and the indignities heaped upon his heroic wife could scarcely be borne by the Minister and his family. When Mr. Monroe decided to risk sending his wife to see Madame Lafayette, he appreciated the decided effect it would have for good or evil. He well knew that either it would meet with signal success, and be of benefit to his unfortunate friend, or render her slight claim to clemency yet more desperate. Enlisted as his feelings were, he determined to risk the die, and Mrs. Monroe was consulted in regard to the plan. To her husband's anxious queries she replied calmly, and assured him of her ability to control and sustain herself.

As the carriage of the American Minister, adorned with all the emblems of rank, halted before the entrance of the prison, the keeper advanced to know the object of the visit. Mrs. Monroe, with firm step and steady voice, alighted and made known her business, and to her surprise was conducted to the reception room, while the official retired to make known her request. After a lapse of time, which to one in her nervous state seemed an age, she heard the footsteps returning, and soon the opening of the ponderous door revealed the presence of the emaciated prisoner, assisted by her guard.

The emotion of the Marchioness was touching in the extreme, and she sank at the feet of Mrs. Monroe, speechless. All day she had been expecting the summons to prepare for her execution, and when the silence of her cell was disturbed by the approach of the gendarmes, her last hope was fast departing. Instead of the cruel announcement, the assurance that a visitor awaited her presence in the receiving room of the prison, and on finding that visitor to be the American Ambassadress, her long-pent feelings found relief in sobs. The reaction was sudden, and the shock more than her feeble frame could bear.

The presence of the sentinels precluded all efforts at conversation, and both hesitated to abuse the unheard-of privilege of an interview. After a painful stay of short duration, Mrs. Monroe rose to retire, assuring her friend in a voice audible to her listeners, for whom it was intended, that she would call the following morning, and then hastened to relieve the anxiety of her husband.

Madame de Lafayette's long-delayed execution had been decided upon, and that very afternoon she was to have been beheaded, but the unexpected visit of the Minister's wife altered the minds of the officials, and to the surprise of all, she was liberated the next morning.

Guess Who Came to Dinner

After General Jackson landed at Blakely, near Mobile [in April 1821], he proceeded up the river about forty miles to a military post under the command of Colonel Brook and called Montpelier. Here he was detained some days, during which time he learned that the Indian Chief Weatherford, who commanded at the destruction and massacre of Fort Mimms, was living but a few miles off. General Jackson remembered the brave conduct of the Chief at the battle of Horse Shoe, where losing most of his warriors, he surrendered alone, remarking that "he had fought as long as he had men, and would fight longer if he could"; and at his suggestion Colonel Brook invited the Chief to dinner the following day. The next day his appearance attracted much attention at the fort, and when dinner was announced, General Jackson escorted him to the presence of the ladies, introducing him to Mrs. Jackson as the Chief of the Creek Indians and the bravest of his tribe. She welcomed him and said that she "was pleased to meet him at the festive board, and hoped that the strife of war was ended forever." "I looked up," the Chief later related, "and found all eyes upon me, but I could not speak a word. I found something choked me, and I wished I was dead or at home." Colonel Brook came to his rescue by replying to Mrs. Jackson, and the dinner passed off pleasantly, but the chief related the occurrence a few years later, and said he "was never caught in such quarters again."

Royal Favorite

In 1852 James Buchanan was sent as Ambassador to the Court of St. James's, and he took his niece, Miss Harriet Lane, with him. And now she became publicly identified with Mr. Buchanan. At dinners and upon all occasions, she ranked not as a niece, or even daughter, but as his wife. There was at first some question on this point, but Queen Victoria, upon whom the blooming beauty had made a deep impression, soon decided that, and Miss Lane was thenceforward one of the foremost ladies in the diplomatic corps at St. James's. Upon every occasion Miss Lane was most graciously singled out by the Queen, and it was well-known that she was not only an unusual favorite with Her Majesty, but that she was regarded with favor and admiration by all the royal family. She was so immediately and universally popular that she was warmly welcomed in every circle and added much to the social reputation Mr. Buchanan's elegant manners won him everywhere. At her home she was modest and discreet, as well as sprightly and genial, and her countrymen never visited their great representative in England without congratulating themselves upon having there also such a specimen of American womanhood.

Constant Companion

Jackie Kennedy began her journey to become one of the most glamorous celebrities of the world when she and the President went to Europe in 1961. Paris went absolutely wild, with newspaper headlines calling her *ravissante* and *magnifique*. The Mayor of Paris, in presenting her with an expensive diamond watch, declared that her visit had been the most awaited event since Queen Elizabeth's visit to the city. Listening, one of Kennedy's aides whispered to the President:

"Queen Elizabeth, hell; they couldn't get this kind of turnout with the Second Coming."

Even the President was impressed by the extraordinary impact his wife made on foreigners; she became an important force in conducting international diplomacy with the Allies. At a press conference held at SHAPE (Supreme Headquarters, Allied Powers, Europe) he opened his remarks: "I do not think it entirely inappropriate to introduce myself to this audience. I am the man who accompanied Jacqueline Kennedy to Paris, and I have enjoyed it."

How to Be Popular

During the tense Vienna summit between John F. Kennedy and Nikita Khrushchev in June 1961, Jacqueline held her own summit with Nina, the distinctly unglamorous wife of the Soviet leader. Letitia Baldrige describes how the First Lady overcame a potential embarrassment:

We were all chatting over coffee in the living room when a chant rose from the square outside the palace. It was filled with people—the Secret Service later estimated the crowd at three thousand. "Jac-kie!" they cried, over and over again, in bursts of rhythmic cadence. In every country, the rhythm had been the same. But here, today, it became increasingly embarrassing that no one mentioned Nina Khrushchev's name. The Russian sat gazing sadly down at her feet, saying nothing. Conversation in the room was impossible, and I could see Frau Schaerf was beginning to be agitated.

Mrs. Kennedy handled the crisis with great diplomacy. She went to the open window to appease the impatient crowd, smiled, and waved at them. The volume of noise became an earsplitting symphony of cheering and applause. After about one minute, she took Mme. Khrushchev gently by the arm and led her back to the window. She held up Mme. Khrushchev's hand for a second, and then the Russian began to wave on her own. The crowd loved it, crying this time, "Jac-kie! Ni-na!" It was almost as if they were obeying the American First Lady's request for courtesy to be shown to her fellow guest.

Under Fire

During a tour of South America in 1958, the Nixons encountered anti-American demonstrators in several places. At one point in Caracas, the Vice President's limousine was blocked by a screaming mob which proceeded to batter the car with pipes and clubs. The local police actually fled and the U.S. Secret Service agents had their guns drawn. Pat Nixon, riding in a car behind her husband's, remained calm and reassured the wife of the Venezuelan Foreign Minister, who was frightened out of her wits, that everything would turn out well. One witness described Mrs. Nixon showing "cold animal courage."

Later, as First Lady, she often encountered anti-Vietnam demonstrators. Once she was showered with bits of paper while one of the protesters explained: "If this was napalm, you would now be dead." On another occasion, visiting a Methodist volunteer help center, she was greeted by a group of young women dressed as witches, chanting:

> Mrs. Nixon, trouble's mixin';
> Millions die, but you don't cry.
> Money to kill against our will:
> People at home are denied their own.
> This nix on you will all come true;
> We'll say no: your kind must go.

When asked later how she felt about the incident, Mrs. Nixon replied: "I was out there doing the very best I could, and if that was the best that they could do, that's sad."

Whisper Campaign

Foreign Minister Andrey Gromyko was chatting with Nancy Reagan at the White House when he suddenly turned to the First Lady:

"Does your husband believe in peace or war?"

"Peace," she replied.

"You are sure?"

"Yes."

As the dour Russian diplomat was leaving to join the President at a working lunch he said to Mrs. Reagan: "Well, you whisper peace in his ear every night."

"I will," she promised. Then added: "I'll also whisper it in your ear."

IN TIME OF WAR

Dolley Rescues George

Unintimidated by the sight of friends and acquaintances making their escape from the city, of the officials of the State and Treasury Departments withdrawing with valuable papers, or even by the sound of guns at Bladensburg, Mrs. Madison calmly awaited the return of her husband. Cool and collected in the midst of confusion and dismay, she made ready for flight should it become necessary. In a letter written to her sister (Mrs. Cutts) on August 23, when the British fleet had sailed up the Patuxent and landed their troops at Benedict, Maryland, about thirty miles southeast of Washington, Mrs. Madison said that the President had gone to join General Winder, and that she had received two dispatches from him desiring her to be ready, at a moment's warning, to enter her carriage and leave the city.

"I am accordingly ready," she wrote. "I have pressed as many Cabinet papers into trunks as to fill one carriage. Our private property must be sacrificed, as it is impossible to procure wagons for its transportation. I am determined not to go myself until I see Mr. Madison safe and he can accompany me. My friends and acquaintances are all gone, even Colonel C—— with the hundred men who were stationed as a guard in this enclosure. French John [a faithful servant] offers to spike the cannon at the gate and lay a train of powder which will blow up the British should they enter the house. To this proposition I positively object, without being able, however, to make him understand why all advantages in war may not be taken."

Among the friends who stopped at the White House the next day to warn its mistress of her danger were Charles Carroll of Bellevue and Mrs. George W. Campbell. Mr. Campbell, then Secretary of the Treasury, was with the President, but his wife, having been told by an official of the War Department that the British would be in Washington in two hours, put on her bonnet and shawl and hastened to urge Mrs. Madison to leave the city. Two messengers also came from Mr. Madison urging flight. After these and other warnings Mrs. Madison consented to set forth without her husband, but not before she had secured the large picture of General Washington by Stuart which was hanging in the dining room, although she says that her kind friend Mr. Carroll was in a very bad humor with her on account of this delay. Of the unscrewing of the picture from the wall she wrote:

"This process was found too tedious for these perilous moments. I have ordered the frame to be broken and the canvas taken out. It is done and the precious portrait placed in the hands of two gentlemen of New York for safekeeping. And now, dear sister, I must leave this house, or the retreating army will make me a prisoner in it by filling up the road which I am directed to take. When I shall again write to you or where I shall be tomorrow I cannot tell."

The financier Jacob Barker was one of those two gentlemen and, writing to the son of the other, Charles Carroll, completes the story of the picture:

"Whether I found your father there [at the White House] or whether he came in subsequently, I do not know; but I do know

161

that he assisted in taking down the portrait of Washington and left the house with the President, leaving the portrait on the floor of the room in which it had been suspended to take care of itself, where it remained until the remnant of our army, reduced to about four thousand, passed by, taking the direction of Georgetown, when the portrait was taken by Mr. [Robert G. L.] Depeyster and myself, assisted by two colored boys, from the said room; and with it we fell into the trail of the army and continued with it some miles. Overtaken by night and greatly fatigued, we sought shelter in a farmhouse. No other person assisted in removing or preserving the picture."

In relating his experiences with this portrait, Mr. Barker was wont to speak of the interest shown by the inmates of the farmhouse when they saw it, one colored servant exclaiming, as she beheld the familiar features of the great General, that the city wouldn't have been taken if he'd been about.

Peace

The President and Mrs. Madison were back in Washington, at the Octagon (Colonel Tayloe's Octagon House, where the Madisons stayed while the White House was restored after having been burned by the British), when in February 1815 a carriage thundered down Pennsylvania Avenue bringing news of the Treaty of Ghent.

In the hours of rejoicing that followed the arrival of the peace commissioners, hospitality reigned in the house, which was crowded with visitors until midnight. Mrs. Madison received in the large parlor to the right of the entrance hall, while in the dining room to the left, good cheer was dispensed with a liberal hand. Tradition relates that the household servants were not overlooked in the general merrymaking, as Miss Sally Coles flew to the basement stairs, crying, "Peace, peace," while the distribution of meats and drinks in their quarters was so bountiful and the good cheer was partaken of so joyously that French John was incapacitated for service for some days.

While the President and his Cabinet officers were engaged

with the commissioners, Mrs. Madison flitted from room to room and from guest to guest, her face reflecting the happiness that warmed every heart. Whatever mistakes the President may have made were forgotten in the gladness of the hour, and more than one writer has said that Mrs. Madison was at that time the most popular person in the United States. Friends old and new gathered around her to offer their congratulations, the soldiers marching home stopped before the house to cheer her, and the special Ambassador from Great Britain, Sir Charles Bagot, declared that the wife of the republican President looked every inch a queen.

Mrs. Jackson Lays Down the Law

In July 1821 Rachel Jackson witnessed the occupation of Pensacola by her husband. Writing to her friend Elizabeth Kingsley, Mrs. Jackson describes her work among the inhabitants:

Three weeks the transports were bringing the Spanish troops from St. Mark's in order that they should all sail to Cuba at the same time. At length they arrived, but during all this time the Governor of this place and the General [Jackson] had daily communications, yet his lordship never waited on the General in person. After the vessels returned from St. Mark's, the General came within two miles of Pensacola. They were then one week finishing the preliminaries and ceremonies to be observed on the day of his entrance into the city. At length, last Tuesday was the day. At seven o'clock, at the precise moment, they hove in view under the American flag and a full band of music. The whole town was in motion. Never did I see so many pale faces. I am living on Main Street, which gave me an opportunity of seeing a great deal from the upper galleries. They marched by to the government house, where the two Generals met in the manner prescribed, then His Catholic Majesty's flag was lowered, and the American hoisted high in air, not less than one hundred feet.

O how they burst into tears to see the last ray of hope departed of their devoted city and country—delivering up the keys of the archives, the vessels lying at anchor, in full view, to waft them to their distant port. Next morning they set sail under convoy of the *Hornet*, sloop of war, *Anne Maria*, and the *Tom Shields*. How did the city sit solitary and mourn. Never did my heart feel more for any people. Being present, I entered immediately into their feelings. Their manners, laws, customs, all changed, and really a change was necessary. My pen almost drops from my hand, the effort is so far short, so limited to what it might be.

Three Sabbaths I spent in this house before the country was in possession under American government. In all that time I was not an idle spectator. The Sabbath profanely kept; a great deal of noise and swearing in the streets; shops kept open; trade going on, I think, more than on any other day. They were so boisterous on that day I sent Major Stanton to say to them that the approaching Sunday would be differently kept. Yesterday I had the happiness of witnessing the truth of what I had said. Great order was observed; the doors kept shut; the gambling houses demolished; fiddling and dancing not heard anymore on the Lord's day; cursing not to be heard. What, what has been done in one week!

The Colonel's Wife

During the Civil War, Rutherford Hayes served as a major of the Twenty-third Ohio Volunteers. He was four times wounded, was promoted to Colonel, and served with distinction until the close. Mrs. Hayes spent two summers and a winter taking care of her husband's soldiers, and they loved her for her motherly ministrations to them in their hours of sickness and mental dejection. The following characteristic story of the future First Lady was told by one of the soldiers:

It was the first of our being out, when we had as yet known but little of the hardships of war. One day Mrs. Hayes arrived in camp, but the fact was not generally known. James Saunders was a member of my company. Jim, as he was called, was a tall, lean, unsuspecting, awkward country boy—a good soldier, but not overly smart in detecting a joke. Consequently the boys used frequently to sell him quite badly; but he took it all in good part. For some time there had been sad need of some means of mending our clothes. This need was being discussed the next day after

Mrs. Hayes' arrival, and Jim was especially strong in his expressions of need for someone to mend his blouse, which really was in a very unpresentable condition.

"Why, Jim," said one of the boys, "didn't you know that there is a woman in camp whose business it is to mend the boys' clothes?"

"No," said Jim, in astonishment. "Where is she?"

"Up in the Colonel's tent," said the other. "I was there and had her fix my coat yesterday, and she did a smackin' good job, too."

"Golly!" said Jim. "I'll go up then, this very afternoon, and git my blouse doctored. That is very handy, indeed."

True to his word, Jim called around at the Colonel's tent, and, with his hat under his arm, presented himself, with his awkwardest bow, at the entrance. He was received with marked politeness by the Colonel, and the boys who were lurking about appreciating the joke awaited developments. In a few moments Jim again appeared outside in his shirtsleeves, and the radiant smile that lit up his honest features showed that he had not been rebuffed, at least. Calling him aside, where a group of the boys were gathered, the following conversation took place:

"Well, Jim, did you find your woman?"

"Of course, I did. She was just settin' there, and she's a mighty good-looking woman, too."

"What did you say?" all chuckling.

"Why, when I went in I told the Colonel that I heerd there was a woman there to do sewing for the boys, and as my blouse needed mendin' and buttons sewed on, I had come to git it done. He kind of smiled, and turned to the woman settin' there and asked her if she could fix the blouse for me, and she said she could as well as not, as she had nothing special on hand. So I took it off and left it, the Colonel tellin' me to call 'round this afternoon and git it. You all seem to laugh, but I don't see anything funny. If she is here to do the sewing, why not do mine?"

This was too much. The boys all broke out into a loud chorus of laughter, and as soon as it subsided, one of them said:

"Jim, don't you know that that woman is the Colonel's wife?"

"I don't care; she's a lady anyhow," as though that didn't follow, "and I am going to git my blouse, just as she told me to."

And he did go, and was again received in that manner which made him forget himself and his awkwardness, and she restored his blouse to him in perfect repair.

This little incident was all that was needed to fix the affections of all the boys upon the Colonel's wife, and whenever she appeared again in camp, she was certain to receive the warmest welcome.

Mother of the Regiment

Thirteen years later, when the Colonel and his wife were celebrating their silver wedding anniversary at the White House, the only present they would accept was a gift to Mrs. Hayes from the officers of the Twenty-third Ohio Volunteer Infantry, consisting of a silver plate embedded in a mat of black velvet and enclosed in a richly ornamented ebony frame. The present was given in memory of kindness received at the hands of Mrs. Hayes in the field, and it was inscribed on its face:

To the Mother of the Regiment.

To Thee, Mother of ours, from the 23d O.V.I. To Thee, our Mother, on this silver troth, we bring this token of our love. Thy boys give greeting unto thee with burning hearts. Take the hoarded treasures of thy speech, kind words, gentle when a gentle word was worth the surgery of an hundred schools to heal sick thought and make our bruises whole. Take it, our mother: 'tis but some small part of thy rare beauty we give back to thee, and while love speaks in silver, from our hearts we'll bribe Old Father Time to spare his gift.

Above the inscription is a sketch of the log hut erected as Colonel Hayes' headquarters in the valley of of the Kanawha, during the winter of 1863 and 1864, and above it the tattered and torn battle flags of the regiment.

Rover

During World War II, Eleanor Roosevelt, who had already traveled more than any other First Lady, extended her visits around the far-flung battlefields of the world. "Rover"—the code name bestowed on her by FDR—could turn up unannounced anywhere; soldiers stationed at Espíritu Santo in the New Hebrides were given orders not to shower naked in the rain, in case Mrs. Roosevelt was suddenly to make an appearance. The First Lady usually traveled alone, wrote Joseph Lash, in order not to take up extra space: "She made long flights in uncomfortable planes, rode in jeeps, walked miles through camp kitchens, hospitals, and warehouses, inspected Red Cross installations, smiled upon thousands of military patients. She got up before 6:00 A.M. in order to eat breakfast with the enlisted men, because she did not want to spend all her time with officers." Sometimes the highest-ranking officers found her difficult to manage at first, but they, too, were swept off their feet:

She was anxious about her meeting with Admiral Halsey. Most of the men in the hospitals in the Fijis were casualties from the great battles that had taken place in the Solomons. Her heart was set on going to Guadalcanal, which for her was the symbol of the war in the South Pacific and of all the hardships and suffering to which American boys were being subjected. How could she look wounded men in the eye in the future and say she had been in the South Pacific but had not been to Guadalcanal? She felt as strongly about going there as Franklin had about going to the front in the First World War when he had insisted on visiting a battery of 155s under fire and even firing one of its guns. But he had been unwilling to give her a firm "yes" and left the decision up to Halsey.

The conqueror of the Japanese fleet in the South Pacific also classed Eleanor Roosevelt as a "do-gooder" and "dreaded" her arrival. What were her plans, he asked almost as soon as she had stepped from the plane. "What do you think I should do?" she countered, hoping to get her way by subordinating herself to his wishes. But the Admiral was wise to that feminine tactic.

"Mrs. Roosevelt," he said, "I've been married for thirty-odd years, and if those years have taught me one lesson, it is never to try to make up a woman's mind for her." He suggested that she spend two days in Nouméa, proceed to New Zealand and Australia, and then return to Nouméa for two days on her way home. She agreed, and the Admiral began to relax when she produced a letter from the President that said he had told his wife that he was "leaving the decision wholly up to the Area Commanders" as to where she should go. "She is especially anxious to see Guadalcanal and at this moment it looks like a pretty safe place to visit," the President concluded.

"Guadalcanal is no place for you, Ma'am!" Halsey brusquely responded.

"I'm perfectly willing to take my chances," she said. "I'll be entirely responsible for anything that happens to me."

"I'm not worried about the responsibility, and I'm not worried about the chances you'd take. I know you'd take them gladly. What worries me is the battle going on in New Georgia at this very minute. I need every fighter plane that I can put my hands on. If you fly to Guadalcanal, I'll have to provide a fighter escort for you, and I haven't got one to spare."

Eleanor looked so crestfallen that Halsey found himself adding, "However, I'll postpone my final decision until your return. The situation may have clarified by then."

By the time she departed for New Zealand, Admiral Halsey had become her most ardent partisan in the theater:

"Here is what she did in twelve hours: she inspected two Navy hospitals, took a boat to an officers' rest home and had lunch there, returned and inspected an Army Hospital, reviewed the Second Marine Raider Battalion (her son Jimmy had been its executive officer), made a speech at a service club, attended a reception, and was guest of honor at a dinner given by General Harmon."

And, the Admiral might have added, pecked away at her typewriter in the dead of night, doing a column. Halsey's report continued:

"When I say that she inspected those hospitals, I don't mean that she shook hands with the chief medical officer, glanced into a sun parlor, and left. I mean that she went into every ward, stopped at every bed, and spoke to every patient: What was his name? How did he feel? Was there anything he needed? Could she take a message home for him? I marveled at her hardihood, both physical and mental; she walked for miles, and she saw patients who were grievously and gruesomely wounded. But I marveled most at their expressions as she leaned over them. It was a sight I will never forget."

Almost needless to add, Mrs. Roosevelt did get to Guadalcanal.

GOOD WORKS

Giving from the Heart

Mrs. Dolley Madison, though so fond of social festivities, set apart certain mornings for visits to the poor and continued the custom even after she left the White House.

Whenever Mrs. Grant heard of anyone in distress, she not only helped such person with gifts of money and material necessities, but often she insisted that the distressed man or woman or child be brought to the White House in order that she might personally learn the person's needs.

Doorkeeper Thomas Pendel believed that no First Lady would ever surpass the charitable impulses of Lucy Hayes:

"How kindhearted she was. Always had a kind word to say to the humblest employee at the White House. Notes would come to the White House time after time from the destitute and poor wanting help. She would have me come upstairs and see her, and would say, 'Mr. Pendel, here is some money, and here is a note. Take this, and find out where they live, and give it to them.'

"On one occasion, out on Massachusetts Avenue, there was a

young girl, about twenty-two years of age, down with consumption, and Mrs. Hayes said to me, 'Mr. Pendel, I want you to take these oranges up to that young lady and give them to her.' The doorkeepers at the White House fared well, for hardly an evening passed but we were told to go into the parlor and take the magnificent bouquet that was standing there."

Personal Attention

Mrs. McKinley's thoughtfulness for others was very marked. She was most solicitous concerning the welfare of all who were around her and whom she met as the hostess of the White House. When sorrow came or affliction of any kind, she never failed to send flowers and kind, cheering messages to the suffering ones. In the Ladies' Aid Society of the Metropolitan Church she was always one of the most interested helpers. Each Sunday she sent to the church altar flowers from the White House greenhouses, which she had personally picked, and she always had them sent to some poor invalid, to brighten a sickroom, after church service was over. The finest blooms in her conservatories she culled and sent to the sick and the hospitals, sending with them some appetizing dainty from her own kitchen. She told the wife of a Senator that she had knitted with her own fingers 3,000 yarn slippers, every pair of which had been given outright to the poor. Mrs. John A. Logan described her friend's charities:

"Mrs. McKinley's greatest charm was her perfect sincerity and thoughtfulness for others. No day passed over her head without her doing something for someone. If she hears of an affliction of any kind overtaking anyone—no matter how much a stranger— she will immediately order something sent to that person, if nothing more than a bunch of flowers or a cheering message; in some way she conveys her sympathy and good wishes. Her friends endeavor to keep from her knowledge many instances of illness or sorrow, because she immediately makes a personal matter of them, and is untiring in her interest until all is well again."

Martha Washington, our first wartime
knitter (*Library of Congress*)

Abigail Adams, in Gilbert Stuart's
portrait (*Library of Congress*)

Dolley Madison (*Library of Congress*)

Rachel Donelson Jackson (*Library of Congress*)

Mary Todd Lincoln (*Library of Congress*)

Frances Folsom Cleveland (*Library of Congress*)

Roosevelt family group at Oyster Bay, 1907 (*left to right*): Kermit, Archie, T.R., Ethel, Edith, Quentin, and Ted (*Courtesy Department of Library Services, American Museum of Natural History*)

Helen H. Taft (*Courtesy William Howard Taft National Historic Site*)

Edith Bolling Galt, who was to become the second Mrs. Woodrow Wilson, seen here at a Navy football game in October 1915 (*The Bettmann Archive*)

Florence and Warren Harding, circa 1920 (*The Bettmann Archive*)

Mrs. Coolidge (*left*) and Mrs. Hoover as they left the White House for the 1929 inaugural ceremonies (*The Bettmann Archive*)

Lou and Herbert Hoover at a
football match, November 1929
(*The Bettmann Archive*)

Eleanor and Franklin Roosevelt greeting farmers near Fremont, Nebraska,
September 1935 (*The Bettmann Archive*)

Edith Wilson (*seated*), Bess Truman (*left*), and Eleanor Roosevelt, at a 1955 Democratic party dinner in Washington (*The Bettmann Archive*)

Jacqueline Kennedy with Soviet Premier Nikita Khrushchev, during a reception at the Schönbrunn Palace in Vienna, 1961 (*The Bettmann Archive*)

Former First Lady Mamie Eisenhower (*right*) makes a nostalgic visit to the White House at a luncheon given by Lady Bird Johnson in 1967 (*The Bettmann Archive*)

Pat Nixon shows off a stuffed panda given her by her staff in 1972, commemorating the two live pandas presented to the Nixons during their visit to China (*The Bettmann Archive*)

Betty Ford, accompanied by Tony Orlando, belts out a song during the 1976 Republican National Convention (*The Bettmann Archive*)

Amy, Lillian, and Rosalynn Carter at the 1976 Democratic National Convention (*The Bettmann Archive*)

Nancy Reagan addresses a conference of the National Federation of Parents for Drug-Free Youth, October 1982 (*The Bettmann Archive*)

In the Presence of Greatness

In 1946 Eleanor Roosevelt took her friend, the attorney Fanny Holtz-mann, across the Hudson from Hyde Park to the Wiltwyck School for Boys. The school at Esopus was an interracial center for troubled young-sters that was one of Mrs. Roosevelt's favorite causes. As Edward Berkman narrates in his biography of Fanny Holtzmann, Mrs. Roosevelt believed in getting her hands dirty:

Arriving at the school, Mrs. Roosevelt was instantly surrounded by a dozen small residents, mostly black. Every one of them was clamoring for her attention—and, Fanny noticed, every one of them got it. The former First Lady addressed each boy by name, bestowing a word of praise here, a smile of recognition there.

Then she led Fanny through rickety halls into the main dor-mitory. Bedding was in wild disarray. One corner was a jumble of old baseball gloves, leftover bicycle parts, and discarded clothes. From the lavatory beyond came a powerful stench of small boys in their most casual manifestations.

Mrs. Roosevelt noticed Fanny's dismay. "We have a hard time getting help from Harlem. Nobody wants to look after deprived problem children; it's pleasanter to work in the sunny kitchens of the wealthy. Actually, this doesn't smell any different from a dormitory at an exclusive boarding school. Little boys are all alike."

She went to a closet and took out cleaning equipment: pail, mop, scrub brush. Fanny, at her elbow, inquired if she could help.

"My dear, it looks to me as if you're about to throw up. But you can give me a hand changing these sheets. I'll take care of the rest."

Together they replaced several soiled bed sheets. Then the President's widow moved on into the lavatory, where, dropping to her hands and knees, she methodically scrubbed the floor.

It was a scene Fanny would never forget, "an act of humility, responsibility, love. There, in that washroom for forgotten little boys, I felt in the presence of greatness."

Tribute

At a fund-raising luncheon for the Eleanor Roosevelt Foundation in 1964, Lady Bird Johnson recalled how the former First Lady had come to another lunch organized by Mrs. Johnson's Seventy-fifth Congress Club in 1939. The money raised then was to buy a wheelchair for a crippled boy: "Only one person would benefit," said Mrs. Johnson in her speech, "but where else do you start except with one person? Mrs. Roosevelt was always ready to *start*. And one person was important to her."

Lassie Go Home

Conservation and beautification of the environment were Lady Bird Johnson's main passion in the White House and afterward. Her press secretary, Liz Carpenter, describes an episode in the pursuit of her pet project:

The White House was constantly a forum for Mrs. Johnson's favorite project—conservation. And one time the dogs got into the act when Lassie, the most famous bark on TV, came to the White House for a ceremony.

Secretary of Agriculture Orville Freeman felt that in Lassie he had a newsworthy recruit for his campaign to keep the national forests clean, just as Smokey the Bear kept them from disappearing in flames. "Let me bring Lassie over one day to meet Mrs. Johnson," Secretary Freeman said. "It would really boost the new anti-litter poster 'Help Lassie Keep America Beautiful.' "

If Tom Mix could bring his favorite horse, Tony, to the White House during the Coolidge Administration, I saw no reason why Freeman couldn't bring Lassie. So I assigned Cynthia Wilson to handle the dog show. With foresight, she arranged the animal summit meeting in the East Garden, where there are no hydrants. Mrs. Johnson would meet Lassie, the litter dog, and unveil the new poster.

To make this the social event of the Year of the Dog, there

would be tea and cookies after the ceremony. The planning moved along smoothly, and the event was widely publicized in advance. Not since Princess Margaret came for dinner had so many people called demanding an invitation.

Another problem was our own white collie, Blanco, whose image was, of course, jealously guarded by Mr. Bryant. Blanco looked very much like Lassie.

Came the great day for Lassie's party, and Cynthia Wilson was determined that Blanco would not steal the show from Lassie. In the process of extensive briefings from Lassie's trainer, she had discovered evidence of a Hollywood credibility gap.

"Lassie is not really a lassie at all. Lassie is a male dog," she said. "And the trainer warns us to keep all other male dogs away. Males do not mix with males."

She gleefully reported this message to Mr. Bryant, hoping he would keep Blanco, a temperamental dog at best, in the background. After all, what had Blanco ever done for litter?

I had been worried about getting press coverage of the Lassie presentation, because the President had a very newsworthy schedule that day. I needn't have worried. The whole West Wing—some forty photographers and seventy reporters—abandoned the President and his affairs of state and invaded the East Garden with cameras to capture each wag of the tail and microphones to record every bark.

Seeing all this equipment from the communications media roll into the garden was too much for Mr. Bryant. He appeared with Blanco newly bathed and brushed. Cynthia glared at him, and I motioned for him to stay back behind the holly tree, out of sight.

Meanwhile, Lassie performed nobly. He trotted up to Mrs. Johnson with a nosegay of flowers, carrying it in his mouth. He picked up several pieces of paper that his trainer tossed on the ground and showed he knew a trash can when he saw one.

The cameras ground. The reporters kept a running record on this historic event. Mrs. Johnson smiled approvingly. Secretary Freeman glowed. Hollywood press agents rubbed their hands in glee. And Mr. Bryant sulked behind the holly tree.

But right after the ceremony, Mr. Bryant got his revenge. He brought Blanco up importantly. I was surprised he hadn't arranged for the Marine Band to herald their entrance. Blanco descended on Lassie, and for three tense minutes, there was silence. They were eyeball-to-eyeball. Then, a low growl from Blanco. Cynthia envisioned a lawsuit if Blanco so much as touched one hair of the million-dollar TV dog. I envisioned head-lines that said: DOGFIGHT LITTERS WHITE HOUSE LAWN.

"Get that dog out of here," I said to Mr. Bryant more sharply than I have ever spoken to anyone in my life.

Both Mr. Bryant and Blanco tucked their tails and left. Mr. Bryant sulked for two weeks. So did Bill Moyers, the President's press secretary, who opened the next day's papers to see that White House coverage had literally gone to the dogs.

Clout

Rosalynn Carter became champion of mental health as a result of an incident during her husband's gubernatorial campaign in Georgia. Visiting a factory very early in the morning, she got into conversation with a woman just finishing the night shift. She had to work at night, because during the day she had to be at home to care for her daughter, who was mentally retarded. This woman's problems stayed with Rosalynn, and she told her husband that he must do something for the mentally retarded. After his election, she persisted until he set up the Governor's Commission to Improve Services for Mentally and Emotionally Handicapped Georgians. Rosalynn was appointed as one of the four commissioners, and she became a well-known activist on behalf of the mentally ill. During Carter's presidential campaign, she took her cause nationwide. When she visited a Chicago halfway house for mental patients, Rosalynn was asked how she managed to get the relatively lavish resources for outpatient clinics in Georgia. "Jimmy was Governor," she said, smiling.

Drugs

Diana McLellan chronicles how Mrs. Reagan became involved with the chief public issue she made into her own cause:

When Nancy Reagan decided to take on drug abuse as her crusade, she did not know what awaited her. As late as the fall of 1981, on a visit to New York to watch son Ron Junior dance with the Joffrey Ballet, she stopped at Phoenix House, a twenty-four-hour drug-treatment center. (It was about to face a twenty-five percent cut in federal funding, thanks to the Reagan budget.) Her distress was evident but unfocused. She told five young drug addicts of her fear that America would lose a whole generation, as "brains are going to be mush."

It was not until her tour in February 1982 that reporters noted that her emotions were now engaged. Donnie Radcliffe of *The Washington Post* reported an extraordinary scene at a Florida drug center. For two and one-half hours, kids in a free-floating rap session told what their lives on drugs were really like. The accounts of how they had lied, cheated, stolen, fought, hated, and run away—how they had overdosed; how they had smoked and popped and sniffed and mainlined pot, cocaine, uppers, downers, PCP, acid, THC, hash, hash oil, mushrooms, insecticides, D-Con powder, gasoline—formed a moving and horrifying litany.

Nancy was stirred beyond anything she had expected.

She "puddled up." Her voice trembling, she looked around at the group and said that her heart was full—"So many things I'd like to say to you, if I can only get through them. We only make this trip once and that one you ought to make as wonderful, as full, as interesting as you possibly can."

She became interested in the clinical effects of drugs. Back at Children's Hospital in Washington, she revealed that as a child she had gone to Northwestern University, "where my father was a professor of neurosurgery, and watched him cut a brain."

The doctors had her rapt attention.

Computers can now measure the effects of popular drugs on the brains of children after about six months, they told her, but "a dramatic way" to spread the word around was required—something like the White House's public backing.

By now, Nancy was hooked.

The following month, the White House, which has seen some strange sights, saw one of its strangest. For a meeting there of the Drug Use Prevention Program, a dazzling display just outside the elegant Blue Room showed visitors an awesome array of forbidden substances—cocaine, heroin, uppers, downers, and several different breeds, colors, and classes of marijuana.

These were backed up with an impressive jumble of bongs, cutting equipment, and other paraphernalia usually seen in murkier surroundings.

As the final fillip, there was a show of drug-hiding and smuggling equipment, ranging from Frisbees with secret compartments to toy dope trucks and shoes with special smuggle-a-hit heels.

"I hope it doesn't give Nancy ideas," grinned one Washington scribe, no stranger to the substances on parade.

7

A HEARTBEAT
AWAY

SUPPORTING CAST

At Valley Forge

During the long years of the War of Independence, at times the anxiety and the absence from her husband became intolerable for Martha Washington:

She met the Commander in Chief at his winter headquarters at Cambridge, after an absence of nearly a year, in December 1775, and continued during the Revolution to go each winter to his headquarters. In early spring she returned to her home, leaving behind her only child, whose desire to remain with his adopted father obtained from her a reluctant consent.

The next winter she passed at Morristown, New Jersey, where she experienced some of the real hardships and sufferings of camp life. The previous season, at Cambridge, the officers and their families had resided in the mansions of the Tories, who had deserted them to join the British; but at Morristown she occupied a small frame house, without any conveniences or comforts, and, as before, returned in the spring, with her daughter-in-law and children.

Valley Forge, during the last months of 1777 and the early part of 1778, was the scene of the severest sufferings, replete with more terrible want than any ever known in the history of the Colonies.

During all this season of horrors, Mrs. Washington remained

with her husband, trying to comfort and animate him in the midst of his trials. Succeeding years brought the same routine, and victory and defeat walked ofttimes hand in hand.

Power Behind the Throne

Mrs. Polk, intellectually, was one of the most marked women who ever presided in the White House. She never astonished or offended her visitors by revealing to them the depth or breadth of her intelligence; nevertheless she used that intelligence as a power—the power behind the throne. Never a politician, in a day when politics, by precedent and custom, were forbidden grounds to women, Sarah Polk was thoroughly conversant with all public affairs and made it a part of her duty to inform herself on all subjects which concerned her country or her husband.

She was her husband's private secretary and, probably, was the only lady of the White House who ever filled that office. She took charge of his papers, he trusting entirely to her memory and method for their safekeeping. If he wanted a document, long before labeled and pigeonholed, he said: "Sarah knows where it is"; and it was Sarah's ever-ready hand that laid it before his eyes.

Clipping Service

Eliza Johnson refused to play the part of White House hostess, but her influence over her husband during his troublesome presidency was said to have been extraordinary. Although she appeared only once in public, she kept busy in her room, reading all the newspapers and magazines. She clipped articles she thought the President should see, which she separated into two batches. She gave Andrew Johnson only the good news in the evening, so he could sleep well, waiting until breakfast to give him the bulk of the bad press.

Advocate

While General Grant was in command at Cairo, just after the battle of Belmont, and while his promotion to a major generalship was being discussed, a relation of his said to Julia Grant:

"Ulysses may get along as a brigadier, but he had better be satisfied with that and not seek to rise higher."

"There is no danger of his reaching a position above his capacity," she replied indignantly. "He is equal to a much higher one than this, and will certainly win it if he lives." And this was the recognition she always gave him, and to this fearless advocate of his worth he was indebted for much of the material help he had received from both his and her family.

Behind Every Successful Man

One shivery, snowy night in the winter of 1905, Secretary of War and Mrs. William Howard Taft bundled up in their warmest coats and rode in their carriage to the White House.

They dined alone with President and Mrs. Theodore Roosevelt by candlelight. The table talk was gay and animated, ranging from the new electric lights to Edward Arlington Robinson's newest poem, from the growing controversy over prohibition to the latest political intrigue.

The amiable Taft was feeling especially amiable; he had finally been persuaded by Mrs. Taft to go on a diet and was secretly delighted that he had already lost fifteen pounds. Mrs. Taft, who was inclined to be serious-minded and intense, was unusually lighthearted because a front-page story in the morning's *Washington Post* had mentioned her husband as a leading possibility for the Republican presidential nomination in 1908, since Roosevelt had already announced that he would not try for a third term.

After dinner President Roosevelt led his old friends into the library while his wife went off to tuck in the children for the night. He closed the library door behind them and draped himself comfortably in a big easy chair. He smiled at the Tafts. Then, suddenly, with an innate sense of drama, he made a wide sweep with his hands to form a circle. "This is my crystal ball," he said.

Gazing mystically into his "ball," Roosevelt intoned in a deep, faraway voice:

"I am the seventh son of a seventh daughter, and I have clairvoyant powers. I see a man weighing three hundred and fifty pounds. There's something hanging over his head. . . . I cannot make out what it is. . . . At one time it looks like the presidency. Then again it looks like the chief justiceship!"

"Make it the chief justiceship," said Taft promptly.

"Make it the presidency," said Mrs. Taft.

Mrs. Taft had one ambition since childhood, and that was to someday be First Lady of the land. When she was seventeen she spent a week at the White House with her older sister, as guests of President and Mrs. Rutherford Hayes, who were close friends of her parents. When she returned home to Cincinnati, young Nellie, as she was called, promised herself that she would only marry a man who could become President and take her back to live in that glamorous white mansion.

Through the years, Mrs. Taft prodded the husband she had selected toward the goal she had set for him. The judicial life that spelled comfort and dignity to Taft spelled boredom to her— "an awful groove" that she thought "quite too settled." She became his chief political adviser, his severest critic, and always the dominant influence in his life.

On March 4, 1909, when Taft was inaugurated, *The Washington Post* commented: "There is every reason why she [Mrs. Taft] should feel satisfaction in her husband's success, for had it not been for her determination to keep him from becoming a Supreme Court Justice he would not have been able to accept the nomination. . . . 'I want you to be in line for the presidential nomination,' she told him, and he followed what turned out to be excellent and timely advice."

The new First Lady herself was quoted that day as saying, "It always has been my ambition to see Mr. Taft President of the United States, and naturally when the ceremonies of the inauguration were in progress I was inexpressibly happy."

But Taft got his wish, too. After being defeated by Woodrow Wilson (helped greatly by his former friend Teddy Roosevelt's splitting of the vote) Taft retired to play golf and teach law, until Warren Harding appointed him Chief Justice in 1921.

Plus Ça Change

Having made him President, Helen Taft attended every one of her husband's Cabinet meetings. When the press accused her of influencing public policy, she said that she went along only to keep her husband awake.

Readiness Is All

Mrs. Harding often boasted that she "had made Warren Harding." Mrs. Taft attended important conferences in the White House until she became an invalid, and she was always deeply interested in her husband's political career. Mrs. Wilson was a power behind the scenes in her husband's last days. But although members of the household considered Mrs. Coolidge an important part of the administration, she scarcely knew from hour to hour what she was expected to do. She was always ready with her hat on, waiting for a last-minute summons to accompany the President anywhere. When Ike Hoover would ask her if she was going with her husband on a certain mission she would reply: "I do not know, but I am ready."

After they had been in the White House for two weeks, she felt she needed some clue to his movements. "Calvin, I wish you would have your Secret Service men give me your engagements," she told him mildly.

"Grace, we don't give that out promiscuously," he replied.

The President's Conscience

Eleanor Roosevelt, while denying having any real influence on public policy, exercised her right of free speech in the White House to the fullest extent. Her biographer, Joseph Lash, describes the aftermath of the 1944 campaign:

Although the President's popular margin was reduced in comparison to the 1940 returns, his victory was substantial and included a sizable increase in Democratic strength in Congress. To Eleanor, victory immediately posed the question: "What for?" When they returned to Washington she put that question to the President and Harry Hopkins in a talk she had with them about the next four years and which Hopkins recorded:

"Mrs. Roosevelt urged the President very strongly to keep in the forefront of his mind the domestic situation because she felt there was a real danger of his losing American public opinion in his foreign policy if he failed to follow through on the domestic implications of his campaign promises. She particularly hoped the President would not go to Great Britain and France and receive great demonstrations abroad for the present, believing that that would not set too well with the American people.

"She impressed on both of us that we must not be satisfied with merely making campaign pledges; the President being under moral obligation to see his domestic reforms through, particularly the organizing of our domestic life in such a way as to give everybody a job. She emphasized that this was an overwhelming task and she hoped neither the President nor I thought it was settled in any way by making speeches."

Of this Hopkins note [Robert] Sherwood wrote that Eleanor was known as the President's "eyes and ears" but that there were many others who reported to him. The unique function she performed for her husband was "as the keeper of and constant spokesman for her husband's conscience."

Her allegedly radical influence upon the President had been an issue in the campaign, a "phony" one she said. She had never had any real power or influence, she maintained. In any case, "these aren't the things people make decisions about. But the election showed that the people on the whole believe even a woman has a right to do what she believes is the right thing."

A Tower of Strength

Eleanor Roosevelt's strength was most manifest when she was told by Steve Early that FDR had died unexpectedly in Warm Springs. Although she later claimed that she did not remember having uttered these words, they were nonetheless typical of Mrs. R.: "I am more sorry for the people of this country and of the world than I am for ourselves." And The New York Times wrote: "A lesser human being would have been prostrated by the sudden and calamitous tidings, but Mrs. Roosevelt at once entered upon her responsibilities." Her biographer, Joseph Lash, describes Eleanor Roosevelt at this one of her finest moments:

She sent for Vice President Harry Truman. Her cable to her sons—HE DID HIS JOB TO THE END AS HE WOULD WANT YOU TO DO—became the order of the day for a stricken people and their government. She asked Steve Early to hold up the announcement of the President's death for fifteen minutes so that Henry Morgenthau could have a doctor break the news to his wife because she did not want her ailing friend to hear the news over the radio.

The Vice President, who did not know why he had been summoned to the White House so urgently, soon arrived and was ushered into Eleanor's sitting room. Anna and John Boettiger were with her, as was Early. Eleanor came forward and placed her arm gently on the Vice President's shoulder.

"Harry," she said quietly, "the President is dead."

For a moment a stunned Truman could not bring himself to speak. Finally, finding his voice, he asked, "Is there anything I can do for you?" He would never forget, he later wrote, her "deeply understanding" reply.

"Is there anything *we* can do for *you*?" she asked. "For you are the one in trouble now."

Who Commands the Commander in Chief?

General Eisenhower may have been Supreme Allied Commander and later Commander in Chief; yet there was a higher power both he and Chief Usher J. B. West came to recognize:

President Eisenhower had scheduled a stag luncheon for business associates his second week in office. Alonzo Fields pulled out a menu from his "appropriate for stag" file, and we set about our usual preparations to serve fifty in the State Dining Room.

Two days before the luncheon, Ann Whitman, General Eisenhower's personal secretary, called the Usher's office. "The President wants to see the menu for the luncheon," she informed us. Fields sent it over immediately, and back it came by return messenger, "Approved DDE."

The morning of the luncheon, when I went upstairs for Mrs. Eisenhower's bedside conference, she looked over the day's menus.

"What's this?" she asked. "I didn't approve this menu!"

"The President did, two or three days ago," I quickly explained.

Mrs. Eisenhower frowned, shaking her head in annoyance.

"I run everything in my house," she said. "In the future all menus are to be approved by *me* and not by anybody else!"

And Who Decides Who Is Right?

The First Lady's power is derived from her position in the marriage. Even in such a balanced relationship as that of Rosalynn and Jimmy Carter, her power comes from supporting his policies, as journalist Ralph Martin pointed out in a Ladies Home Journal *article about the Carters in the White House:*

She probably is the President's main adviser. There's no one else he trusts more implicitly, no one whose judgment he respects more than hers. No one else can tell him, as she can, "This just doesn't fit in with what people expect of you, Jimmy Carter."

"Everything they've done has not been the case of Jimmy Carter doing it with a *supportive* wife," press secretary Jody Powell points out. "It has been Jimmy Carter and Rosalynn Carter doing it together as a *team*." She gets a steady stream of her husband's circulating memos, on which he scribbles, "Ros, what think?" And White House staffers often hear him interject, "Well, Rosalynn thinks that . . ."

"When we have an argument," she says, "I listen to his point of view. If he's right, then I agree to do it his way. And if I'm right, then we'll do it my way."

And That's the Truth

A journalist once asked President Truman if it was true that in the heat of the moment he had called a certain general "squirrel head." "No, I never said that," and the President looked to his wife to back him up. "Really?" Bess said with a sweet smile. "It sounds just like you."

POLITICS

Advice

As a previous dispute with England grew worse, Abigail Adams advised her husband that it was time for the colonies to separate from the mother country:

Braintree, 12 November 1775

The intelligence you will receive before this reaches you, will, I should think, make a plain path, though a dangerous one, for you. I could not join you today, in the petitions of our worthy pastor, for a reconciliation between our no-longer parent state, but tyrant state, and these colonies. Let us separate; they are unworthy to be our brethren. Let us renounce them; and instead of supplications as formerly, for their prosperity and happiness, let us beseech the Almighty to blast their counsels, and bring to nought all their devices.

Those Democrats

Dr. Manasseh Cutler, who spent many evenings at the house of the Secretary of State and delighted in the gracious manners and spirited conversation of Mrs. Madison, said that upon one occasion this usually amiable woman expressed herself quite forcibly upon the dishonesty of Democrats. Dr. Cutler remarked, inquiringly, "You do not believe all the Democrats are dishonest?" "Yes," she said, "I do—every one of them!" This unequivocal rejoinder provoked a merry laugh, in which the grave little Secretary of State [James Madison] joined heartily.

But normally Dolley kept herself out of politics. During the debates of the war with the British she wrote:

"The mornings are devoted to Congress, where all delight to listen to the violence of evil spirits. I stay quietly at home (as quietly as one can be who has so much to feel at the expression for and against their conduct)."

Mrs. Madison's "their" is doubtless intended to refer to her husband and his advisers, as her own "conduct" could not have been questioned. Indeed, although Mr. Blaine spoke of Mrs. Madison as a "political force," her influence was simply that which a good and gracious woman always exerts upon the life about her. No general discussion of political questions was encouraged in her drawing room, and the letters of the President's wife, with the exception of expressions of uneasiness at the prospect of war, are confined to social and family matters.

Repartee

Entertaining her husband's political enemies is one of the more difficult tasks of the President's wife. According to a nineteenth-century account, Sarah Polk handled it with humor:

Shortly before his departure from the Capital, Mr. Henry Clay attended a dinner party, with many other distinguished gentlemen of both political parties at the President's house. The party is said to have been a very pleasant affair—good feeling abounded, and wit and lively repartee gave zest to the occasion, while Mrs. Polk, the winning and accomplished hostess, added the finishing grace of her excellent housewifery in the superior management of the feast. Mr. Clay was, of course, honored with a seat near the President's lady, where it became him to put in requisition to those insinuating talents which he possessed in so eminent a degree, and which are irresistible even to his enemies. Mrs. Polk, with her usual and affable manner, was extremely courteous to her distinguished guest, whose good opinion, as of all who share the hospitalities of the White House, she did not fail to win.

"Madam," said Mr. Clay, in that bland manner peculiar to himself, "I must say that in my travels, wherever I have been, in all companies and among all parties, I have heard but one opinion of you. All agree in commending, in the highest terms, your excellent administration of the domestic affairs of the White House. But," he continued, directing her attention to her husband, "as for that young gentleman there, I cannot say as much. There is some little difference of opinion in regard to the policy of his course."

"Indeed," said Mrs. Polk, "I am glad to hear that my administration is popular. And in return for your compliment, I will say that if the country should elect a Whig next fall, I know of no one whose elevation would please me more than that of Henry Clay."

"Thank you, thank you, Madam."

"And I will assure you of one thing. If you do have occasion to occupy the White House on the fourth of March next, it shall be surrendered to you in perfect order from garret to cellar."

His Better Half

Woodrow Wilson's second wife came closest among First Ladies to acting as the President of the United States. Her first venture into politics was not greeted well, according to an anonymous gossip:

Some time ago, she ventured to attend a meeting of Democratic women in Baltimore. That started it! The Whispering Gallery was in fine form, and it echoed and re-echoed with murmurs, exclamations, and strange asseverations. "He has sent her over to spy out the land!" was the theme played, with variations, on

189

the vibrant chords of women's tongues. Bad politician as he may be, Woodrow Wilson knew better than to send his wife on such an errand. He once said that she had better political judgment than he had. On hearing this, one woman remarked: "That isn't a matter of much pride."

Fish Story

An unnamed Congressman once sent an aide with a very large fish over to the Hoover White House. The fish was supposed to have been a present from Maine, and Mrs. Hoover had it sent to the kitchen. Then the Congressman arrived and revealed that he had sent the fish over so that he could be photographed with it and the President. By the time the fish was located, its head was missing. Mrs. Hoover, somewhat embarrassed, did some fast thinking. She had the fish taken to Lillian Parks, the White House seamstress, who sewed back the head. The photograph was then taken and, according to Mrs. Parks, nobody in Maine could have told the difference.

Better Than Wyoming

Although she married into one of the most political families in America, Mrs. Kennedy was never much interested in politics. Once during the 1960 campaign a reporter was trying to estimate for her the sizable victory her husband was likely to score in New York State. "Really?" she responded. "That's important, isn't it? How nice."

We Must Stop Meeting Like This

During a political luncheon, Jacqueline Kennedy was seated several places away from JFK—then still a Senator. When asked to speak, the normally shy and apolitical wife remarked: "This is the closest I've come to lunching with my husband in four months."

We're Also Holding Your Mother

Once in the White House, Jacqueline Kennedy quickly caught on. In the early months of his administration, Kennedy was facing opposition to his New Frontier school bill. One of the young Republican senators putting up a fight was an eligible bachelor who had his eye on Letitia Baldrige, the First Lady's social secretary. He was strolling one day on a Washington street when suddenly the presidential limousine pulled up and the Senator was startled to see the First Lady lean out. "I thought you were going to be nice to us," Mrs. Kennedy shouted out from her perch on the jump seat, while her husband was hugely enjoying the episode in the back. "Because if you're not, I won't let you take out Tish Baldrige anymore."

CAMPAIGNS

Prayer

Abigail Adams, writing to her husband in February 1797, upon his election as the second President of the United States:

My thoughts and meditations are with you, though personally absent; and my petitions to heaven are that the things which make for your peace may not be hidden from your eyes. My feelings are not those of pride or ostentation upon the occasion. They are solemnized by a sense of the obligations, the important trusts, and numerous duties connected with it. That you may be enabled to discharge them with honor to yourself, with justice and impartiality to your country, and with satisfaction to this great people, shall be the daily prayer of yours.

Disinterested Devotion

"Aunt Rachel," as Mrs. Jackson was called by her husband's personal friends, had accompanied him to Washington when he was there as a Senator from Tennessee. She was a short, stout, unattractive, and uneducated woman, though greatly endeared to General Jackson. While he had been in the army she had carefully managed his plantation, his slaves, and his money matters, and her devotion to him knew no bounds. Her happiness was centered in his, and it was her chief desire to smoke her corncob pipe in peace at his side. When told that he had been elected President of the United States, she replied, "Well, for Mr. Jackson's sake I am glad of it, but for myself I am not." A few weeks later she was arrayed for the grave in a white satin costume which she had provided herself with to wear at the White House.

Ambition Fulfilled

The Republican Convention at Chicago verified Mrs. Lincoln's prophecy of being the wife of a President. It assembled the 16th June, 1860, and after a close contest between the two favorites of the Republican party—Governor Seward and Mr. Lincoln—the latter was declared unanimously nominated as a candidate for the presidency. In Springfield, Mrs. Lincoln waited in her own home for the result of her prediction, and when at noon the cannon on the public square announced the decision of the convention, breathless with expectancy, she scarcely dared to ask the result. Her husband, in the excitement of the moment, did not forget her, but putting the telegram in his pocket, remarked to his friends that "there is a little woman on Eighth Street who has some interest in the matter," and walked home to gladden her heart with the good news. That Friday night must have been the very happiest of her life, for few women have ever craved the position as she did, and it was hers! Crowds of citizens and strangers thronged to her home all the afternoon, and the roar of cannon and the wild, tumultuous shouts of excited men filled the town with a deafening noise.

All the Way with LBJ

According to Liz Carpenter, who executed the logistics for it, Lady Bird Johnson's Whistlestop campaign

was a salvage operation in the wake of the Civil Rights Act of 1964. The bill had been engineered by LBJ and signed three months before the Lady Bird Whistlestop rolled through Dixie. Our star attraction was a Southern-bred First Lady. We were supposed to blow kisses and spread love through eight states and make them like it, forget about Barry Goldwater, and vote for "that nigger-lover in the White House." Miraculously we held half the South for the Democrats.

Mrs. Johnson had always said placidly, "Lyndon is the kind of man who stretches you."

Well, she can say that again. We stretched ourselves over 1,682 miles, 47 stops, and four "slowdowns" from October 6th to the 9th. Do you know you can get votes just by slowing down and waving?

"Don't give me the easy towns, Liz," she said. "Anyone can get into Atlanta—it's the new, modern South. Let me take the tough ones."

Thanks a lot, Mrs. Johnson!

That meant the places neither LBJ nor HHH could get in and out of with their hides on—or they couldn't take the time to visit because it was a lost cause. Ours was simply a holding operation.

"But we must go," Mrs. Johnson insisted. "We must let them know that we love the South. We respect them. We have not turned our backs on them. I don't think there's much chance of carrying it for Lyndon, judging by the letters I get from my Alabama cousins. But at least we won't lose by default."

After a noisy send-off by the press and the President, the hard campaigning began. The First Lady had an early chance to show her mettle:

Our first trouble in the South came in Columbia, South Carolina, and it was so surprisingly ugly, it left all of us aghast.

There was a tremendous crowd waiting at the station as Governor Donald Russell introduced, in gallant and glowing terms, the First Lady. And then, before she could even begin talking, there was a rumble, a drumbeat, and a chant from a group of boys bunched together, heckling, "We want Barry! We want Barry!"

Shocked, the crowd looked to see how the First Lady would handle this startling discourtesy. She did not disappoint them. One hand raised gently, she said, "My friends, in this country we are entitled to many viewpoints. You are entitled to yours. But right now, I'm entitled to mine."

It worked. That time it worked, and every network that evening carried the filmed story of the First Lady's courage. Newspapers all over the country remade their editorial pages. And at Republican headquarters in Washington, Barry Goldwater's top aides denounced the attack on the First Lady and tried to deter heckling, for they knew it did them no good.

The Eyes of Texas

During the 1960 campaign, Lady Bird covered 35,000 miles, mainly in the South, for her husband and the Democratic ticket. Bobby Kennedy later acknowledged her by saying: "Lady Bird carried Texas for us."

Betty's Husband

Betty Ford was such an asset to her husband's presidential campaign that it became almost an embarrassment. When she got the first campaign button that said "Betty's Husband for President," she actually hid it, in case he might not like it. But soon thereafter Gerry Ford himself brought home a button with the same slogan to tease her, and they both had a good laugh about it.

Running Her for Office

Rosalynn Carter became a good campaigner through practice:

On the plane Rosalynn glances at notes for her speech, then recalls the early days of her husband's campaign when just the thought of making a speech made her physically ill. Jimmy suggested that she use a few notes instead of trying to memorize every word. It worked. Her delivery improved, her confidence and poise grew.

One speech, she says, reminiscing, stands out in her memory. It was an introduction for Jimmy, and she talked about their early years, their work together as a family. She noticed that Jimmy was listening to her more intently than usual. His eyes teared, then suddenly he jumped up, grabbed her, kissed her, and asked the crowd, "How many of you would like to have this woman as First Lady?"

And May the Best Man Win

Betty Ford's thoughtfulness extended to her husband's political enemies. During the 1976 presidential campaign, just before the final televised debate between the candidates at William and Mary College, the First Lady left a scribbled note on candidate Jimmy Carter's rostrum. It read:

"Dear Mr. Carter, may I wish you the best tonight. I'm sure the best man will win. I happen to have a favorite candidate, my husband, President Ford. Best wishes, Betty Ford."

THE PUBLIC ROLE

HOSTESS

Protocol

During Jefferson's presidency, Mrs. Madison, then wife of the Secretary of State, shared the duties of being official hostess at the White House with the President's daughter, Martha Randolph. The British Ambassador and his wife, Mr. and Mrs. Merry, were invited to dine with President Jefferson:

When dinner was announced, Mrs. Madison happened to be standing and talking to the President at some distance from Mrs. Merry, and he offered his arm to her and conducted her to the table, where she always presided when no members of his family were present. This attention to the wife of the Secretary of State was considered by Mrs. Merry as an insult. President Jefferson had abolished all etiquette in regard to official precedence when he went into office, and Mrs. Merry knew this, but she never forgave the occurrence and never afterward went to the White House.

Mrs. Madison regretted being the innocent cause of such a trouble, but she was spared further notoriety by the absence of the British Minister or his family ever afterward at the President's reunions. The affair was not, however, destined to end here, for after the first clamor had subsided, the President, through another Foreign Minister, inquired if Mr. and Mrs. Merry would accept an invitation to a family dinner. It was understood that they would accept, and Mr. Jefferson wrote the invitation himself. Mr. Merry addressed a note to the Secretary of State to know if he was invited in his private or official capacity; "if in the one, he must obtain the permission of his sovereign; if in the other, he must receive an assurance in advance that he would be treated as became his position."

[After the original incident] such a stir was made by the angry Ambassador that Mr. Madison wrote to Mr. Monroe (who had succeeded Mr. King as our Minister to England), apprising him of the facts, to enable him to answer an expected call of the British government for official explanations. Mr. Monroe, however, got his first information from a friendly British under secretary, who intimated that he would soon probably hear of the matter through a different channel. The Minister was delighted. Within a very short period, the wife of an English under secretary had been accorded precedence over his own, under analogous circumstances. He had no great fund of humor, but the absurdity of the whole affair, and the excellent materials in his possession for a reply to a call for explanations, struck him in a most amusing light. Shaking with merriment, he hinted to his informant the satisfaction the call would give him. He never afterward heard a lisp on the subject.

A few years later the British got some satisfaction by burning down the White House.

Gate-Crasher

In a famous letter to his friend Henry Brevoort, Washington Irving describes how, badly shaven and uninvited, he attended one of Dolley Madison's levees:

I arrived at the Inn about dusk; and, understanding that Mrs. Madison was to have her levee or drawing room that very evening, I swore by all my gods I would be there. But how? was the question. I had got away down into Georgetown, and the persons to whom my letters of introduction were directed lived all upon

Capitol Hill, about three miles off, while the President's house was exactly halfway. Here was a non-plus enough to startle any man of less enterprising spirit; but I had sworn to be there, and I determined to keep my oath. So I mounted with a stout heart to my room; resolved to put on my pease blossoms and silk stockings; gird up my loins; sally forth on my expedition; and like a vagabond knight-errant, trust to Providence for success and whole bones. Just as I descended from my attic chamber, full of this valorous spirit, I was met by my landlord, with whom, and the headwaiter, by the bye, I had held a private cabinet counsel on the subject. Bully Rook informed me that there was a party of gentlemen just going from the house, one of whom, Mr. Fontaine Maury of New York, had offered his services to introduce me to "the Sublime Porte." I cut one of my best opera flourishes; skipped into the dressing room, popped my head into the hands of a sanguinary Jacobinical barber, who carried havoc and desolation into the lower regions of my face; mowed down all the beard on one of my cheeks, and laid the other in blood like a conquered province; and thus, like a second Banquo, with "twenty mortal murthers on my head," in a few minutes I emerged from dirt and darkness into the blazing splendor of Mrs. Madison's drawing room. Here I was most graciously received; found a crowded collection of great and little men, of ugly old women and beautiful young ones, and in ten minutes was hand and glove with half the people in the assemblage. Mrs. Madison is a fine, portly, buxom dame, who has a smile and a pleasant word for everybody. Her sisters, Mrs. Cutts and Mrs. Washington, are like the two Merry Wives of Windsor; but as to Jemmy Madison—ah! poor Jemmy!—he is but a withered little apple-John.

Memory

Dolley Madison was said to be, during Mr. Madison's administration, the most popular person in the United States, and she certainly had a remarkable memory for names and faces. No person introduced to Mrs. Madison at one of the crowded levees at the White House required a second introduction on meeting her again, but had the gratification of being recognized and addressed by his or her own name.

Do as You Please

On General Jackson's election to the presidency he appointed Major Donelson his private secretary and invited Mrs. Donelson to officiate as mistress of ceremonies at the Executive Mansion. To settle a delicate question of precedence between Mrs. Jackson, Jr., and Mrs. Donelson, who were both inmates of the President's House and nieces of General Jackson, he said to Mrs. Jackson, "You, my dear, are mistress of the Hermitage [General Jackson's house in Florida] and Emily is hostess of the White House." Both were satisfied with this decision, and ever afterward Mrs. Donelson occupied the first position in the President's Mansion. Beloved as a daughter by Mrs. Jackson, and intimately associated with her for years, she was also an honored and dear friend at the time of her death; and her tenderness and sympathy did much to mitigate the poignancy of the General's bereavement. He always called her "my daughter," and often when wearied with the cares of office would seek relaxation amid her family circle. Arbiter in politics, he deferred all matters of etiquette to her, and when she would appeal to him to settle any knotty social point, he would reply, "You know best, my dear. Do as you please."

Wildflower

Of lively imagination, Emily Donelson was quick at repartee, and had that gift possessed by so few talkers of listening gracefully. Thrown in contact with the brightest and most cultivated intellects of the day, she sustained her part; and her favor was eagerly sought by the learned and polished. A foreign minister once said to her: "Madam, you dance with the grace of a Parisian. I can hardly realize you were educated in Tennessee." "Count, you forget," was her spirited reply, "that grace is a cosmopolite, and like a wildflower, is much oftener found in the woods than in the streets of a city."

Duty

As a good hostess, Mrs. Polk was even willing to read a book outside her own religious interests:

One morning a lady found her reading. "I have many books presented to me by their writers," said she, "and I try to read them all; at present this is not possible; but this evening the author of this book dines with the President, and I could not be so unkind as to appear wholly ignorant and unmindful of his gift."

At one of her evening receptions a gentleman remarked, "Madame, you have a very genteel assemblage tonight." "Sir," replied Mrs. Polk with perfect good humor, but very significantly, "I have never seen it otherwise."

Burden

A hundred years ago the social life of Washington placed such heavy demands upon the women of official and private life that Mrs. Grant, widow of the President, made a statement:

I will most cordially endorse a concerted movement on the part of the social leaders of Washington to arrange that the hours now given to evening entertainments shall be fewer, and so more in accordance with the laws of nature.

Mothers of young girls now absolutely dread their entrance into society because of the great drain on their strength which social life means.

I think the older members of the world of fashion can obviate all this. Have no entertainment, dance, dinner, or reception which will extend later than midnight.

The Party Wasn't Over

Early in their first summer at the White House, the Hardings threw open the grounds and held their first garden party. It was a magnificent success. The weather was perfect, the green lawn a velvet carpet splashed with gay colors—the red uniforms of the band, the bright frocks and hats and parasols. It was a distinct change after the seclusion that followed President Wilson's long sickness.

Mrs. Harding tried one innovation that afternoon. In order to indicate the close of the party the band played "The End of a Perfect Day." However, someone had previously announced that this was Mrs. Harding's favorite melody, so it was a pointless allusion so far as the guests were concerned. It was played a second time, but the hint failed to penetrate the pleasure-sodden minds of the party. In the ballroom, where the dancing was in progress, the end of the party was once more proclaimed. At last it seemed to dawn on some that the oft-repeated tune had a suggestion of finality, and the crowd gradually dispersed. "Are you going to establish that as a definite custom for the termination of White House functions?" one woman asked. "Not after this!" said Mrs. Harding, laughing.

Shocking the Help

Franklin Delano Roosevelt's inauguration brought not only a New Deal to the country, but also an energetic hostess who did not care much for tradition to the White House. At first this caused confusion among the staff, as Alonzo Fields, who became Chief Butler during this period, relates:

March 4, 1933, my first inauguration, was not only a hard, long day but one filled with mixed emotions and confusion. No one had a plan of what to do except that we did have a menu from Mrs. Roosevelt. For luncheon she had ordered fifty covers, and bouillon, salmon salad, chicken salad, whole-wheat and white-bread-and-butter sandwiches, coffee and tea and plenty of milk. She added ice cream and cake.

There were to be three thousand covers for tea with assorted sandwiches, buttered nut bread, tea, coffee, punch, cake, and cookies. The dinner menu was oyster stew, crackers, scrambled eggs and sausages, fried potatoes, creamed chicken, peas, buttered rolls, buttered biscuits, jellies and jams, charlotte russe, and coffee.

For luncheon she didn't want any tables set up, but just to have a few tables nearby. We had a buffet in the center of the dining room. It was a sick-looking table with the chicken salad, salmon salad, bread-and-butter sandwiches, coffee, tea, and plenty of milk.

The President came into the dining room on Mr. James Roosevelt's arm. We hustled a table to a spot he requested. Encarnación served the President his bouillon and I rushed over with Mrs. Roosevelt's, but when I reached her she merely smiled and moved away to the table and started serving tea and coffee to the guests.

I stood there holding her bouillon. Well, we were flabbergasted. A First Lady, with all the help we had, rushing off to serve the guests, and the help didn't know what to do! She was really in our way and the order of service was disrupted. No one gave any priority to the President. The guests took what they wanted and we just tried to do our best and acted as if we knew what it was all about.

Someone asked for ice cream before the bouillon had been finished. In fact, we never knew what was what after the First Lady started serving at the buffet table. The guests finished with their lunch and were leaving without waiting for the President to finish.

Encarnación said, "I don't understand these people. They eat ice cream with their bouillon."

Before we had finished serving the oyster stew, Mrs. Roosevelt said, "We will have the coffee and tea and milk with the dinner."

So Connie said to me, "Mr. Fields, you were right."

I said, "Yes, Connie, these people are going to throw Old Man

Protocol and formality right out the window, from what little I have seen."

Well, the guests finished their dinners just as they willed, saying, "I must be going." Sometimes Mrs. Roosevelt would say, "Franklin, Joe"—or Jane—"is leaving now." The President would smile and say, "Well, Joe, it was good of you to come. We'll see you later. Have a good time."

This was going on all through the dinner—and to think that just twenty-four hours earlier no one would have thought of leaving the table before the President!

Smoking

The Hoovers were Quakers and occupied the White House during Prohibition, so some of the thirstier guests would fill up with some home brew before setting out for the White House. Smoking was permitted according to sex, and would sometimes lead to disaster. Chief Butler Fields witnessed one of these:

Mrs. Hoover would politely tell ladies that the President didn't approve of women smoking. The President was a cigar smoker. This reminds me of an incident during the serving of tea in the Green Parlor for Lady Astor and His Lordship. The President seldom attended teas. In fact, he didn't drink tea. So when we were alerted that he would be present we always prepared orangeade for him.

He arrived after the tea had been in progress for a few minutes. He greeted Lady Astor and His Lordship and apologized for being tardy. I served the orangeade to the President as usual. When he had finished he placed the glass on a little serving table and asked permission to smoke, which naturally was granted. He pulled out a cigar, took off the wrapper, and tossed it into the empty glass, although an ashtray was nearby. Encarnación did not see the wrapper in the glass. He approached the President and inquired if he cared for another glass of orangeade. Before I could signal, Connie had filled the glass. The President lifted it to drink and saw the wrapper. Without hesitating, he took the wrapper out with his fingers and drank the orangeade, then placed the wrapper in the ashtray. Poor Connie nearly had a stroke. He was afraid Mrs. Hoover had seen the incident, for there was little she missed in a breach of service.

One of Mrs. Roosevelt's first acts of social change was to lift the ban on ladies smoking. Though Mrs. Roosevelt did not really smoke, she would ask for the cigarettes to be passed and would take one and go through the motions of smoking. Anyone knew she did not really know how to smoke. After she had established the custom of ladies smoking in the White House she stopped taking the smokes when they were passed.

Democracy

Eleanor Roosevelt also took immediate steps to broaden the social spectrum of her invitees list. Some functions remained exclusive, such as the movie-stars luncheons or the one organized by Cabinet wives for the Senate ladies. But she also gave enormous tea parties, instituting what the staff called "the double-header tea." Whereas her predecessors were content with having on a few occasions a few hundred people for the whole afternoon, Mrs. Roosevelt thought nothing of inviting four or five hundred people for 4:00 P.M. and another group of the same size for 5:00 P.M. She also invited people from many different walks of life, something that did not entirely please the Washington social elite. Chief Butler Fields repeats a story circulating during the early days of the Roosevelt era about a lady who had been invited to a White House reception and consequently had let her maid have the afternoon off. In the receiving line just ahead of her she was astonished to see her maid, who had received a separate invitation. The society matron suddenly was seized with malaise and left in a hurry.

Royal Visit

Perhaps because of their radical republican traditions, Americans are peculiarly susceptible to the glamour of royalty. In 1964, King Hussein of Jordan visited the White House. Lady Bird Johnson confided to her diary on April 14:

207

There was a presentation of gifts. We gave the King a gold clock with the U.S. Seal and engraved inscription, a vermeil pen stand with two gold pens, also with seal and inscription, and a camera and a book of Lyndon's speeches, called *A Time for Action*. Sometimes I am vaguely unhappy that our gifts seem less imaginative and less meaningful than the gifts that foreign monarchs make to us. This was one of those times, for His Majesty gave to me two bracelets from the time of the patriarch Abraham and a little oil-burning lamp that might have been used at any time during a thousand years of biblical history. To both of us he gave a magnificent Bible, bound in mother-of-pearl and elaborately carved. Following the presentation came the always-thrilling removal of the colors, the forming of the line, and the marching downstairs to the tune of "Hail to the Chief."

The King sat on my right and his beautiful English—he was educated at Sandhurst—made conversation easy, although I can't say there was any time I felt I had made real contact with him. We spoke about his having piloted the plane (a 707) on the way over. I approached gingerly the subject of water, and he said that many of the springs of the Jordan River rose within Israel. For the first time I asked the guest of honor to sign my menu. The autograph was in Arabic; I couldn't read it but the King graciously added "Hussein I."

We went to the East Room after dinner and heard the Dave Brubeck Quartet render four numbers of avant-garde jazz, planned because we had been told that the King was a jazz fan. Afterward we went into the Blue Room for dancing. Since the King had had a long hard trip, he danced only long enough to be polite and took his departure.

Altogether, I would say it was a successful, not superb evening, but I wish I could look at it through the eyes of some of the guests and not always through my own.

Next day a society columnist said, "Not one of the 151 guests were seen to yawn once, which may be somewhat historical in review of presidential entertainment."

MEETING PEOPLE

Identity Crisis

Each First Lady developed her own way of relating to visitors to the White House. Chief Butler Fields watched Mrs. Eisenhower becoming adapted to the job:

It was important to Mamie Eisenhower to be set apart from the throngs. After she'd stood in her first receiving line at the White House, she asked for a platform "so everyone can see me."

Down in the carpenter's shop, we built a small platform, elevating her about a foot, so that the tiny First Lady could look her visitors in the eye as she shook hands. We covered the stand with an Oriental rug and hauled it out for her second reception, for the DAR [Daughters of the American Revolution].

But it didn't work. "We almost lost me," she laughingly told me the next day. "They nearly jerked me off the platform."

So at the next reception, for the wives of conventioneering Shriners, she stood on the landing of the grand staircase, overlooking the Green Room, and waved to more than two thousand ladies as they passed by. Except for a few hurt feelings from unshaken hands, this arrangement seemed to work all right. A few days later, receiving fifteen hundred Republican women, she stood on the bottom step facing the lobby, and four top Republican ladies stood on the second step, immediately behind her.

She rested for ten minutes after greeting each group of two hundred, while they were served tea. When she came back downstairs to meet the second group, she stopped by my office.

"Would you please have the social aides speak to the ladies standing behind me, and ask them to step back a couple of steps? They're so close nobody knows who is *me*!"

Moving Right Along

First Ladies spend much time meeting people at ceremonial functions. One of Edith Bolling Wilson's early visits to a women's club was captured by an anonymous Washington gossip:

When Mrs. Wilson Number Two came to the White House, there was the usual rush of clubs and organizations to entertain her and run an eye over the new Lady of the Mansion. One national organization gave a reception in her honor, but they didn't have a clubhouse then. They held their social sessions in a room behind a tailor's shop.

Desiring to make it as impressive as possible, the committee requested the tailor to move his pressing board and close the door, so that in passing into the clubroom the First Lady might not be suffocated by the steam rising from a half-pressed pair of trousers. The tailor, a born Democrat, wanted to see all that was going on. So he kept the door open and continued the sacred rite of pressing trousers, watching for the White House entourage through a veil of of vapor which arose from the moist cloth.

At last she came, flanked by two women secretaries to act as buffers. Furniture and fittings had been hastily borrowed to add to the beauty and comfort of the clubroom. There was a settee. In that settee was a broken spring. Beside that settee was a vigilance committee of one, specially appointed to keep Mrs. Wilson from sitting on that broken spring. But she did. The vigilance committee had for one sad moment relaxed, and there was a—plonk. Mrs. Wilson had sat down. She was with many apologies and some effort assisted to arise and accommodated in a more secure and seemly setting.

Then the procession formed and the introductions began. You know how it is. You mumble your name, or somebody in advance mumbles it for you, and the guest shakes hands and endeavors to accommodate each with an individual smile. One woman paused to have a little chat and held up the whole line. "I have been connected with Lady Blank's hospital in Canada," she volunteered, recounting her war sacrifices. "Have you, really?" said

Mrs. Wilson, smiling. Her face is very pleasant when she smiles and her interest is aroused. The woman still stood in front of her. "Yes, indeed, I have," she said, and diving a hand into her pocket, she produced a white veil. "And this is the veil I wore the day I saw her, and I want you to accept it," thrusting the crumpled treasure into Mrs. Wilson's hand.

One of the buffers on her flank quickly relieved Mrs. Wilson of the embarrassing gift and hid the precious gossamer from sacrilegious eyes. Mrs. Wilson murmured strange phrases of gratitude. There was a determined effort at the rear of the line. A forward movement crowded the generous donor off the center of the stage, and the program proceeded.

The People's House

President Jackson held public receptions which anybody might attend, with or without invitation. This custom was in accordance with the opinion that the Executive Mansion belonged to the people, and therefore the people should have the privilege of entering the mansion at any time when the President gave notice that he would be "at home." The result was that such a great number of people crowded into the White House, whenever a reception was held, that often those who had been formally invited could not get into the mansion at all.

After Lincoln's assassination, access to the mansion became much more regulated. Except for the New Year's Day receptions, when as many as nine thousand people were greeted by the First Family, invitations to the White House became restricted more and more to political and government circles. From Jackson down to McKinley, various Presidents made attempts to limit the number of persons who should attend White House receptions. Cards were issued which allowed the bearer to attend all receptions for the whole season. But all such attempts were in vain, the people continuing to pour into the mansion whether they held a card of invitation or not.

President McKinley proceeded to take steps to correct the abuse that had been so long endured by other Presidents. He ordered that cards should be sent to certain persons, that they should specify which reception the guest was to attend, and that only those who held such cards should be admitted. Theodore Roosevelt made the reformation more pronounced by having cards of admission included in each invitation, which had to be shown to the attendant at the White House entrance on the nights of the receptions.

All these reforms were necessary to bring order to the White House receptions, since before that time, chaos and confusion reigned whenever the President or his wife received.

Workout

More than one President had said, after leaving the White House, that one of the hardest duties he had to perform was that of handshaking. Each President has had his own peculiar, individual way of grasping the hand of a guest. Some used first the right hand and then the left, alternately, in shaking hands. Others used only the right hand. Some wore a glove on the left hand, others wore no glove at all.

At one reception President Lincoln shook hands with so many people that the next day his own hands were covered with blisters. According to Thomas Pendel, the White House doorkeeper:

> I crowded my way through the hallway where the jam of people was very compact, into the Blue Parlor, with a glass of water for Mr. Lincoln. He drank it, and seemed to enjoy it very much. The perspiration was just rolling down his face as he grasped the hands of the passing throng, as though he had been splitting rails as of yore. Everything passed off very nicely that night, and next morning, the Sabbath, Simon Cameron called upon the President. Mr. Cameron was received in the Blue Parlor. After a while they came out and stood in the grand corridor opposite, engaging in earnest conversation. The President said, "Cameron, something occurred to me last night at the reception that never did before." He held his hands up and said, "Cameron, between every one of these fingers is a blister from the shaking of hands."

During the celebration of the Washington Centennial, in 1900, one newspaper recorded the fact that President McKinley broke all records by clasping 4,816 palms in one hour and forty-five minutes.

When Mrs. Cleveland became the youngest First Lady ever to preside at the White House "she did what no other wife of a President attempted," according to a contemporary journalist. "At receptions she would take a step forward and shake hands with the caller, returning to her position before saluting the next in line. This task is one which only a woman of tremendous physical endurance could carry out successfully. At one New Year's reception, for example, nine thousand persons greeted the President and his wife. So that Mrs. Cleveland took nine thousand steps and shook hands nine thousand times on each of these occasions."

Looking Back

A few months after becoming First Lady, Lady Bird Johnson invited the legendary Alice Roosevelt Longworth, who was nearing eighty, to the scene of her childhood:

It was one of those afternoons I had promised myself—one of those completely unofficial things, no duty at all, just pleasure. Mrs. Longworth has lived this life I've loved, in this town I've loved, and seen so much of it—has observed it with such a caustic wit and such close-up range, that I yearned to spend an hour with her. And it was a grand one! I rushed downstairs hoping to meet her at the front entrance to accord her the dignity that is due her age and position—but, alas, I was just a moment late. She had on her stiff black hat, which is a trademark with her, and a big smile. We came upstairs and sat in the family living room.

It was no trouble to persuade her to reminisce about the days when she was in the house. She told us that it was true that when one of her little brothers had been sick, they had taken his pony up in the elevator to his room because it would surely help make him well! I can understand that so well, because Luci really needed our beagles Him and Her at hand one day not long ago when she was sick.

To show how much this town has changed—that same brother rode his horse, unattended by any Secret Service person, to school a few miles from the White House. She told us about attending a Republican dinner for President Eisenhower—one of the appreciation dinners where several Senators were deploring the sad state of social life, when people jumped in swimming pools with their clothes on and did the "Twist" in the stately halls of the White House. She laughed and she talked about the time her father had an American wrestler and a Japanese practitioner of jujitsu in the East Room, stripped to their waists, engaged in the respective styles of battling, to see which one would come off best. I guess one of the main things I like about Alice Longworth is her spirit and vitality at seventy-nine or thereabouts. She also mentioned a time when she herself jumped into a swimming pool with her clothes on, but it was on board ship and she had on the white, washable summer clothes that were the fashion for strolling the deck in that day.

I don't know whether I would like to be around when Mrs. Longworth is describing her visit later on to somebody else, because I don't know how we appear in her eyes.

Equal but Separate

Few examples can illustrate more vividly how far race relations have progressed—and needed to progress—in the United States than the fuss raised over Mrs. Hoover's inviting to tea Mrs. De Priest, wife of a black Congressman from Illinois. This account is by a member of the domestic staff:

Mrs. Hoover had decided to invite all the Congressional ladies to a series of teas and the families of the different Senators and members of the House were allotted to four groups and invited accordingly, the Cabinet ladies being asked to all the parties. The name of Mrs. De Priest was put aside for future consideration when these groups were made up. Everyone concerned realized that it was an unusual situation. Should Mrs. De Priest be included? The decision was postponed, for there was no precedent to go by.

Thus the four parties of Congressional ladies came and went and Mrs. De Priest was invited to none of them.

In the meantime the discussion as to what to do continued. The social secretary who had charge of these affairs took the position that she must be invited, since the parties were of an official nature. Precedents were sought, but none could be found that definitely applied. The nearest approach seemed to be the Booker Washington affair in the Roosevelt Administration. Mrs. Hoover seemed to have an open mind and was willing to be guided by whatever course was mapped out for her. However, when it was at last decided in the affirmative, she seemed hesitant and began to figure how it could be done.

After much discussion pro and con, she decided to give an extra party for Mrs. De Priest. A few chosen guests would be informed in advance of the situation.

All arrived on schedule with a look of expectancy on their faces. They were evidently prepared for almost anything and appreciated that they were taking part in a most unusual affair. The police officers on the outside and the doormen on the inside had been cautioned to be careful when a colored lady should present herself and say she had an appointment with Mrs. Hoover, lest they create a scene by refusing her admittance.

The guests assembled in the East Room. Mrs. Hoover was to receive in the Green Room and pass the guests on to the Red Room for tea. Mrs. De Priest was introduced to the others present and the reception immediately began. Being the lowest in rank of the official ladies, she had to await her turn while the others were being shown in.

After a few minutes of conversation with Mrs. Hoover, Mrs. De Priest moved on to the Red Room, where she was served a cup of tea in regular form. It can be stated that Mrs. De Priest conducted herself with perfect propriety. She really seemed the most composed one in the room. She certainly acted her part.

In a short while Mrs. Hoover retired from the room, and Mrs. De Priest in perfect form made her exit, no doubt to the relief of all and yet leaving behind a feeling of admiration at the way she conducted herself.

Swept Away

Ten years before she became mistress of the White House, Rosalynn Carter, the girl from Plains, met an almost-real prince:

Of all the dinners at the White House, I remember best the one the Johnsons gave for Princess Margaret, who was then married to Lord Snowdon. I was seated at Mrs. Johnson's table. Lord Snowdon was of course on her right. The dinner was very grand. At the end of dinner President Johnson rose and made a kind, thoughtful toast to the Royal visitors. Princess Margaret, according to protocol, responded, and then we all went into the East Room for dancing.

Before the Royal pair arrived in Washington, there had been a great play in the Washington papers about what swingers they were. The Snowdons were always out, we were told, in London's most fashionable nightclubs, dancing the night away.

When Lord Snowdon asked me to dance (I think Meyer Davis and his orchestra were playing that evening) I was glad I knew how to do the frug because I was sure Lord Snowdon would want to dance all the latest steps. Before long the clasp of my gold and turquoise bracelet gave way and it fell to the floor. Lord Snowdon picked up the bracelet, put it into his pocket, and we danced our restrained frug a little bit longer. I wasn't really that good, and to my surprise he wasn't much better, but it was fun anyway.

(This was the same party at which Henry Ford's then-wife Cristina was dancing round and round and her dress fell away on top. She startled her dancing partner more than somewhat.)

I knew it was up to me to get my partner back to Princess Margaret so that he could dance with her or with other guests. I didn't want Lord Snowdon to be stuck and no one appeared to be going to cut in. So I said that I'd loved our dance and perhaps we might go along, or words to that effect, and we went over to where Princess Margaret was sitting at the side of the dance floor with Vice President Hubert Humphrey and others.

As we came up to them, I had thought to say some bit of trivia about what a good dancer Lord Snowdon was, but as I got closer I saw her expression. I can only say it gave serious competition to that Gorgon who turned people to stone with a glance. It was the real Royal Freeze. I think for some reason Princess Margaret had been peeved from the beginning of the evening. Now she was furious because her husband had appeared to have been having a good time dancing and she had been sitting out, although undoubtedly she had been asked to dance.

Anyway, Lord Snowdon's presence of mind was undisturbed, because he remembered to reach into his pocket and give me my bracelet as I turned and fled.

Fame

Lynda Bird told the story of her mother shopping at an Austin department store when she noticed a woman who had been a longtime campaign worker for LBJ. As she was in a hurry, and was pretty sure that the woman had not noticed her yet, Lady Bird was debating in herself whether to go over and greet her. She finally decided to do so, giving a Texas-size hello. The party worker looked at Lady Bird for a moment: "Do I know you, dearie?" she asked.

Plain Speaking

Mike Wallace's wife liked to tell the story about the time Mrs. Truman attended a Grange meeting at Independence with a friend whose husband was making a speech about how to conserve the soil. He ended his lecture with the exhortation to the assembled farmers: "Now remember—what you need is manure, manure—and more manure." Bess Truman's friend was embarrassed and whispered to her: "Oh, dear, I've been trying to get him to say fertilizer!" At which point Mrs. Truman whispered back to her: "And I've been trying to get Harry to say manure!"

THE PRESS

Signs of the Times

The press was united in its applause for quiet Mrs. Coolidge. Her friendly face brought warmth to a picture that had long been chilling. She was said to match Dolley Madison in charm and tact, to be "quick at repartee and full of fun," to be an accomplished dancer and better informed on baseball than most men. Actually she had presidential orders not to dance in public "but when [my son] John comes home I just keep him busy dancing with me," she confessed.

Another prohibition that she felt keenly was her husband's ban on riding. For the first time in her life she had an opportunity to learn to ride. Dwight F. Davis, then Secretary of War, aided and abetted her in her secret plan to take lessons at Fort Myers in Virginia. She joyfully bought her riding togs and he accompanied her to the riding hall for her first lesson. It was a happy morning. But the press got wind of the story, with predictable results. They were breakfasting when the President noticed the headline: MRS. COOLIDGE TAKES UP RIDING. She was described as looking more like a debutante in her jaunty tan habit and boots than like the First Lady of the land.

He stared across at her with a look of surprise, mingled with anxiety and disapproval, and quickly dashed her adventurous spirit with the flat announcement: "I think you will find that you will get along at this job fully as well if you do not try anything new." Ten years later she wrote feelingly—or perhaps with her tongue in her cheek—of this moment that it had had the "semblance of a death notice."

The President had no objection to specific news items involving official appearances, but no personality stories, quotations, or personal interviews were permitted. The day of the free interviews with First Ladies had not yet arrived. Once when she was giving the newspaperwomen a luncheon under the giant magnolia tree planted by Andrew Jackson in memory of his wife, Rachel, she was asked for a speech. Without any change of expression she raised her graceful hands and gave a five-minute talk in the language of the deaf, but without uttering a sound.

Women Only

Soon after the inauguration of her husband, Eleanor Roosevelt announced that she would hold a weekly press conference just for women journalists. It caused a stir; it had been the custom for the White House secretaries to give information about the First Lady's activities. According to a couple of contemporary Washington journalists:

The opening conference was jammed with cynical women feature writers, hard-boiled spinsters with faces like battle-axes but hearts full of goo for humanity, ritzy society editors, and awed girl-reporters giggling and chewing the stubs of much-bitten pencils. On this assemblage, wriggling ecstatically and devouring every word with rapt attention, Mrs. Roosevelt produced an extraordinary effect. Her real accomplishments were neglected while the sob sisters hurled irrelevant and frequently personal questions. On one occasion, while Mrs. Roosevelt was discussing her inspection of government homestead projects, a woman reporter inquired brightly, "What has happened to the sofa that used to be in the Green Room?"

Another time, during a conference dealing with resettlement problems [related to the Subsistence Homestead program, started in 1933, whereby $25 million was spent to resettle 25,000 urban poor on farms], Jack, a White House setter, ran into the room wagging his tail. "Oh, please tell us about Jack," begged one press girl. That ended resettlement for the time being.

Male reporters had at first joined the opposition to Mrs. Roosevelt's weekly conferences for women, because they feared their competitors would get many "scoops." It turned out differently. So multitudinous and so varied were the accomplishments of the President's wife that word of many of her exploits leaked out to masculine ears. Men columnists began scooping the girls' meetings. One pretty young creature took her time about writing a certain important item, and a male colleague scored a front-page story. The next conference of Mrs. Roosevelt resembled an indignation meeting. The girl-reporter demanded that the group formally expel the woman responsible for the leak. Mrs. Roosevelt smiled tolerantly. "I quite approve of your plan," she said, "but how will you find the source of the leak?"

The conference adjourned without an answer.

Glad You Asked

When Bess Truman moved into the White House, she knew she did not even want to try to follow in her predecessor's footsteps. Eleanor Roosevelt had been the most politically active First Lady, and she remained in the public limelight until her death, as one of the outstanding personalities of the century. One of Mrs. Truman's first changes was to discontinue the regular press conferences and contacts that Mrs. Roosevelt had instituted as a way of furthering her causes. In the summer of 1947, after more than three years of silence, reporters respectfully submitted a list of questions to Mrs. Truman's secretaries. Several months elapsed before Mrs. Truman replied, and the press eagerly reprinted meager samples:

Q. *What innate or acquired qualities does she think would be the greatest assets for a First Lady?*
A. Good health and a well-developed sense of humor.
Q. *Does she think there will ever be a female President in the United States?*
A. No.
Q. *Would she want to be President?*
A. No.
Q. *Does she keep a scrapbook of her husband's activities?*
A. Yes.
Q. *Of her daughter Margaret's?*
A. Yes.

Q. *Of her own?*
A. No.

Q. *Does she keep a diary?*
A. No.

Q. *Is she disturbed by unfavorable criticism of the President?*
A. After twenty-five years in politics, she is learning to live with it to some extent.

Q. *How does she react to criticism of Margaret's singing?*
A. No comment.

Q. *Has she found ways of lightening the burden of social functions, such as entertaining hundreds of guests?*
A. So far she has not felt it a burden.

Q. *Does she ever, in the course of her duties, get stage fright?*
A. No comment.

Q. *Does she ever have to pinch herself to remind herself that she is First Lady?*
A. No comment.

Q. *If she had a son would she try to encourage him to be President?*
A. No.

Q. *Would she be going to the Democratic Convention in 1948?*
A. She would not miss a Democratic Convention if she could help it.

Q. *What would she like to do when her husband is no longer President?*
A. Return to Independence, Missouri.

Make This Cup Pass from Me

Although she started her professional career as a press photographer, Jacqueline Kennedy developed an early aversion to her ex-colleagues' prying into her life. Realizing what difficulties her shyness caused her husband's press office, she once gave Pierre Salinger a photograph with the inscription: "To Pierre, from the greatest cross he has to bear."

Wanderer

When she moved into the White House, Mrs. Kennedy continued to pursue her private interests: riding to the hounds in Virginia, going to the ballet in New York City, visiting friends in Palm Beach. Commenting on her pattern of absences from Washington, one radio columnist signed off: "Good night, Mrs. Kennedy, wherever you are."

Wish

Following the funeral of President Kennedy, Lady Bird Johnson was continually asked by the press when she would be moving into the White House. Finally, exasperated, the new First Lady told her press secretary, Liz Carpenter, to make known her feelings on the subject: "I would to God I could serve Mrs. Kennedy's comfort; I can at least serve her convenience."

Hue and Cry

Lady Bird Johnson had the misfortune of following suddenly on the heels of Jacqueline Kennedy, the most glamorous First Lady in history. Chicago journalist Maggie Daly found her lacking in any special flair: "She looks like every well-dressed woman of means." The Parisian press, which Jackie Kennedy had completely captivated, was particularly disappointed with her successor: "Lady Bird does not evoke any particular feelings," wrote *L'Express*. "Who cares about a gray lady bird?" A BBC executive in London embroidered the color metaphor even further by exclaiming with disgust: "She's so—beige!"

And That's a Promise

Although Pat Nixon did not carry much political weight, she won personal allegiance from one tough group of people whose favor eluded her husband to the end. After her first press conference as First Lady, one of the journalists asked Mrs. Nixon as she was already leaving:

"Do you like to talk to the press?"

"Well, you know, I really do," Mrs. Nixon answered. She could have left it at that, but she went on, with obvious sincerity: "I admire the press. It isn't easy to go out day after day and get news. You deserve a medal, and I'm going to give it to you."

"You mean," asked one reporter, "that you're not going to call us harpies when you leave the White House?"

"Certainly not," Mrs. Nixon promised. And she smiled sweetly.

The Deep End of the Pool

Two Washington reporters describe some press frolics from the Nixon era:

Out-of-town trips are considered the icing on the cake by almost all reporters. They are not only a chance to get out of Washington and "see the world first-class," but they are also a chance to get to know the President and the First Lady far better than is usually possible in Washington. Trips never fail to etch themselves indelibly on the memories of reporters, especially the "pool people."

A "pool person" is a reporter chosen by one of the press secretaries to accompany the President or First Lady, or both, on Air Force One, or in a helicopter, chartered plane, etc., while the rest travel in the accompanying press plane.

The reason for the pool is not only to allow the principals to breathe without the full rapacious pack of a hundred or more newsmen and women bearing down upon them, but to permit the press to function with efficiency. Pool people travel in a car behind the Secret Service when they land at an airport, while the rest of the press generally arrives at its destination by bus. To keep it fair, representation on the pools alternates each time among the different major news media, except that the AP and the UPI are always included.

Some of the women's pool reports are pretty hilarious. ABC's redheaded glamour girl, Marlene Sanders, an out-of-towner who travels often with First Ladies, says that the most memorable things about White House coverage for her are the "hysterical" pool reports; and Lenore Hershey, managing editor of the *Ladies' Home Journal*, the writer who ghosted Perle Mesta's column in *McCall's* for years, says the pool reports on Mrs. Nixon's trip to the West Coast were the funniest things she has read in her long journalistic career.

One she undoubtedly had in mind was given on a bus, speeding along a California freeway in Los Angeles, after Mrs. Nixon had made a nighttime visit to the Wesley Social Service Center in Watts, where volunteers teach such skills as sewing, music, and weight lifting to the area's underprivileged youngsters.

Kandy Shuman Stroud of *Women's Wear Daily* stood at the front of the swaying bus to give the first pool briefing.

"Mrs. Nixon went into the weight-lifting room and fourteen-year-old Junior Olympic Champion Raymond Morgan raised a 215-pound weight into the air. Mrs. Nixon gasped, 'How he got it up I'll never know!' "

Photographers in the back of the bus were the first to laugh. Within seconds the female reporters and the bus driver were howling, too.

Kandy, a puzzled look on her face, stood waiting for the laughter to die down. A photographer called, "What else did Mrs. Nixon say, Kandy?"

"She said, 'I don't think I could get it down.' "

(Pause for uproarious laughter.)

"Mrs. Nixon told him, 'You're just great, you certainly get up perspiration.' Then she said, 'I haven't seen a weight lifter in a long time.' "

"You're making that up!" cried Wauhillau La Hay.

Ending her part of the briefing, Kandy said, "Mrs. Nixon then went into the music room next door."

"Thank God!" exclaimed Wauhillau.

When reporters and photographers piled off the bus in front of the hotel, the driver told them, "I certainly hope I get to drive you folks tomorrow."

CONTROVERSY

Criticism

During the Civil War the regular White House receptions and dinners were suspended. In a Southern city with the government of the Northern cause under siege inside it, Washington society was deeply divided. Finally Secretary of State Seward persuaded President Lincoln to give an evening reception for the Cabinet, the Diplomatic Corps, and the Capital's social circles. The event, held on February 5, 1862, gave rise to strong criticism of Mrs. Lincoln:

The President and Mrs. Lincoln received their guests in the East Room, where he towered above all around him and had a pleasant word for those he knew. Mrs. Lincoln was dressed in a white satin dress with low neck and short sleeves. It was trimmed with black lace flounces, which were looped up with knots of ribbon, and she wore a floral headdress, which was not very becoming. Near her was her oldest son, Mr. Robert Lincoln (known as the Prince of Rails), and Mr. John Hay, the President's intellectual private secretary. In addition to the East Room, the Red, Green, and Blue Parlors (so named from the color of their paper-hangings and the furniture) were open and were ornamented with a profusion of rare exotics, while the Marine Band, stationed in the corridor, discoursed fine music.

A magnificent supper had been provided in the State Dining Room by Maillard, of New York, but when the hour of eleven came, and the door should have been opened, the flustered steward had lost the key, so that there was a hungry crowd waiting anxiously outside the unyielding portal. Then the irrepressible humor of the American people broke forth—that grim humor which carried them through their subsequent misery. "I am in favor of forward movement!" one would exclaim. "An advance to the front is only retarded by the imbecility of the commanders," said another, quoting a speech just made in Congress. To all this General McClellan, himself modestly struggling with the crowd, laughed as heartily as anybody. Finally the key was found, the door opened, and the crowd fed.

The table was decorated with large pieces of ornamental confectionery, the center object representing the steamer *Union*, armed and bearing the "Stars and Stripes." On a side table was a model of Fort Sumter, also in sugar, and provisioned with game. After supper promenading was resumed, and it was three o'clock ere the guests departed. The entertainment was pronounced a decided success, but it was compared to the ball given by the Duchess of Richmond, at Brussels, the night before Waterloo. People parted there never to meet again. Many a poor fellow took his leave that night of festivity forever, the band playing, as he left, "The Girl I Left Behind Me."

The Abolitionists throughout the country were merciless in their criticisms of the President and Mrs. Lincoln for giving this reception when the soldiers of the Union were in cheerless bivouacs or comfortless hospitals, and a Philadelphia poet wrote a scandalous ode on the occasion, entitled "The Queen Must Dance."

Exhibition

Mary Lincoln remained controversial after her husband's death:

Mrs. Lincoln created an excitement in the autumn of 1867 by offering for sale, in a small upstairs room on Broadway, in New York, what purported to be her wardrobe while she was at the White House. Ladies who inspected it said that the object of this exhibition could not have been to realize money from the sale of the collection. With the exception of some lace and camel's-hair shawls, and a few diamond rings, there was nothing which any lady could wear, or which would not have been a disgrace to a secondhand clothes shop; the dresses—those that had been made up and worn—were crushed, old-fashioned, and trimmed without taste. The skirts were too short for any but a very short person, and of the commonest muslins, grenadines, and bareges; all were made extremely low in the neck, and could not be available for any purpose. There were some brocaded silk skirts in large, heavy patterns, which had been made but not worn, but these were unaccompanied by any waists, while the price put upon them and the other articles was exorbitant.

The opinion was that the exhibition was intended to stimulate Congress to make Mrs. Lincoln a large appropriation. Those Republicans who had subscribed to the fund of one hundred thousand dollars paid to Mrs. Lincoln after the death of her lamented husband were very angry. The general opinion was that the exhibition was an advertising dodge which some of Mrs. Lincoln's indiscreet friends had persuaded her to adopt.

Thurlow Weed created a decided sensation by taking up the cudgels in defense of his party, and published a letter stating that the Republicans, through Congress, "would have made proper arrangements for the maintenance of Mrs. Lincoln had she so deported herself as to inspire respect." He further intimated "that no president's wife ever before accumulated such valuable effects, and that those accumulations are suggestive of 'fat contracts and corrupt disposal of patronage.' " He continued that "eleven of Mr. Lincoln's new linen shirts were sold" almost before the remains, which were shrouded in the twelfth, had started "for that bourne from whence no traveler returns." Not only was Mr. Weed censured in this country, but in England the *London Telegraph* said: "To attack Mrs. Lincoln is to insult the illustrious memory of Abraham Lincoln, and to slander a gentle lady. She is entitled to more than 'respect' from the American people. They owe her reverence for her very name's sake."

Breach of Trust

Sometimes the White House's open-door policy to the press backfired. Marie Smith of The Washington Post *made the seemingly innocuous request to interview Zephyr Wright, Lady Bird Johnson's family cook:*

This was one of the few occasions when Liz Carpenter was outsmarted, for when she gave permission for Marie to talk with Zephyr, she had no idea that Zephyr was going to "tell it like it was." Under a headline proclaiming ZEPHYR WANTS OUT OF THE KITCHEN Marie wrote that Mrs. Wright was looking forward to retirement, that she considered the White House a prison, and that the tension of working there for five years had caused her to become a compulsive eater whose weight had increased from 130 to 210 pounds.

Zephyr never knew when she would serve meals, she told Marie. "Sometimes the President buzzes that he will come to lunch in ten or fifteen minutes and is bringing twenty-five people with him." That wasn't the worst of it; sometimes he would have dinner guests and she would be told to serve dinner at eight-thirty, but "Mr. Johnson didn't bring his guests to the dining room until ten, eleven, or twelve at night." It's difficult to hold popovers, one of LBJ's favorite foods, she said, so this caused the boss to bellow at her one night when the three-hour-old popovers were almost burned.

Among other secrets Mrs. Wright revealed were: that President Johnson had gone from 184 to 212 pounds, that he loved everything fattening, and that when she, on orders of the White House physician, cooked him low-calorie meals and something else for guests, "he ends up eating both."

Hopelessly Devoted to Him

Some of the early attacks on Nancy Reagan as First Lady were accusations that her transfixed gaze of devotion in listening to her husband's speeches was somehow an act. Mrs. Reagan defended herself to journalist Susan Granger: "I can't really digest what someone is saying unless I look directly at him. I've often wondered what those same people would have said if I'd been looking at my plate or counting the house!"

But most of the time she did not fight back against what she considered unfair attacks on herself or the President, except in private: "I have my own way of dealing with them. I take a long, hot bath, during which I have a marvelous imaginary conversation with the person who wrote the article about my husband. All the words come as they should if you ever had the opportunity, which you don't, and the other person can't answer you back. You get out of the tub feeling marvelous!"

Reversal

Washington Post *columnist Diana McLellan, who had retailed much of the malicious gossip about Nancy Reagan, describes the First Lady's conquest of the press:*

As it was Nancy Reagan's clothes and her act that dragged her into the war with the press, it was to be her clothes and her act that were to turn the tide of battle.

The miracle happened in late March 1982—almost a year after her husband had been shot.

It happened at the Gridiron Club's ninety-seventh annual dinner and show.

The satirical show is put on by the cream of the Washington press corps for themselves and Washington's most powerful movers-and-shakers. Its stated aim is to "singe but not burn" the White House and the out-of-power party.

Nancy's miracle began halfway through the 1982 show. There had been a satirical number about Nancy's clothes, sung with gusto, to the tune of "Secondhand Rose."

Suddenly, from behind a rack of clothes onstage, peeped Nancy herself.

"Let me see that score!" she cried.

The audience craned. It could not believe its ears, or its eyes. On she swept, dressed in bag-lady finery—feathered hat, dangling beads, pantaloons and yellow boots, clutching a plate painted to look like the new White House china. The assemblage stood to applaud the sheer courage of her presence.

She threaded her way on stage, swung into motion, and warbled in a smoky voice:

Secondhand clothes, I'm wearing secondhand clothes,
They're all the thing in the spring fashion shows.
Even my new trench coat with fur collar Ronnie bought for ten
   cents on the dollar!
The china is the only thing that's new.
Even though they tell me that I'm no longer queen

Did Ronnie have to buy me that new sewing machine?
Secondhand clothes, secondhand clothes
  I sure hope Ed Meese sews.

And then she smashed the plate.

It was masterful. The assembly rose to roar its approval.

Her husband, caught completely unawares, declared himself a stage-door Johnny.

The miracle was, so was the Washington Establishment.

"I have never seen anyone given such an ovation!" raved Judge John Sirica, the Iceman of Watergate, writing to Mrs. Reagan's press secretary. "I wish every American could have seen it."

Librarian of Congress Daniel Boorstin wrote to congratulate Nancy on her "brilliant and delightful performance," and likened it to "William Jennings Bryan's 'Cross of Gold' speech—one of the most brilliant events in American political history."

Even the press tossed aside its spears and left with thin smiles. They had caught the act. They knew that few among their own number would have dared risk failure among foes. Nancy had risked, and won.

She had shown she could make fun of herself. Now the press was willing to take her seriously.

TRAVEL

At Sea

In 1784 Abigail Adams crossed the Atlantic to join her husband, who was representing the infant United States in France. She wrote her sister, Mrs. Cranch:

On board ship *Active*, Latitude 44, Longitude 34, Tuesday, 6 July 1784. From the Ocean.

MY DEAR SISTER,

  I have been sixteen days at sea, and have not attempted to write a single letter. 'Tis true, I have kept a journal whenever I was able;

but that must be close locked up, unless I was sure to hand it to you with safety.

'Tis said of Cato, the Roman Censor, that one of the three things which he regretted during his life was going once by sea when he might have made his journey by land. I fancy the philosopher was not proof against that most disheartening, dispiriting malady, seasickness. Of this I am very sure, that no lady would ever wish a second time to try the sea, were the objects of her pursuit within the reach of a land journey. I have had frequent occasion, since I came on board, to recollect an observation of my best friend's, "that no being in nature was so disagreeable as a lady at sea," and this recollection has in a great measure reconciled me to the thought of being at sea without him; for one would not wish, my dear sister, to be thought of in that light by those to whom we would wish to appear in our best array.

Our sickness continued for ten days, with some intermissions. We crawled upon deck whenever we were able; but it was so cold and damp that we could not remain long upon it. And the confinement of the air below, the constant rolling of the vessel, and the nausea of the ship, which was much too tight, contributed to keep up our disease. The vessel is very deep loaded with oil and potash. The oil leaks, the potash smokes and ferments. All adds to the *flavor*. When you add to all this the horrid dirtiness of the ship, the slovenliness of the steward, and the unavoidable slopping and spilling occasioned by the tossing of the ship, I am sure you will be thankful that the pen is not in the hand of Swift or Smollett, and still more so that you are far removed from the scene.

Our accommodations on board are not what I could wish, or hoped for. We cannot be alone, only when the gentlemen are thoughtful enough to retire upon deck, which they do for about an hour in the course of the day. Our staterooms are about half as large as cousin Betsey's little chamber, with two cabins in each. Mine had three, but I could not live so. Upon which Mrs. Adams's brother gave up his to Abby, and we are now stowed two and two. This place has a small grated window, which opens into the companionway, and by this is the only air admitted. The door opens into the cabin, where the gentlemen all sleep, and where we sit, dine, &c. We can only live with our door shut, whilst we dress and undress. Necessity has no law; but what should I have thought on shore, to have laid myself down to sleep in common with a half a dozen gentlemen? We have curtains, it is true, and we only in part undress, about as much as

231

the Yankee bundlers; but we have the satisfaction of falling in with a set of well-behaved, decent gentlemen, whose whole deportment is agreeable to the strictest delicacy, both in word and action.

An American in Paris

From Paris Abigail wrote her niece about some disagreeable experiences:

This lady I dined with at Dr. Franklin's. She entered the room with a careless, jaunty air; upon seeing ladies who were strangers to her, she bawled out, "Ah! mon Dieu, where is Franklin? Why did you not tell me there were ladies here?" You must suppose her speaking all this in French. "How I look!" said she, taking hold of a chemise made of tiffany, which she had on over a blue lutestring, and which looked as much upon the decay as her beauty, for she was once a handsome woman; her hair was frizzled; over it she had a small straw hat, with a dirty gauze half-handkerchief round it, and a bit of dirtier gauze, than ever my maids wore, was bowed on behind. She had a black gauze scarf thrown over her shoulders. She ran out of the room; when she returned, the Doctor entered at one door, she at the other; upon which she ran forward to him, caught him by the hand, "Hélas! Franklin"; then gave him a double kiss, one upon each cheek, and another upon his forehead. When we went into the room to dine, she was placed between the Doctor and Mr. Adams. She carried on the chief of the conversation at dinner, frequently locking her hand into the Doctor's, and sometimes spreading her arms upon the backs of both the gentlemen's chairs, then throwing her arms carelessly upon the Doctor's neck.

I should have been greatly astonished at this conduct, if the good Doctor had not told me that in this lady I should see a genuine Frenchwoman, wholly free from affectation or stiffness of behavior, and one of the best women in the world. For this I must take the Doctor's word; but I should have set her down for a very bad one, although sixty years of age, and a widow. I own I was highly disgusted, and never wish for an acquaintance with any ladies of this cast. After dinner she threw herself upon a settee, where she showed more than her feet. She had a little lapdog, who was, next to the Doctor, her favorite, and whom she kissed. This is one of the Doctor's most intimate friends, with whom he dines once every week, and she with him. She is rich, and is my near neighbor; but I have not yet visited her. Thus you see, my dear, that manners differ exceedingly in different countries. I hope, however, to find amongst the French ladies manners more consistent with my ideas of decency, or I shall be a mere recluse.

Indian Princess

In 1919, Edith Bolling accompanied President Wilson to Paris to sign the Treaty of Versailles that ended World War I. One of the snobbish aristocrats at first refused to invite Mrs. Wilson and the President, telling their mutual friend, the Serbian Ambassador, that since they were only ordinary Americans, she was sick of hearing about them. Mr. Vesnitch then told the Duchess that Mrs. Wilson was "descended from a princess, and of the only aristocracy in America; her grandmother seven times removed was the great Princess Pocahontas." "Why," said the Duchess, "this is very important, and I knew nothing of it at all. Of course I must go and call on Mrs. Wilson at once and give an entertainment in her honor." The First Lady was greatly amused by the Ambassador's account:

After he had gone I made an amusing story of the incident to tell my husband, adding that as my mother was then living at the Hotel Powhatan in Washington I thought I would get a picture postcard of it and send it to the Duchess as the photograph of "my ancestral palace, now used as a hotel for war workers." The Chief Powhatan was Pocahontas's father. Woodrow laughed and said: "Please wait until I finish this job over here before you play jokes on any French lady."

Voodoo Economics

Jacqueline Kennedy visited India at the suggestion of John Kenneth Galbraith, the Harvard economist whom JFK sent as his ambassador to that country. But whenever the First Lady wanted to go off and visit a bazaar, in the hope of finding bargains, the

Secret Service nixed the idea. Instead, a variety of items were brought to her. Jacqueline, who was a careful and shrewd buyer, now found herself at the mercy of a real economist. As she told Joan Braden, who accompanied her on the trip: "Once I spent almost six hundred dollars when I thought I was only spending fifty dollars. Ken Galbraith kept saying, 'Oh, I'm sure that sari is only about five dollars,' or an evening bag 'only ten dollars,' or a piece of raw silk for Jack 'only fifteen dollars'—and when I found out that night what I'd really spent, I nearly died. Only an economist could make such a mistake."

Chinese Puzzle

During President Nixon's historic visit to Peking, Pat Nixon pursued her own brand of quiet diplomacy. In the words of *Time* magazine she "proved herself a master of the very subtle art of being winning and winsome in the role of distaff stage left." Visiting the kitchen of the Peking Hotel, she sampled delicacies like goldfish and baby birds, and dazzled the staff with her skillful wielding of chopsticks. The Nixons had always enjoyed Chinese food and the White House chefs usually served chicken with walnuts a couple of times a month. On her trip, Mrs. Nixon revealed to the press that she had solved the ancient Chinese puzzle of where to put the sticks between courses: "You just place them on someone else's plate."

IN THE
PRESIDENT'S
HOUSE

REAL ESTATE

Finding the Spot

Benjamin Perley Poore, the nineteenth-century Washington "cave dweller," preserved an interesting tradition in his Reminiscences:

General Washington used to pass through Georgetown on his journeys between the North and Mount Vernon, and I have heard my grandfather describe the interest which he took when the "Federal City" was located. On one occasion he rode over to visit David Burns, who owned a farm on which the Executive Mansion and the Departments now stand. Washington agreed with the Commissioners that what is now Lafayette Square should be a reservation, but Burns disliked to donate any more building lots for the public good. Finally Washington lost his temper and left, saying, as he crossed the porch: "Had not the Federal City been laid out here, you would have died a poor tobacco planter." "Aye, mon!" retorted Burns, in broad Scotch, "an' had ye nae married the widow Custis, wi' a' her nagurs, you would hae been a land surveyor today, an' a mighty poor ane at that." Ultimately, however, the obstinate old fellow donated the desired square of ground.

What to Call It

There are several accounts of how the White House got its name. The literalist school has it that the mansion simply happened to be painted white. Another source says: "Its cornerstone was laid October 13th, 1792, and in 1796 General Washington named it *The White House*, while in course of construction, in honor of his wife's old home."

Yet another states that "our First Lady of the White House never lived in the building which now bears that name, bestowed upon it in honor of her early home, *The White House*, where the engagement of Martha Custis and General Washington took place."

From a third source we learn that at first "the house in which the President lived was called *The Palace*, but a strong antimonarchical sentiment frowned on this designation, and finally Congress declared it *The Executive Mansion*, and by that name and *The President's House* it was popularly known until it was burned by the British in 1814. Then, when the blackened freestone walls were repainted white to hide the traces of the fire, it was rechristened *The White House*, a name that has clung to it ever since."

One of President Thomas Jefferson's granddaughters wrote years after she left the mansion:

"My grandfather did not allow the presents proffered by the Tunisian Ambassadors to be brought to the President's House, as it was then called—a name, which it seems, is too plain English to suit modern notions of dignified refinement for it has been superseded by the more stately appellation of Executive Mansion."

The First Occupant

In June 1800 the seat of the federal government was moved to Washington City, a hopeful name for what was still a village. Abigail Adams, the first mistress of the newly built President's House, wrote her impressions about the place to her daughter:

Washington, 21 November 1800

MY DEAR CHILD:—

I arrived here on Sunday last, and without meeting with any accident worth noticing, except losing ourselves when we left Baltimore, and going eight or nine miles on the Frederick road, by which means we were obliged to go the other eight through woods, where we wandered two hours without finding a guide or the path. Fortunately, a straggling black came up with us, and we engaged him as a guide to extricate us out of our difficulty. But woods are all you see from Baltimore until you reach *the city*—which is only so in name. Here and there is a small cot, without a glass window, interspersed amongst the forests, through which you travel miles without seeing any human being. In the city there are buildings enough, if they were compact and finished, to accommodate Congress and those attached to it; but as they are, and scattered as they are, I see no great comfort for them.

The river, which runs up to Alexandria, is in full view of my window, and I see the vessels as they pass and repass.

The house is upon a grand and superb scale, requiring about thirty servants to attend and keep the apartments in proper order, and perform the ordinary business of the house and stables: an establishment very well proportioned to the President's salary. The lighting of the apartments, from the kitchen to parlors and chambers, is a tax indeed; and the fires we are obliged to keep to secure us from daily agues, is another very cheering comfort. To assist us in this great castle, and render less attendance necessary, bells are wholly wanting, not one single one being hung through the whole house, and promises are all you can obtain. This is so great an inconvenience, that I know not what to do, or how to do.

The ladies from Georgetown and in the city have many of them visited me. Yesterday I returned fifteen visits—but such a place as Georgetown appears—why our Milton is beautiful. But no comparisons; if they will put me up some bells, and let me have wood enough to keep fires, I design to be pleased. I could content myself almost anywhere three months; but surrounded with forests, can you believe that wood is not to be had, because people cannot be found to cut and cart it.

Drying Clothes

When Abigail Adams moved her household to Bush Hill, near the seat of the new federal government in Philadelphia, she is said to have pined for her previous home by frequently exclaiming, "This, alas, is not Richmond Hill!" In the wilderness of Washington, she complained to

Mrs. Gallatin and other women friends: "This, alas, is not Philadelphia!" Her eminently practical solution to one of her most pressing problems in her new residence reverberated down the nineteenth century:

It has often been said, and with an undertone of disapproval, that Mrs. John Adams used the East Room for drying clothes. A wiser use was this, surely, although the clothes must have dried but slowly in the moist atmosphere, than to have given the President and his Cabinet officers rheumatism by requiring them to sit in the penetrating dampness of the East Room to transact business of state, as some thrifty housewives of that time would have done.

The ladies of Georgetown and Alexandria, being of a social nature, promptly called upon the President's lady and were received in a hastily improvised parlor at a safe distance from the drying clothes. It soon appeared that these visiting dames required some gaiety in the White House. Mrs. Adams yielded with a good grace, although, as appears from her letters to her daughter, she was in anything but a festive mood. The first drawing room was held on New Year's Day, 1801, Mrs. Adams receiving her guests in the oval room on the second floor, which was afterward used as a library.

Amen

John Adams, before he joined Abigail at their new official residence in Washington, sent her a prayer, which FDR ordered inscribed over the fireplace in the State Dining Room:

"I pray heaven to bestow the best of blessings on this house and on all that shall hereafter inhabit it. May none but honest and wise men ever rule under this roof."

Furnishings

John Quincy Adams found the furniture of the White House in a dilapidated condition. Thirty thousand dollars had been appropriated by Congress for the purchase of new furniture during the administration of Mr. Monroe; but his friend, Colonel Lane, Commissioner of Public Buildings, to whom he had entrusted it, became insolvent and died largely in debt to the government, having used the money for the payment of his debts, instead of procuring furniture. When an appropriation of fourteen thousand dollars was made, to be expended under the direction of Mr. Adams, for furniture, he took charge of it himself. This was severely criticized by the Democratic press, as was the purchase of a billiard table for the White House, about which so much was said that Mr. John Adams finally paid the bill from his own pocket.

A Place Like No Home

When Benjamin Harrison and his family moved into the White House, Mrs. Harrison took a look at the place and did not like what she saw: "We are here for four years," she said, "I do not look beyond that, as many things may occur in that time, but I am very anxious to see the family of the President provided for properly, and while I am here I hope to be able to get the present building put into good condition. Very few people understand to what straits the President's family has been put at times for lack of accommodations. Really there are only five sleeping apartments and there is no feeling of privacy."

Enjoyment

While Mrs. Grant has always denounced the White House as not suitable for a President's residence, Mrs. Hayes was charmed with it. She once took an old friend through it, showed him the rooms, and exclaimed: "No matter what they build, they will never build any more rooms like these!" She had the lumber rooms ransacked, and old china and furniture brought out and renovated, and, when it was possible, ascertained its history. Every evening after dinner she had an informal reception, friends dropping in and leaving at their will and enjoying her pleasant conversation. Often her rich voice would be heard leading the song of praise, while the deep, clear bass notes of Vice President

Wheeler rounded up the melody. She almost always had one or two young ladies as her guests, and she carried out the official program of receptions to the letter.

Attic

Criticism about rebuilding and refurbishing the White House is a constant refrain through successive administrations. Here is an anonymous sniper from earlier in our century:

After her husband's election to the White House, Mrs. Taft seemed to retire from politics and was submerged in furbishing and furnishing the White House. I have an idea that the contents of the attic were greatly increased after her advent.

What! Haven't you heard of the famous attic? My dears, it's a perfect treasure house of antiques. Old four-posters that would make your mouth water and rare pieces discarded by the new-coming Presidents to make way for modern designs.

Stuffed Moose

Edith and Theodore Roosevelt were very proud to have made some major renovations to the White House at the turn of the century and claimed to have restored it to its original design. The inside decoration was another story. Teddy Roosevelt decorated the State Dining Room like a game room with the stuffed trophies of his hunting safaris. Eleanor Roosevelt would tell stories to the dining-room staff about "the days of Uncle Ted and how awful it was to be enjoying a meal and then suddenly look up to find the eyes of a stuffed moose or some other animal staring down at you."

Ghost Stories

The most famous ghost of the White House is that of Abraham Lincoln. Eleanor Roosevelt, who used the Lincoln Bedroom as her office, men-

tioned several times to servants that she had felt the Great Emancipator's presence behind her. And Mrs. Coolidge saw him standing at one of the windows in the Oval Office, where he used to watch the troops leaving for Virginia. Maggie Rogers and her daughter Lillian spanned more than fifty years of domestic service at the White House, and they saw all the ghosts during their time. Lillian Parks wrote in her memoirs:

The ghosts of several First Ladies are supposed to return now and then. Dolley Madison is said to have been an angry ghost when the second Mrs. Wilson ordered her old flower garden dug up, and Abigail Adams is a busy ghost, fooling around with her laundry in the East Room.

Mrs. Hoover had a little fun with the latter story when she gave a shower for one of her three secretaries, who was leaving to be married. She suggested that all the guests bring linen, and all this ghostly array was strung up on a clothesline in the East Room. Shades of Abigail Adams.

Then there has been the ghost of Mrs. Cleveland, who gave birth to the first child of a President to be born in the White House. Some of the moaning such as Mama heard is supposed to be the echo of her childbirth pangs.

Out Damned Spot

Chief Usher J. B. West once found Mamie Eisenhower in a panic:

She never treated the mansion as government property, it was *hers*. And she took such fastidious care of it that we almost believed it was hers. She became truly alarmed if things went wrong.

One such problem rated a 7:00 A.M. phone call to the housekeeper.

"Come up to my bedroom as soon as the President goes to his office!" Mrs. Eisenhower ordered. Miss Walker, alarmed, stopped by my office first. "Perhaps you'd better come up with me," she said. "It sounds like disaster."

It was the earliest we'd ever seen Mrs. Eisenhower. And she wasn't in bed.

But the bed was a mess. All over the sheets, covers, pink dust ruffle, headboard, everything, were big black spots—or, to be exact, dabs and blotches and swipes of indigo.

"What on earth can we do?" the First Lady wailed.

Miss Walker began jerking the sheets off the bed herself. "I'll take these down to the laundry room to soak, and one of the maids will bring up some spot remover for the rest," she said.

Once the housekeeper had disappeared with the soiled linens, Mrs. Eisenhower began to explain.

"You see, my nose was all stopped up," she began, "and I had a jar of Vicks on my bedside table. So during the night when I woke up, I reached over to put some in my nostrils. Well, it seemed to just get drier, instead of moister," she went on, "so I kept applying more and more. I didn't want to wake up Ike, so I didn't turn on the light. Then this morning I discovered that I was using *ink* to cure my cold."

She had begun the conversation very earnestly, but now, knowing that it could all be set right, she began to smile.

"But you should have seen me," she laughed. "Black and blue all over—and the President, too."

I held down a chuckle that rose up in my throat. The President and the First Lady, in all their dignity, covered in ink.

"I don't think anything is permanently damaged," I assured her. "I'm sure it will all come out in the wash."

"Now don't you tell a soul," she admonished, still laughing.

"Certainly not," I promised, and beat hasty retreat. Not since Harry Truman's four-poster broke down had I heard such a good bedtime story.

A Bargain

Some First Ladies had developed expensive tastes long before coming to live at the White House and found the redecorating budget too small for their visions. Some managed to find a way around it, as Kitty Kelley tells of Mrs. Kennedy's efforts:

Despite her pleas that the presidency not be exploited, Jackie was much like Nellie Taft in working out personal arrangements for herself. Mrs. Taft, while First Lady, was allotted only $12,000 for transportation. So she bought White House cars at a cut rate in return for allowing manufacturers to advertise that they were privileged to supply the President. Similarly, Jackie made secret negotiations with Tiffany & Co. to borrow diamonds for the Inaugural Ball in exchange for White House business on state gifts.

When she wanted a $10,000 Oriental rug for the President's private dining room on the second floor, she wrote a memo to the Chief Usher: "I so like the rug but we are short of dollars and I am *enraged* at everyone trying to gyp the White House. Tell him if he gives it he can get a tax donation and photo in our book—if not—good-bye!" The dealer donated the rug.

CHINA

The Problem Begins

One of the early controversies that engulfed Nancy Reagan had to do with the White House china. Soon after moving into the barely finished Executive Mansion, Abigail Adams mentions her china in a letter to her daughter:

The ladies are impatient for a drawing room: I have no looking glasses but dwarfs, for this house; and a twentieth part lamps enough to light it. My tea-china is more than half missing. We have not the least fence, yard, or other conveniences without, and the great unfinished audience room (the East Room) I make a drying room of to hang my clothes in. Six chambers are made comfortable; two lower rooms, one for a common parlor and one for a ballroom.

Ogling the Spoons

The refurnishing of the White House soon after Mr. Van Buren's inauguration was strongly criticized, as was the greater formality of the weekly receptions and the absence of hard cider at these gatherings. Some writers have even stated, in all seriousness, that the lack of the favorite beverage, the redecoration of the White House, and rumors of a silver service and gold use cost him the reelection in 1840.

[During the campaign] the most notable speech was by Mr. Ogle, of Pennsylvania, who elaborately reviewed the expensive furniture, china, and glassware which had been imported for the White House by order of President Van Buren. He dwelt on the gorgeous splendor of the damask window curtains, the dazzling magnificence of the large mirrors, chandeliers, and candelabra; the center tables, with their tops of Italian marble; the satin-covered chairs, taborets, and divans; the imperial carpets and rugs, and above all, the service of silver, including a set of what he called gold spoons, although they were silver gilt. These costly decorations of the White House were described in detail, with many humorous comments, and then contrasted with the log cabins of the West, where the only ornamentation, generally speaking, was a string of speckled birds' eggs festooned about a looking glass measuring eight by ten inches, and a fringed window curtain of white cotton cloth.

Upon one occasion, when Mr. Ogle, who had been a frequent guest at the White House, made some campaign speeches in which the gold spoons figured prominently, a friend asked Mr. Van Buren if Ogle was right about the gold spoons. "He ought to know," replied the President, "he has often had them in his mouth."

Fauna and Flora

Mrs. Hayes, instead of frittering away the liberal appropriations made by Congress for the domestic wants of the White House, expended a large share of them in the purchase of a state dinner service of nearly one thousand pieces, illustrating the fauna and flora of the United States. The designs were executed by Mr. Theodore R. Davis, who had fished in the rivers of the East and West and in the sea, hunted fowl and wild game in the forests, the swamps, and the mountains, shot the buffalo on the plains and visited historic haunts of the Indians in the East, met the Indians in their wigwams and studied their habits on the prairies of the Far West. The designs were made in watercolors, and although in nearly every instance they were bold and striking, they were difficult to reproduce perfectly upon porcelain with hard mineral colors, and to accomplish this successfully it was necessary to invent new methods and to have recourse to peculiar mechanical appliances, but the effort was successful and the set was produced.

The China Connection

Edith Roosevelt was fond of collecting china, even before she became mistress of the White House. With Mrs. Abby G. Baker she put together one of the finest historic collections of porcelain and china in the country. It was exhibited in the East Corridor of the ground floor of the mansion and comprised examples of tableware used by Presidents, their families, and guests from the time of Washington.

According to an account published in 1908:

Each new mistress of the White House provides all or part of a new china service in keeping with her own tastes, and in consequence there are in the closets today no less than parts of half a dozen distinct services, representing the administrations since that of President Lincoln. Some of these services include many pieces, and the styles of decoration cover a wide range of color and design. Of almost all the pieces, however, either the coat of arms of the nation or the national colors are introduced in some manner.

The principal service in the mansion today, and the only complete one, was ordered by Mrs. Roosevelt, who also selected the design for it. It is always used at the State dinners, supplemented by pieces of the sets which still remain in the house. Mrs. Lincoln selected a very beautiful and elaborate set of china, as did also Mrs. Grant, but Mrs. Cleveland and Mrs. McKinley only selected such pieces of china and glass as were necessary to supply the immediate needs of the dining table during their regimes.

The silver and glass service is extremely modest. There is none of the wealth of silver and cut glass so frequently displayed on the tables of many of our multimillionaires. The glasses are cut simply with the President's coat of arms. The spoons and knives and forks are marked democratically, "President's House."

Wayward China

When Nancy Reagan received all the flak about ordering new china, the White House finally saw that it had a problem on its hand. It launched a counteroffensive by hiring a flak catcher. Landon Parvin, one of her makeover image makers, provided Mrs. Reagan with a one-liner she used effectively when asked about her famous new china set. She would reply that, as her special project, she was "setting up the Nancy Reagan Home for Wayward China."

Legacy

Clement Conger, the White House curator responsible in our own times for restoring the White House to its historic stature, paid the following tribute to Pat Nixon:

In the last four months, we were redoing the Queen's Bedroom, the East Sitting Hall, installing new draperies in the family dining room on the second floor, upgrading the collection in the Yellow Oval Room, and doing a garden room on the ground floor. We were working on a silver flatware service and had revived the subject of the Nixon china. After months of looking, we had finally found a gentleman from a New Jersey oil company who said he could raise $200,000 for the china (150 pieces of each, cobalt blue and white), and we had gotten a preliminary design. At that point things were tense; we all knew there was trouble brewing. But Mrs. Nixon was still working as if she were going to stay in the White House.

Six or seven days before August 9, 1974, she called me and said, "I won't explain, Clem, but don't go ahead with the porcelain. Call it off." Her voice was quivering. I knew what she meant. We stopped work on everything. I have worked for six or seven First Ladies, and I admire Mrs. Nixon much more than all the others. She never let the altitude of the job go to her head. She was always just Pat Nixon from Whittier, California. She's so real, so warm, so realistic, so matter-of-fact. She did more for the authentic refurbishing of the White House and its beautification than any other administration in history—and that includes the Kennedys. I only hope that someday she'll be given credit for her accomplishments.

THE STAFF

Touching

Neither her contemporaries nor posterity had much good to say about Mary Lincoln. But long after she had left Washington, she would remember with affection the White House staff. Thomas Pendel, doorkeeper at the White House for thirty-six years, reminisced:

Some years after [Lincoln's death], during the Hayes Administration, a Mrs. Rathbone called on the President and his family. I met her as she was leaving and found that she was the Miss Harris who was in the box with Mr. Lincoln the night he was assassinated. She had just returned from Ohio and said that Mrs. Lincoln was living there, in a town called Poe. She stated that Mrs. Lincoln requested her to inquire how many of the old employees were still in the White House. It touched me much to think that Mrs. Lincoln did not forget her old employees.

She Should Have Been a Realtor

Notwithstanding her constant oversight of her children, her care of her husband, and her interest in many friends, Mrs. Grant had sincerely at heart the welfare of the servants in the White House. She was a very keen, levelheaded woman, possessing in her way as much sound sense as Grant possessed in his. And Mrs. Grant as well saw with unerring eye that not many years would pass before real estate in Washington would increase tremendously in value. During her husband's first administration, Mrs. Grant used to explain to her servants the necessity for them to purchase homes of their own while the city was still small and while modest homes could be obtained at modest prices. She took special interest in this matter, so far as the dining-room servants of the White House were concerned, and practically insisted that each of them should purchase a home for his family.

One of these servants, a colored man named Harris, was slow to take her advice. He did not realize that his mistress knew what she was talking about, and Mrs. Grant was so anxious to take advantage of the opportunity she saw that one day she sent for him and said:

"Harris, if you do not buy a home at once, and commence paying for it while houses are cheap, your opportunity will soon be gone. The time is coming when there will be a great change in real estate values all over the city. Washington will grow into a big place so suddenly that you will never again have the chance that you now possess. If you do not go out and select a home and commence to pay for it, I will buy one for you myself; and I will take out of your wages each month enough to pay the installments."

Harris looked at his mistress, who was speaking so decidedly, and he knew that when Mrs. Grant spoke she meant every word that she uttered. There was no alternative for him to choose. If he and his wife did not select the home they wanted and commence to pay for it, he knew that Mrs. Grant would select a home for him and would buy it on the installment plan just as she had said she would do. And that is the way that Harris came to have a little property of his own in Washington.

Kindness

Despite all her demands and all her commands, Chief Usher J. B. West found Mamie Eisenhower a thoughtful and generous person:

When a State dinner had gone especially well, she was lavish with compliments. And although she squeezed pennies in her household, she was more than generous to her employees. There was a personal touch to her kindness; it was not done by rote or in a perfunctory manner. She came to know a great deal about us all, and her knowing revealed her interest in those who served her, as human beings with lives outside the White House.

On Christmas Eve she invited all the employees up to the second floor, in small groups, to present us our gifts.

She had even bought presents for my wife and my daughters.

One morning she opened a small white box on her bedside table.

"Isn't this pretty?" she said, showing me a pearl-and-rhinestone necklace, bracelet, and earrings set. "I want to give this to your wife for Christmas."

"That's very thoughtful of you," I began. But she hardly heard me. "Now, you should go out and buy her a ring to match."

"I will," I nodded.

"Bring it back and show it to me!"

Realizing that I was in a bind, I hurried to a store on Connecticut Avenue and selected a gold ring with a cultured pearl for Zella. When I brought the ring back for her inspection, Mrs. Eisenhower said, jangling her own bracelet with its "Ike" charms—helmet, tank, five stars, map of Africa—"That's perfect. I couldn't do better if I had shopped for it myself."

251

That Special?

Nancy Howe, Betty Ford's executive assistant at the White House, said about working for her boss: "She's the most special person I've ever known. I feel as if I should give her back my paycheck at the end of each month."

How to Be Indispensable

Ike Hoover was working for the Edison Company when one day in May 1891, during the tenancy of Benjamin Harrison, he was sent to help install the first electric lights in the White House. Because there were many problems with the newfangled invention, the company asked him to stay on the job as electrician.

It took four months to put in all the wiring for the newfangled lighting, and all the electric bells for summoning the staff. The occupants of the White House were friendly and enthusiastic about the enterprise, and Hoover found a way of becoming indispensable. In his memoirs he describes how at first "the Harrison family were actually afraid to turn the lights on and off for fear of getting a shock. They really did not use the lights in their private chambers for a long time. I would turn on the lights in the halls and parlors in the evening and they would burn until I returned the next morning to extinguish them. The family were even timid about pushing the electric bell buttons to call the servants! There was a family conference almost every time this had to be done."

Ultimately, there was one solution for this problem, and soon Ike Hoover installed himself as a permanent fixture.

Recognition Scene

Hoover later joined the ushers' force, and became Chief Usher under President Taft. The Chief Usher in effect runs the President's household and is responsible for all the social engagements at the White House. At the inaugural reception on March 4, 1921, the Coolidges were welcomed at the White House by Chief Usher Ike Hoover. Mrs. Coolidge recognized him and told a reporter:

You know, the first time I came to the White House, I brought my class of deaf-and-dumb pupils. Their affliction was a terrible handicap, and it took much longer to show them round. The delay annoyed the Head Usher, and he grew impatient. Finally, in exasperation, he invited us to leave. I realized, of course, that we had taken more than our share of time and didn't blame him. But, behold! It was the very same man who opened the door to us today—and bade us welcome!

Sign Language

Ike Hoover lasted past the Hoover Administration, having served ten Presidents and their First Ladies. He died in 1933, just a year or so before his planned retirement. His uncompleted memoirs were published under the title 42 Years in the White House. *In his lengthy service at the White House, Ike Hoover found his namesakes the most exacting:*

Not that the hours were longer, for I have put in many more hours under previous administrations. But the Hoovers were dictatorial, attempted to do more than any of the rest, were extensive entertainers, stayed closer to the White House, were much easier of access to the outside world, seemed to know more people, felt they must entertain them, and generally were up and doing all the time. When one adds to this a certain indefiniteness in their ways, one can realize how difficult it was to give satisfactory service.

The Hoovers were great believers in lots of help, domestic and otherwise. Servants simply fell over each other around the White House.

Mrs. Hoover was an interesting and intelligent talker, and spoke very rapidly, especially when she seemed to be a little more intent than usual. She loved to give signals to the help, all sorts of signals for all sorts of purposes. Signs to the waiters to change the service and to vacate the room. Signs to her secretaries and signs to the ushers. These consisted of dropping her handkerchief or her pocketbook, tossing her eyeglasses around her fingers; or perhaps, holding her glasses or her pocketbook in her hand, she would let the hand drop to her side and to the rear a little.

At an afternoon tea party, for instance, Mrs. Hoover would take her position in the Green Room, the guests having previously assembled in the East Room, and the word would be given to me to begin showing the people in. The aides, generally two or three in number, would pick out someone to start the performance. While she would be talking to this party, I would have to stand in the doorway and watch for the signal to inform the aide to bring in the next one. Never until he got the sign did he presume to introduce another visitor. If the party was not agreeable, the sign would come quickly, but more often it was postponed until we became quite embarrassed at keeping others waiting.

Supporting Role

There's an old adage in the theatre that there are no small roles, only small actors. Alonzo Fields never dreamed of becoming Chief Butler at the White House, which is what he was for two decades. Originally he wanted to be a concert singer. Gradually he came to see that he was on a vast stage, if in a supporting role to the man who held the starring part. Occasionally Fields would give a pep talk to the dining-room staff: "Boys, remember that we are helping to make history. We have a small, perhaps a menial part, but they can't do much here without us. They've got to eat, you know." Fields came to the White House staff because Mrs. Hoover remembered him serving tea for his previous employer, Dr. Stratton. After the doctor's sudden death, Fields received the call to work at the White House. This is his account of his first day:

I was assigned a locker and I changed clothes and reported back to the pantry. When I arrived the men were all in a huddle. I could feel the conversation was about me, because upon my appearance the huddle broke up. Connie assigned me to a big tray of flat silverware and a rouge pad. I had never seen so much flatware in my life and said, "Did you have a party last night?" Connie replied, "No, just a daily routine."

After I had my lunch Mr. Neal approached Mr. Rodriguez and said, "Since Fields has his uniform, you might as well take him into the dining room tonight for dinner. As you know, Mrs. Hoover doesn't like men as tall as he is. You might as well get it over with so he can be on his way back to Boston tomorrow."

I kept my poker face and went about my assignments. At last the hour approached and I was assigned to Mrs. Hoover's side of the table. I could feel the tension and I imagined that they were anticipating Mrs. Hoover's saying, "Get that big galoot out of here."

The dining-room doors were open. Candles on the table were lit and the heavy drapes at the windows were drawn. Soon the President and the First Lady would enter through the open door. We stood in our positions near the table. My back was toward the door and, of course, I was ordered not to turn to see who was entering when the signal was received that the President was approaching.

Suddenly the quietness of the silence was broken by Mrs. Hoover's voice: "Fields, I heard that you were here. I'm so glad to see you." Mrs. Hoover went on, "Father, you remember my telling you about Fields, Dr. Stratton's man?" It was the family custom of the Hoovers to address each other as "Father" and "Mother."

The President, nodding, said, "Hello, Fields."

There was an expression of amazement on the faces of the other butlers. No one said a word when we returned to the pantry for a change of service for the next course. Well, the next day the rumors had it that I had been brought there to take over as head man. "So this is the White House," I thought. "The help gossips here just like any other place."

Into the Closet

Like Ike Hoover, Fields found Mrs. Hoover an exacting boss to work for:

The tension in the dining room under the Hoovers was hard to get used to, I confess. In order to pass the scrutiny of Mrs. Hoover, a servant had to be tops. For her the slightest error was an offense. I do not believe it really mattered too much to President Hoover, but this I will say: anyone who had once served under Mrs. Hoover really knew the formalities of service.

During the Hoover Administration the sounding of three bells would send the help hurrying and scurrying for a hiding place. One of the ushers would rush down the stairs with a doorman who would get the elevator and lock it, waiting for the arrival of the President, and the usher would see that no one was in the corridor. There was only one elevator then, and anyone on it other than the First Lady had to jump off as soon as possible. On the second floor, which is the living quarters, there was a closet with a sink near the stairway used by the housemen and maids for their cleaning equipment. If either the President or First Lady came out of their rooms into the corridor the maids, housemen, and butlers would scamper to this closet. They would almost run one another down trying to be first in the closet and out of sight, for if they lingered and were seen they would be warned not to let this happen again.

I am sure the President and Mrs. Hoover never requested such actions, but those in charge preferred to have things done this way. It was really funny to see the help packing into that closet. It was like a cat coming into a room and surprising the mice playing. In those days I, too, pushed my way in, and no question about its being full after I got in!

Secret Service

Guarding the President and his family is a constant worry not only for the Secret Service but the entire White House staff. Mrs. Harding was the first member of a President's family to have her own Secret Service protection. She co-opted one of the men assigned to the President and turned him into a factotum, as Ike Hoover described him: "He acted as a messenger, special watchman, general handyman, and at times almost as a lady's maid." After Mrs. Coolidge came to the White House,

Mrs. Harding's man was replaced with her own Secret Service guard, who got in the President's bad graces and was thrown out. A second man stayed until Mrs. Hoover's arrival. She did not care to have protection but found that by now the law included the protection of the family of the President. This amendment had been made to allow Secret Service men to guard the Coolidge boys without arousing public criticism. Ike Hoover, the Chief Usher, describes an incident involving the Hoovers:

Within a week after the President came to the White House to live, a strange man walked into the dining room, where he was seated at dinner with eight or ten guests. It was startling and almost beyond belief, with a colored doorman and a police officer stationed at the entrance and a Secret Service man and an experienced usher seated not twenty feet away, all with responsibility to see that no stranger entered. Nor must one forget that there was a policeman stationed just outside the door, in the driveway that approaches the porch.

The circumstances as established afterward were as follows: A man without hat or overcoat appeared in the dining room while all were seated at the dinner table. The President looked up and inquired, "What do you want?" The man said, "I want to see you." The President remarked, "I have no appointment with you." The man said, "You better have an appointment with me!" and walked over toward the President, seated at the table. The intruder's hand was extended as if to shake hands. Even the butlers were out of the room when he entered and they returned just as he made his last move. The President just looked, but Mrs. Hoover spoke up and said to one of the butlers, "Get the Secret Service man." With this the other guests became more or less excited, and all began to talk out loud, which drew the attention of the four men who were within earshot. They all rushed for the dining room, but in the meantime one of the butlers had walked over to the intruder and pushed him toward the door from which he had entered. It was here he was found when these guardians of the President reached the spot. Of course there was consternation. How could it have happened?

The possibilities were startling. The man could have done any harm he had seen fit to do.

There were all kinds of questionings, all kinds of excuses, a world of explanations, but to this day it cannot be intelligently explained how it could have occurred.

Bang, Bang

Lillian Parks recalls the most serious breach of security at a presidential residence. The Trumans were staying at Blair House, during the renovation of the White House, when two Puerto Rican nationalists shot one guard and seriously wounded two others:

The President, I knew, was down below taking a nap. I was sitting all alone, making curtains in the front room of the third floor of Blair House, with my portable sewing machine resting partially on the wide windowsill. It was a beautiful All Saints Day—November 1, 1950—and I was thinking about that as I looked across the street at the sunlight on the old State Department Building.

Rose Booker, the new maid, came to the door and said, "Is there anything you would like for me to do to help you?"

I said, "Oh, no, come in and sit down a few minutes."

I guess I was feeling a bit lonesome. Rose sat down, and before we could even talk, we heard this "BANG, BANG, BANG, BANG!"

Both of us jumped up, and Rose said, "What's that?"

I said, "Shots," and did the wrong thing by hoisting the window, because the bullets were whizzing in all directions. Rose and I looked out, and I realized the danger and jumped back and yelled, "Rose, take your head in!"

I was shaking like a leaf as I stood back and watched it all, and later, when Mrs. Truman went down and saw the blood and heard the story, she came back upstairs and cried. Then she pulled herself together and calmly phoned Margaret, who had a concert that night, to tell her everything was "all right," and to go ahead with her singing.

Getting the Sack

When Edith Bolling became Woodrow Wilson's second wife and moved into the White House in 1915, she brought with her a favorite black maid, who was quite a character and liked to talk. When the President and his lady went to Europe for the Peace Commission, Mrs. Wilson took her along on the understanding that her maid was not to talk under any circumstances to anybody. After France, the President's party were invited to stay at Buckingham Palace, where Queen Mary, in an outburst of hospitality, insisted on meeting everybody, including the servants. Mrs. Wilson gave up trying to teach her maid how to curtsy, but she coached her, should the Queen address her, to reply with the words, "Yes, Your Majesty."

Queen Mary came into the reception room and had a few words with each member of the presidential party. When she came to Mrs. Wilson's maid, Her Majesty asked:

"And are your quarters all right?" To which the good-natured servant replied:

"You bet they is, Queen!"

When the Wilsons got home, the President insisted that his wife dismiss her maid. A caretaking job was found for her at the Treasury Department.

AT THE TABLE

Simple Martha

An English manufacturer, who breakfasted with the President's family, wrote:

Mrs. Washington herself made tea and coffee for us. On the table were two small plates of sliced tongue and dry toast, bread and butter; but no broiled fish, as is the custom here. She struck me as being somewhat older than the President, though I understand both were born in the same year. She was extremely simple in her dress, and wore a very plain cap, with her gray hair turned up under it.

Tradition hands down a story about the eating habits of the Washington household. A guest arrived late for dinner, and the meal was already in progress. He was profuse in his apologies. George Washington smiled. "We have a cook," he said, "who does not ask if the guest has arrived, but if the hour has arrived."

Simplicity

It was President Kennedy who once remarked at a dinner given to a large group of distinguished Nobel laureates that the last time such a concentration of intellect gathered at the White House must have been when Thomas Jefferson dined alone. Jefferson's simplicity was proverbial. A typical invitation to dine at the White House read as follows:

> Th. Jefferson requests the favor of Mr. and Mrs. Smith to dine with him on Tuesday next (26th) at half after three, and any friends who may be with them.
>   April 25: 1803.
>   The favor of an answer is asked.

According to his secretary, Jefferson once invited an eccentric printer and publisher, who wrote in answer to the President: "I won't dine with you, because you won't dine with me."

Incongruous Food

Thomas Jefferson might have been unceremonious, but he was not stinting with his hospitality. Edmund Bacon, the steward from Monticello, in his recollections, said of the President's dinners that the table was "chock-full" every one of the sixteen days he was visiting him. The dinner was at half past three or four o'clock; and although there was no more form or ceremony observed than at a family dinner, Mr. Bacon said that the guests usually sat and talked until night, and he, finding it tiresome, would "quit when he got through eating."

Dr. Cutler recorded many dinners at "His Democratic Majesty's," at which the bill of fare, jotted down for the amusement of his daughter, proved that the entertainment was generous, if somewhat incongruous—fried eggs and fried beef being given place upon a board that was graced by the more distinguished company of turkeys, ducks, and rounds of beef, "the new foreign dish macaroni," ices, and various fancy dishes, among them "a new kind of pudding, very porous and light, inside white as milk or curd, covered with cream sauce."

The Virginian

Foreigners were inclined to smile at Dolley's somewhat rustic notions of entertainment. Jackson, the British Minister, wrote home of his amusement when, during a conference with President Madison, a Negro servant brought in a tray plentifully laden with punch and seedcake. The wife of another foreign minister laughed at the size and number of the dishes on Mrs. Madison's table and remarked sneeringly that the dinner was very like a "Harvest home supper."

Of course Dolley soon learned that the prodigal hospitality was being ridiculed by those from abroad but she preserved her good nature and her good sense. "The profusion of my table is the result of the prosperity of my country," she said proudly, "and I shall continue to prefer Virginia liberality to European elegance."

The State Dinner

According to a nineteenth-century account:

At a state dinner the table is always profusely decorated with flowers, and the "first course" is invariably a soup of French vegetables. No general conversation prevails at the state dinner. If the lady and gentleman elected to go in together happen to be agreeable to each other, they have a "nice time." If not, they have a stiff and tiresome one. Exquisite finesse is needed to fitly pair these mentally incongruous diners. Mike Walsh once horrified the shrinking and saintly Mrs. Franklin Pierce at a state dinner by the story of his going "a-fishing on Sunday"; while Hon. Mr. Mudsill of Mudtown has been known to regale dainty Madame Mimosa, of Mignonette Manor, between the courses, with his hatred of flummeries and French dishes, and his devotion to pork and beans and slapjacks.

The President and his wife receive the guests in the Red Room at seven o'clock. Mrs. President is always attired in full evening dress, with laces and jewels, and her lady guests likewise, while each gentleman rejoices in a swallowtail, white or tinted gloves, and white necktie. The President leads the way to the state table with the wife of the senator the oldest in the office, while Mrs. President brings up the rear of the small procession with the senatorial husband of the President's lady companion. Six wineglasses and a bouquet of flowers garnish each plate. From twelve to thirty courses are served, and the middle of the feast is marked by the serving of frozen punch. After hours of sitting, serving, and eating, the procession returns to the Red Room in the order that it left it. Then after a few moments of conversation, it disperses—its honored individuals more than once heard to say in private, "Such a bore." Yet what an ado they would make if not invited to discover for themselves the tiresome splendor and fit of indigestion attendant upon a state dinner.

Paying for It

From the same period (1874):

The State Dining Room, and its state dinners, are controlled entirely by "Steward Melah, the silver-voiced Italian," who was graduated from Everett House, the Astor House, and the St. Charles, New Orleans, to the higher estate of superintending "goodies" for the palates of diplomatists, princes, and members of Congress in the White House. The government pays Professor

Melah for his services, but the President pays for the dinners, and he is expected to continue giving them till every foreign dignitary and home functionary, from the highest diplomat to the most obscure member of Congress, is invited. Mrs. Lincoln's presuming to abolish the time-honored but costly state dinner of the White House increased her unpopularity to an intense degree.

The average state dinner costs about seven hundred dollars. The one given to Prince Arthur, of England, cost that sum, without including the wines and other beverages. The dinner proper consisted of twenty-nine courses. The President puts a sum of money into the hands of the steward, and his expenditure is supposed to be in proportion to the official rank and grandeur of the invited guests. It is said that Professor Melah wrings his hands in distress when he is about to set the State table for a supreme occasion, and exclaims to the lady of the White House, who may be looking on: "Why Madam, there is not silver enough in the White House to set a respectable free-lunch table."

Temperance

Soon after Mrs. Hayes reached the White House she was visited by the wife of a minister of Washington and asked to forbid the use of wine in the mansion during her stay there. Mrs. Hayes heard the request with polite surprise and replied in these words: "Madame, it is my husband, not myself, who is President. I think that a man who is capable of filling so important a position, as I believe my husband to be, is quite competent to establish such rules as will obtain in his house without calling on members of other households. I would not offend you, and I would not offend Mr. Hayes, who knows what is due to his position, his family, and himself, without any interference of others, directly or through his wife." This reply, in the face of the fact that Mrs. Hayes was a strong temperance woman, a Methodist, and very likely as entirely decided in her mind then as later regarding the subject, is a pleasing evidence of the earnest self-respect of the President's wife.

However, Mrs. Hayes soon won herself the nickname of Lemonade Lucy when she did not serve anything stronger at official functions to the ever-thirsty Washington society.

Lifesaver

Washington society managed to circumvent Mrs. Hayes's "Ohio idea," as it was called. Her prohibitionist views brought her into direct conflict with Mr. Evarts,

who, as Secretary of State, refused to permit the Diplomatic Corps to be invited to their customary annual dinner unless wine could be on the table. This Mrs. Hayes refused to allow, and all of the state dinners while she presided over the hospitalities of the White House were ostensibly strictly temperance banquets, although the steward managed to gratify those fond of something stronger than lemonade. True, no wineglasses obtruded themselves, no popping of champagne corks was heard, no odor of liquor tainted the air fragrant with the perfume of innocent, beautiful flowers. The table groaned with delicacies; there were many devices of the confectioner which called forth admiration. Many wondered why oranges seemed to be altogether preferred, and the waiters were kept busy replenishing salvers upon which the tropical fruit lay. Glances telegraphed to one another that the missing link was found, and that, concealed within the oranges, was delicious frozen punch, a large ingredient of which was strong old Santa Croix rum. Thenceforth (without the knowledge of Mrs. Hayes, of course) Roman punch was served about the middle of the state dinners, care being taken to give the glasses containing the strongest mixture to those who were longing for some potent beverage. This phase of the dinner was named by those who enjoyed it "the Life-Saving Station."

Logistics

Although Ida McKinley was a complete invalid when she moved into the White House, she insisted on remaining the center of attention. She attended public functions and accompanied her husband on trips, despite the logistical nightmares caused by her frequent seizures. At formal dinners William McKinley would sit next to his wife, so that when an attack came, he would throw over her face a white handkerchief he always had ready for the purpose. William Howard Taft was once engaged in conversation with the President when he heard a hissing sound. Before he could really determine what was happening, McKinley had already covered his wife's rigid face, and continued talking as if nothing unusual had happened. After the seizure passed, Ida relaxed again, took off the kerchief, and joined in the conversation.

Playing for Their Supper

Musical events have long been a part of White House entertainment. The Tafts instituted the custom of having each state dinner followed by a musicale. Their successors have made it a tradition, and these days such events are regularly broadcast on television. How musicians were selected and treated is described here from a member of the White House staff during the Hoover years:

The artists appearing at musicales are never paid. This rule is absolute. Generally they are anxious to come; more offer their services than can be utilized. This applies especially to the vast number who wish to advertise their wares. Every sort of freak wishes to appear before the President and his wife. Members of Congress and others often make appeal for this, that, or the other prodigy from their districts.

For many years the custom has been to permit the art department of Steinway and Sons, New York, to pass judgment on these matters. All requests for a chance to sing or play at the White House are referred to them, and often they appear before a representative of that firm to try out their talents. The Steinway firm receives no compensation for this other than the advertisement of their piano, which is always used on these occasions. They not only select the artists, having submitted in advance a list of possibilities for any musicales to the President's wife, but they pay their expenses to and from Washington and during the time they are there. Many of the most famous musicians are really anxious to be of service to the President and his wife, so there is no need to accept other than the very best. They invariably consider it a great honor to perform for the head of the nation and any company he may select.

Yet, generally speaking, these famed artists get very little consideration for the free service they render. During the Taft and Wilson administrations they were presented with gold medals, costing about fifty dollars each. No others were so considerate. Of recent years they have been presented with an autographed photograph of the President and his wife. The privilege of singing or playing, and a little supper afterward, has been about their only reward.

Food for Thought

Eleanor Roosevelt proved to be such a good news source that Emma Bugbee, who had been sent by the *New York Herald Tribune* to report on the First Lady's inauguration activities, was kept in Washington by her Republican employers for four months. "Well, if it's going to be like that," Emma's office said, after their reporter had lunched with Mrs. Roosevelt and had been taken through the living quarters of the President's family, something Mrs. Hoover had not done until the final months of her husband's regime, "you had better stay down." Another Monday the press conference became a classroom in diets—patriotic, wholesome, and frugal; the women learned the recipe for Martha Washington's crab soup and for dishes that Andrew Jackson ate in the days "when the onion and herb were as important as the can opener." Sheila Hibben, the culinary historian whom Eleanor had invited to the news conference, even ventured a theory of history about White House menus: "The more democratic our Presidents have been, the more attention they paid to their meals." The lecture on the wholesome, inexpensive dishes that other First Ladies had served their husbands led up to an announcement that with the help of Flora Rose of Cornell, Eleanor had served "a 7-cent luncheon" at the White House—hot stuffed eggs with tomato sauce, mashed potatoes, prune pudding, bread, and coffee. In London a woman read this menu and exclaimed to a friend that "if Mrs. Roosevelt can get her kitchen staff to eat threepenny, ha'penny meals, she can do more than I can with mine!"

Let Them Eat Crab

During the deep recession of the first Reagan Administration, a desperately poor woman wrote to Nancy Reagan asking for advice about how she could feed herself and her family on her reduced food stamps. By an unfortunate error, a member of the First Lady's staff sent her a recipe for making the President's favorite California dish: a casserole with crabmeat and artichokes.

Penny Wise

Both Rosalynn and Jimmy Carter were thrifty in their housekeeping, but they received little praise for it.

When Jimmy Carter invited members of Congress to the White House for egg-and-bacon breakfasts and then billed them $4.75 apiece, they were outraged. Carefully, they kept track of his expenses. The first year, they noted, he spent only $1,372 of his $50,000 entertainment allowance. By 1979, Congress quietly ruled that all unspent presidential entertainment monies were to be returned to the Treasury.

Simple but Good

Sudden changes of administration at the White House made for stress within the staff that had to adapt quickly to new tastes and different methods of housekeeping. Chief Butler Fields chronicles the change following President Roosevelt's death in office:

The Trumans did not care for elaborate meals. Neither did the Roosevelts; but unlike the Roosevelts, the Trumans demanded better-cooked food, for Mrs. Truman is a very good cook and she knew and appreciated good cooking.

I had noticed when we served hot rolls that Mrs. Truman would look at the rolls, break one open, and then put it aside. At first I thought that perhaps the rolls were not hot. So the next time I took special care to see that they really *were* hot. But again she did the same thing. So I said to one of the men,

"I am sure I know why Mrs. Truman doesn't eat the rolls. She wants rolls fresh from the oven, not warmed-over bakers' rolls."

Well, when I went into the housekeeper's office next morning to talk over menus with her and the cook, I sensed that they were waiting for me. Right off they told me that my boys were letting the rolls get cold before serving them. They wanted to get a small heating unit just to keep the rolls from getting cold. The cook said the bread was always hot when she sent it up and she was not going to be blamed for our carelessness.

I turned to Mrs. Nesbitt and asked,

"Do you mean to say that Mrs. Truman has been asking for hot rolls all this time? Well, no wonder she has not been eating the bread. In fact, no one has. Hot bread doesn't mean warmed-over bakery bread. If you people have forgotten how to bake rolls and bread, then you had better learn. The First Lady wants hot bread from the oven, not warmed-over bakery rolls."

From then on the kitchen posed a problem, for they had been too long on one routine and were not very willing to change. Mrs. Nesbitt had much the same attitude. She was talking to me one day about what Mrs. Truman wanted and said,

"I just told her that you don't do things that way. I said Mrs. Roosevelt never did things that way."

"What did she say?" I asked.

She replied, "Nothing. She just looked at me. You know I have been told that I must see to it that she keeps things going around here."

"Well," I said, "I hope you know what you are doing. Mrs. Truman must be a very patient woman, for I am sure that, being a woman, you know what it means to have your own way of keeping house compared with some other woman's way."

I never really knew what happened and I never asked anyone about it, but it was not very long after our conversation that Mrs. Nesbitt retired.

Leftovers

Fields also lived through the changing of the guard from the Truman to the Eisenhower era:

After we had listened to the President's acceptance speech the Chief Usher called my office and told me that Mrs. Eisenhower wanted tea at 4:30 P.M. for two or three hundred people.

"Can you do it?" he asked.

I said, "As far as food is concerned, we can serve two or three thousand. The menus are ready. All we have to do is prepare the sandwiches, and the kitchen and pantry can easily do that."

By 4:30 we had set up for three hundred people in the State Dining Room, when Mrs. Eisenhower sent orders from the reviewing stand to have sandwiches and fifty cups of tea and coffee sent out to the stand.

Then at 5:00 P.M. we were told there would be only about fifty people for tea after the parade. So we cut the table down and at 6:00 P.M. the President and Mrs. Eisenhower, Vice President and Mrs. Nixon, and fewer than twenty others arrived for tea. They did not stay long or eat much, for the dinner hour was near and a dance was to follow. But everything was going along fine until Mr. Nixon said to Mrs. Eisenhower, "What are you going to do with all this food that is left?"

Mrs. Eisenhower turned and looked at the table. Like so many critics, the Vice President did not know the story behind the scene and I thought, "Of all things—for a man to bring up a question like this!" Well, I knew then [in 1961] that Mr. Nixon was going to have to grow up, for there would be bigger and more important things for him to do than to watch the leavings from a tea party.

AFTERMATH

LEAVING

Free at Last

In a letter to her mother, Julia Tyler described the final days of her husband's administration:

The last word had been spoken—the last link is broken that bound me to Washington, and I should like you to have witnessed the emotions and heard the warm expressions that marked our departure. Let me see—where shall I begin? I will go back to Saturday, though I shall have to be very brief in all I say. Saturday, then, the President approved the Texas treaty, and I have now suspended from my neck the immortal golden pen, given expressly for the occasion. The same day we had a brilliant dinner party for Mr. and Mrs. Polk. I wore my black-blonde over white satin and in the evening received a large number of persons.

On Sunday, the President held a Cabinet council from compulsion; on Monday a Texas messenger was dispatched; on Sunday evening Mrs. Semple arrived; on Monday, in the morning, we concluded our packing, Mrs. Wilkins and Mrs. Mason came up to my bedroom, and sat a little—while I made my toilette—offering their services in any way. At five in the afternoon, a crowd of friends, ladies and gentlemen, assembled in the Blue Room to shake hands with us and escort us from the White House. As the President and myself entered they divided into two lines, and when we had passed to the head of the room, surrounded and saluted us. General Van Ness requested them to stand back and himself stepped forward and delivered "on behalf, and at the request of many ladies and gentlemen citizens of Washington, a farewell address."

It remained for a newspaper reporter to divine what Julia Tyler really might have felt on the occasion:

Mrs. Tyler was looking charmingly beautiful. She was dressed in a neat and beautiful suit of black with light black bonnet and veil. I never saw any woman look more cheerful and happy. She seemed to act as though she had been imprisoned within the walls of the White House and was now about to escape to the beautiful country fields of her own native Long Island.

Miserable

Both Tafts very much wanted a second term in the White House. When former President Roosevelt announced that he was so unhappy with Taft's conduct in office he would oppose him for the Republican nomination in 1912, Taft was surprised. His wife wasn't, however. She had feared Roosevelt long before her husband thought that his old friend could have any ground for political grievance.

Mrs. Taft had never completely trusted Roosevelt's support of her husband, dating from their struggle over the Supreme Court appointment. When she heard Roosevelt's announcement, she turned to Taft disgustedly. "I told you so four years ago, and you would not believe me," she said.

"I know you did, my dear," Taft sighed. "I think you are perfectly happy now. You would have preferred the Colonel to come out against me than to have been wrong yourself!"

But Mrs. Taft was not perfectly happy to be right in this case, because Roosevelt's split with the Republican party caused her husband's defeat. While Taft and Roosevelt, running on his own Bull Moose party ticket, divided the Republican votes, Democrat Woodrow Wilson was elected President.

Mrs. Taft was so miserable on the day of Wilson's inauguration that she did not even say good-bye to her staff. A reporter asked her daughter Helen if her mother was relieved to be free of her responsibilities of the White House. Helen replied, "Mother was never much for relief. She always wanted something to be happening."

Independence

When he was a young journalist, A. E. Hotchner was told that Bess Truman was a hard person to get to. Not long after the Trumans had retired from Washington, the young writer tried to arrange, through her husband's secretary, to see the former First Lady. It didn't work, so he decided to drive to Independence, Missouri.

I parked down the block from the Trumans' white frame house and walked toward the entrance. As I did, a car pulled up and Mrs. Truman, carrying a bag of groceries, got out, along with a man with a telltale Secret Service insignia on his lapel.

"Hello, Mrs. Truman," I said.

"Hello," she said pleasantly.

"I'm very pleased to see you. My name's Hotchner, I'm a writer, originally from St. Louis, and I'd very much like to talk to you. I phoned your husband's secretary but . . ."

"What was it about?"

"Just wanted to write about your life now—what happens to you and Mr. Truman when you change your address from Sixteen Hundred Pennsylvania Avenue to a little town in Missouri."

"Well, no harm in that. Come on up on the porch." She gave the bag of groceries to the housekeeper, who came to meet her, and we sat in comfortable chairs on the porch. It was hot, and she fanned herself with a painted bamboo fan. I asked her if she missed living in the White House. From what I had read about her, I had the impression that she was taciturn and not easy to talk to, but that certainly wasn't true. She spoke openly and pleasantly.

"Well, I certainly miss the White House today, I can tell you.

I have just spent the afternoon trying to find a yardman, but I had no luck. I do some of the gardening myself—I work hard at my roses—but how nice it would be to have a few of those White House gardeners caring for our grounds.

"We have a power mower and I spent the early part of the summer trying to induce Mr. Truman to use it. Finally he did. Eleven o'clock of a Sunday morning, with all the Methodists and Baptists going by our house on the way to church, Mr. Truman got out on our front lawn in his shirtsleeves and began cutting the grass. When I looked out of the window and saw him I was horrified.

" 'Harry! Come in here this minute,' I called to him. 'You know what those churchgoers are saying.' There's no doubt in my mind he planned the whole thing deliberately to exonerate himself from ever touching that mower again. And he hasn't.

"This house doesn't look very big, but we have fourteen rooms, and it would be extremely pleasant to have some of the wonderful staff we had in the White House to help run it. I certainly miss them. We only have our maid, who has been with us for twenty-eight years, and occasional cleaning help. Despite the fact that *Collier's* magazine recently said that I shop by phone and avoid the stores, the truth is that I drive to the grocer's like most of the other housewives in Independence, and I choose the meat and vegetables that look best. We have a couple of very good department stores where I do most of my other shopping.

"Now in this respect I don't know whether I miss the White House or not. It's true that this kind of chore wasn't a part of my life there—Mabel Walker, the housekeeper, would bring the menu to my desk at nine o'clock each morning and it would simply be a matter of approving it or changing it a bit—but I don't really mind having to shop, whereas there were certain White House chores that I did mind.

"What I minded most were the big receptions, where hundreds and hundreds of strange hands had to be shaken, and sometimes there were afternoon receptions and evening receptions on the same day. I do not miss them one bit.

"The mountain of daily mail that had to be answered with the help of my secretary and her staff—that's another task I certainly don't miss. The day-in, day-out schedule of appointments that kept me living by the clock—also not missed one bit. I was recently asked whether, when I now read in the papers about some function or activity taking place in the White House, or when I see a photo of Mrs. Eisenhower engaged in some activity which I once performed, whether I feel a twang of nostalgia. Well, I most certainly don't. I never enjoyed that side of White House life.

"But there are some things about the White House that I miss very much. The lovely cut flowers, fresh every morning, that filled the second-floor rooms. The new books that the Library of Congress sent over every week. (I am an avid reader and here in Independence I am limited by what our library has on its shelves.) And I miss our good friends, who would come regularly to visit, and whom we have known ever since we first came to Washington back in 1935. We know people here in Independence, but we are not 'connected' with them, as you are with friends.

"When my husband and I recently returned to Washington for a brief visit, I was reminded how much I enjoy and how much I miss the physical beauty of the city. The wide, tree-lined avenues, the splendid buildings, the thrilling monuments—they lifted my heart the way they did the first time I saw them.

"Then, too, the theatre, concert, and other cultural life of Washington is sorely missed by both Mr. Truman and myself. We have a very good Philharmonic in nearby Kansas City, and occasional theatre, but it cannot compare with the cultural climate of the capital. I do not miss Washington social life in its formal sense, but I do miss the informal social life I had with our many friends.

"I miss, too, certain aspects of my job as First Lady. It was a challenging, intensely interesting position, and I rather enjoyed tackling its many problems.

"Here in Independence, life is easier, slower, much more relaxed. People smile more. We have the luxury of undemanded time, but we also have the occasional dullness that goes with it.

I am not much of a joiner, never have been, and clubs take little of my time. I go to church regularly, but I don't work in any of the groups. I play a little bridge, but not on fixed afternoons. The mail is still mountainous, but I have no secretarial help, so when I get snowed under I send an SOS to Mr. Truman's office.

"We entertain occasionally, but usually in small groups. I have had as many as fourteen for sit-down dinner, and thirty for a buffet, but they were exceptions. My husband and I rarely go out in the evening since his operation, for he is quite tired when he gets home from the office. He has as many daily callers as he had in the White House, and he has his book to work on as well.

"Occasionally some of our Washington friends stop off to see us on their way west, and those are wonderful occasions. We talk about Washington and the things and people we miss there.

"For the truth is, I have two loves, and I would be happiest if I could live half-time in Washington, and half-time in Independence. My husband and I lived in the Capital for a long time, and there are days when I miss it so much I feel blue."

Mrs. Truman's housekeeper came to the screen door and said that Mr. Truman was on the phone. We both stood up, and I thanked her for her kindness in inviting me on the porch to have a chat.

"Not at all," she said. "It's nice to talk to someone from the outside world once in a while."

Disgrace and Dignity

Her final day in the White House must have been the hardest of Pat Nixon's life. She had spent her most productive years helping her husband reach the presidency, often subordinating her wishes and identity to his. Now she had to watch him leave in disgrace, the first President ever to resign.

"I hope I'll never go through another day like that," says [White House Curator Clement] Conger. "There was a terribly emotional farewell with the staff. The President even came out in his pajamas and hugged them all." Many observers wondered why, in his farewell speech, the President mentioned his mother but not his wife. Explains Helen Smith: "If he had said 'my wonderful Pat,' she would have broken down completely. She had a tremendous rein on herself. I think if any word had been spoken she wouldn't have made it."

As she walked swiftly to the helicopter that was to take them from the White House to Andrews Air Force Base, where they would begin their flight to San Clemente, California, Mrs. Nixon's eyes never left the ground. Friends, including Louise and Roger Johnson, were waiting to say good-bye at Andrews. It was again a silent farewell. "We just gave them a big hug," says Louise Johnson. "Pat was drained. But there was no letting down. I don't think any of them would have let go. They're too proud. It was a matter of dignity."

Colonel Ralph Albertazzi, the pilot of Air Force One, recalls flying over Jefferson City, Missouri, at the precise moment Gerald Ford took the oath of office. Most of the passengers on the presidential jet were listening to Ford being sworn in, but neither Pat Nixon nor her husband picked up the earphones attached to their seats.

TRAGEDY

Omens

Jane Appleton Pierce had been an invalid from childhood: her father had died young from consumption, and she contracted the disease in her teens. Although she married a Congressman, she had always hoped to take Franklin away from politics, which she thought was bad for their family life. When their first son died, a tragedy she blamed on politics, Mrs. Pierce began her campaign to persuade her dynamic husband to resign his Senate seat. He was building an enormously successful law practice in Concord when his friend President Polk offered him a Cabinet appointment to become Attorney General. Pierce gave his wife's health as the reason for turning the post down.

In 1852, while his wife was visiting relatives, Franklin was running a dark-horse campaign with the help of his political friends. On Jane's return in early June, they were taking a peaceful ride around the Mt. Auburn cemetery in Cambridge, Massachusetts, when a rider brought the breathless news from the Democratic Convention in Baltimore that Franklin Pierce had won the nomination of his party. Jane, who had been kept completely in the dark about her husband's back-room machinations, immediately fainted. Her foreboding about the effect of politics on the Pierce family was still to bear its most terrible fruit.

On the morning of January 6, 1853, the President-elect, the future First Lady, and their only surviving child, the effervescent Benjamin, were just leaving the train station in Boston when their railroad car became uncoupled and headed for a ravine. Although Jane and Franklin escaped with minor injuries, they witnessed the horror of their son being crushed to death. Neither parent recovered from this tragedy, which cast a shadow over the inaugural and the whole of Pierce's presidency. Though he had been elected with brilliant promise as the youngest President until that time, his tenure was undistinguished and considered largely ineffective. Jane Pierce tried valiantly to battle her illness and the endless social chores of her office, and though widely admired by Washington society, she was openly called "the Shadow of the White House."

Shock

The afternoon of the day on which President Lincoln was shot he was out driving with his wife, and she subsequently remarked that she never saw him so supremely happy as on this occasion. When the carriage was ordered she asked him if he would like anyone to accompany them, and he replied: "No; I prefer to ride by ourselves today." During the ride his wife spoke of his cheerfulness, and his answer was: "Well, I may feel happy, Mary, for I consider this day the war has come to a close"; and then added: "We must both be more cheerful in the future; between the war and the loss of our darling Willie, we have been very miserable."

His household was very miserable from that awful night.

The grief manifested by little Tad, the youngest son, on learning that his father had been shot was touching to behold. For twenty-four hours he was inconsolable. He frequently said that his "father was never happy after he came here," and asked questions of those about him as to their belief in his being in heaven. He seemed resigned when this idea fastened itself strongly in his mind, and in his simplicity he imagined that his father's happiness in heaven made the sun shine brightly.

Mrs. Lincoln never recovered from the shock. After the death of the President she remained in the White House five weeks, too ill to depart. The remains of her husband were borne back to Illinois, through towns, villages, and hamlets, bearing every outward token of woe, and the cortege was met at each stopping place by thousands of mourners who paid their respects to the great dead. Robert Lincoln, the eldest son, accompanied the remains, and after all the honor had been paid the body of the martyred father, he returned to remove his mother to their future home.

The White House was like a public building during these sad weeks. The officials were embarrassed under the extraordinary circumstances, and the mansion was given over to servants. The soldiers on duty there had no other authority than to keep out the rabble, and no one felt justified in taking charge of the house while Mrs. Lincoln remained. The new President, Mr. Johnson, disavowed any inclination to hasten her departure; and when at last Mrs. Lincoln removed from the building, it was in the condition to be expected after the hard usage it had received subsequent to the tragedy.

The Final Moments

A close-up view of Mrs. Lincoln's state of mind just before, during, and following her husband's assassination is reflected in a letter from Anson G. Henry to his wife, written on April 19, 1865. Henry had been Lincoln's physician and close friend in Springfield. Lincoln made him Surveyor General of Washington Territory at the beginning of his administration; he happened to be visiting Washington and looking for further advancement at the time of tragedy.

I was in Richmond on the night of his assassination. The next day in the afternoon I went down to City Point and met the sad news. I was so stunned by the blow that I could not realize that he was dead until I saw him lying in the Guest Chamber cold and still in the embrace of Death. Then the terrible truth flashed upon me, and the fountain of tears was broken up and I wept like a child refusing to be comforted, remaining riveted to the spot until led away by those who came in for the purpose of placing the body in the coffin. I felt that a mountain load had been suddenly lifted from my heart. I had never before realized the luxury of tears, and I never before wept in the bitterness of heart and soul, and God grant that I may never have cause to so weep again.

After recovering my composure, I sought the presence of poor heartbroken Mrs. Lincoln. I found her in bed more composed than I had anticipated, but the moment I came within her reach she threw her arms around my neck and wept most hysterically for several minutes, and this completely unmanned me again, but my sympathy was to her most consoling, and for a half hour she talked very composedly about what had transpired between her and her husband the day and evening of his death, which I will tell you when we meet. She says he was more cheerful and joyous that day and evening than he had been for years. When at dinner he complained of being worn out with the incessant toils of the day, and proposed to go to the theatre and have a laugh over the Country Cousin. She says she discouraged going, on account of a bad headache, but he insisted that he must go, for if he stayed at home he would have no rest, for he would be obliged to see company all the evening as usual. Finding that he had decided to go, she could not think of having him go without her, never having felt so unwilling to be away from him. She sat close to him and was leaning on his lap when the fatal shot was fired, his last words being in answer to her question, "What will Miss Harris think of my hanging on to you so"—"She won't think anything about it," and said accompanied with one of his kind and affectionate smiles. Yes, that look and expression is stamped upon her soul too indelibly to ever be effaced by time, and its recollection will never fail to soothe and comfort her in her hours of darkest affliction.

Restraint

Following President Garfield's assassination, a newspaper described his widow's bearing:

Mrs. Garfield bore the trying ordeal with great fortitude, and exhibited unprecedented courage. She gave way to no paroxysms of grief, and after death became evident, she quietly withdrew to her own room. There she sat, a heartbroken widow, full of grief, with too much Christian courage to exhibit it to those around her. She was, of course, laboring under a terrible strain, and despite her efforts, tears flowed from her eyes, and her lips became drawn in her noble attempt to bear the burden with which she had been afflicted. Miss Mollie (the President's daughter) was, naturally, greatly affected, and bursts of tears flowed from her eyes, notwithstanding her noble efforts to follow the example of her mother.

Grandeur

Reporter Helen Thomas watched Jacqueline Kennedy's enormous presence that fateful day her husband's body was brought back from Dallas:

A policeman tipped me off that the Kennedy casket would be brought into the White House a few hours past midnight. I was told that when Jackie had got off Air Force One, Angier Biddle Duke, the U.S. Chief of Protocol, rushed up to her and asked: "Is there anything I can do for you?"

"Yes," she said, "find out how Lincoln was buried."

I remember Jackie's Spartan courage and control that weekend. Kennedy's funeral had unparalleled grandeur and Mrs. Kennedy had masterminded it. She had always seemed to think of herself as a a queen and in November 1963 she carried herself with majesty. To the family she said, "We must just get through this."

Remembering Camelot

Jacqueline Kennedy wrote in a memorial issue of Look *magazine:*

It is nearly a year since he has been gone.

On so many days—his birthday, an anniversary, watching his children running to the sea—I have thought, "But this day last year was his last to see that." He was so full of love and life on all those days. He seems so vulnerable now, when you think that each one was a last time.

Soon the final day will come around again—as inexorably as it did last year. But expected this time.

It will find some of us different people than we were a year ago. Learning to accept what was unthinkable when he was alive changes you.

I don't think there is any consolation. What was lost cannot be replaced.

Someone who loved President Kennedy, but who had never known him, wrote to me this winter: "The hero comes when he is needed. When our belief gets pale and weak, there comes a man out of that need who is shining—and everyone living reflects a little of that light—and stores up some against the time when he is gone."

Now I think that I should have known that he was magic all along. I did know it—but I should have guessed that it could not last. I should have known that it was asking too much to dream that I might have grown old with him and seen our children grow up together.

So now he is a legend when he would have preferred to be a man. I must believe that he does not share our suffering now. I think for him—at least he will never know whatever sadness might have lain ahead. He knew such a share of it in his life that it always made you so happy whenever you saw him enjoying himself. But now he will never know more—not age, nor stagnation, nor despair, nor crippling illness, nor loss of any more people he loved. His high noon kept all the freshness of the morning—and he died then, never knowing disillusionment.

Farewell

The second wife of President Benjamin Harrison never became First Lady. The widowed general married Mary Dimmick, his first wife's favorite niece, after retiring from public life. Her farewell to her husband was interrupted by another mourner, according to a contemporary newspaper account:

In the parlor of the Harrison home in Indianapolis, March 6, 1901, in a casket draped with a banner of the Legion of Honor, lay the earthly shell of the man and statesman, General Benjamin Harrison. Into this room came the woman whom the still, cold mortal there had made a widow. She came to be alone with him, probably for the last time. The rest of that day and the next he would be claimed by the representatives of the city, state, and nation. While she stood in the darkened chamber, by the bier of her dead, the door opened without noise, and a bent form, still shivering after exposure to the chill air of the morning, entered. He was a grizzled, gray old soldier, in a faded uniform. Unaware of another living presence, he shuffled to the casket, leaned over the still face, tears streaming down his wrinkled cheeks. "Colonel," he whispered hoarsely, touching the bloodless hand on the dead leader's coat—"Colonel."

Just then there was a gentle tugging at his sleeve, and a soft voice said, "I am Mrs. Harrison. You are welcome."

"Do pardon my intrusion," said the old soldier, drawing his coat sleeve across his eyes. "I felt I couldn't live out the few years left to me unless I saw my old Colonel alone, like this, just once more. I marched with him from Atlanta to the sea, and I've come one hundred miles from home to give him a last salute." As he slowly retreated he raised his hand, soldierlike, to his brow.

Taking Over

On October 2, 1919, Woodrow Wilson suffered a stroke that paralyzed him. For the next eighteen months, the second Mrs. Wilson, Edith Bolling, took charge of the White House—and, some claimed, of the executive branch of the government. She defended her actions in her memoirs:

Once my husband was out of immediate danger, the burning question was how Mr. Wilson might best serve the country, preserve his own life, and if possible recover. Many people, among them some I had counted as friends, have written of my overwhelming ambition to act as President; of my exclusion of all advice, and so forth. I am trying here to write as though I had taken the oath to tell the truth, the whole truth, and nothing but the truth—so help me God.

I asked the doctors to be frank with me; that I must know what the outcome would probably be, so as to be honest with the people. They all said that as the brain was as clear as ever, with the progress made in the past few days, there was every reason to think recovery possible. Dr. Dercum told me of the history of Pasteur, who had been stricken exactly in this way, but who recovered and did his most brilliant intellectual work afterward. He sent me a copy of a remarkable book, *The Life of Pasteur.*

But recovery could not be hoped for, they said, unless the President were released from every disturbing problem during these days of Nature's effort to repair the damage done.

"How can that be," I asked the doctors, "when everything that comes to an executive is a problem? How can I protect him from problems when the country looks to the President as the leader?"

Dr. Dercum leaned toward me and said: "Madam, it is a grave situation, but I think you can solve it. Have everything come to you; weigh the importance of each matter, and see if it is possible by consultations with the respective heads of the departments to solve them without the guidance of your husband. In this way you can save him a great deal. But always keep in mind that every time you take him a new anxiety or problem to excite him, you are turning a knife in an open wound. His nerves are crying out for rest, and any excitement is torture to him."

"Then," I said, "had he better not resign, let Mr. Marshall succeed to the presidency and he himself get that complete rest that is so vital to his life?"

"No," the doctor said, "not if you feel equal to what I suggested. For Mr. Wilson to resign would have a bad effect on the country, and a serious effect on our patient. He has staked his life and made his promise to the world to do all in his power to get the Treaty ratified and make the League of Nations complete. If he resigns, the greatest incentive to recovery is gone; and as his mind is clear as crystal he can still do more with even a maimed body than anyone else. He has the utmost confidence in you. Dr. Grayson tells me that he has always discussed public affairs with you; so you will not come to them uninformed."

So began my stewardship. I studied every paper, sent from the different Secretaries or Senators, and tried to digest and present in tabloid form the things that, despite my vigilance, had to go to the President. I myself never made a single decision regarding the disposition of public affairs. The only decision that was mine was what was important and what was not, and the *very* important decision of when to present matters to my husband.

Positively Pat

Paul Keyes, former producer of the television comedy show "Laugh-In," was a close friend of the Nixons. He happened to be at the White House during one of the turning points in the Watergate scandal, the day when the President announced the resignation of his two aides, H. R. Haldeman and John Ehrlichman. That evening, while Nixon was conferring with his most trusted friends, Pat Nixon, with some help from her daughter Tricia, took charge of the telephones which were ringing until past midnight. Mrs. Nixon took one call after another—some came from as far away as Thailand—and spent many minutes reassuring them. "She was calm, comforting, and positive," Paul Keyes recalled later. "God knows she was positive! If I had a problem, I'd like my wife to be like Mrs. Nixon." Then he paused, with comic timing, and added: "Of course, my wife *is*, but we don't have his problems."

Ordeal

When Richard Nixon was operated on for phlebitis, his physician, Dr. John Lungren, was also astonished by Mrs. Nixon's composure:

She behaved in remarkable fashion throughout the whole ordeal. She realized the President was close to death, but she had an amazing ability to handle the situation. There were tears, of course, but always in private. What floored me was that she wanted to reassure me. The press was always insinuating that nothing was the matter with the President. I've been a physician for twenty-six years, and that was pretty difficult for me to go through. But she would say she wanted me to know that she and the family had complete faith in me. She said it was up to God and our ability to handle the situation.

Holding On

Mrs. Reagan told Good Housekeeping *magazine the anguish of how she learned that an attempt had been made on her husband's life:*

I was attending a luncheon, but for some reason I suddenly felt that I wanted to leave before it was over. I'd never had that kind of feeling before. I excused myself and hurried home. I was on the third floor of the White House when a Secret Service man beckoned to me and said, "There's been a shooting at a hotel. Your husband wasn't hit, but other people were and he went to the hospital."

I started running toward the elevator and said: "I want to go to the hospital." The Secret Service man told me it would be better to stay at the White House. But I insisted and was downstairs and in a car in minutes. I was very apprehensive. It seemed strange to me that Ronnie would be at the hospital if he wasn't hurt.

Mike Deaver, White House deputy chief of staff, met me at the door. He said, "Your husband was hit." I said, "I want to see him right away." Mike said, "You can't, they're working on him."

A few minutes later they took me into the emergency room. Ronnie was lying on a table with an oxygen mask over his face. He lifted it and said, "Honey, I forgot to duck." I could see blood on his lips and I wanted to stay with him, but the doctors told me I had to leave. They put me in a tiny room with one desk and one chair. The next hours are a blur. There were a lot of people running around, and a policeman was saying, "Get those people away," and I was thinking: I have to hold on to myself.

Blame

Amid the anguish of his family, President Taylor died at the White House, July 9, 1850. When it was known that he must die, Mrs. Taylor became insensible, and the agonized cries of his family reached the surrounding streets.

After he became President, General Taylor said that "his wife had prayed every night for months that Henry Clay might be elected in his place." She survived her husband two years, and to her last hour never mentioned the White House in Washington except in its relation to the death of her husband.

ALONE

Waiting for the Call

Martha survived George Washington only by about thirty months. The Reverend Manasseh Cutler, visiting her in 1802, found her looking much older than when he had last seen her as First Lady in Philadelphia, but "very little wrinkled and remarkably fair for a person of her years. She spoke of the General with great affection, and observed that, though she had many favors and mercies, for which she desired to bless God, she felt as if she was become a stranger among her friends, and could welcome the time when she should be called to follow her deceased friend."

That Way Madness Lies

After the death of her son Tad, in July 1871, Mrs. Lincoln's mental state deteriorated. Her behavior finally forced Robert Lincoln to ask the state of Illinois to certify her insane. The following is an extract from the hearings in May 1875, as reported in a Chicago newspaper:

Dr. Isham testified that on March 12 he received a telegram from Mrs. Lincoln, at Jacksonville, Florida, as follows: "My belief is my son is ill: telegraph: I start for Chicago tomorrow." Mr. Lincoln was perfectly well, and the telegram rather startled witness then; wired her to that effect, and Mr. Lincoln sent a telegram telling her to remain in Florida until she was perfectly well; received another telegram one hour and a half after receipt of the first; it read: "My dearly beloved son, Robert T. Lincoln—rouse yourself and live for your mother; you are all I have; from this hour all I have is yours. I pray every night that you may be spared to your mother."

Robert T. Lincoln, the petitioner, then took the witness stand. His face was pale; his eyes bore evidence that he had been weeping, and his whole manner was such as to affect all present. His mother looked upon him benignly and never betrayed the emotion which must have filled her breast during the recital of the unfortunate and regretful scenes they were parties to. He testified that there was no reason his mother should think he was sick unless that she had seen some newspaper paragraph. He had not been sick in ten years. He did not want any money from his mother. He owed her money, that is, he had some in his hands in trust for her. Mother arrived from the South on March 15. When witness entered the car in which she was she appeared startled. She looked well and not fatigued after her journey of seventy-two hours. Asked her to come to witness's home. She declined and went to the Grand Pacific. Had supper together, and after it sat talking. She told him that at the first breakfast she had after leaving Jacksonville, an attempt was made to poison her. Occupied a room adjoining hers that night. She slept well that night, but subsequently was restless. Several nights she tapped at witness's bedroom door; she would be in her night-gown. Told her to go back to her room. Twice in one night she roused him up. One night she aroused him and asked that she might sleep in his room. He gave his mother his bed, and he slept on the lounge.

Here witness gave vent to his feelings in tears, and the scene was most touching. He continued: Then I got Dr. Isham to attend her.

On April 1, she ceased tapping at witness's room door, for witness told her she must not do it or he would leave the hotel. On that day he went to her room. She was not properly dressed. She left the room under some pretext, and the next thing he knew she was in the elevator going down to the office. Called back the elevator and endeavored to induce her to return to her room. She regarded witness's interference as impertinent; declined to leave the elevator. Just then the bell rang several times. She was not in a condition of dress to be seen, and witness gently forced her out of the elevator by putting his arm around her waist. Maggie Gavin assisted him, and they got her into her room. She screamed, "You are going to murder me," and would not let Maggie Gavin leave the room to do her work. After a while she said that the man who had taken her pocketbook promised to return it at three o'clock. Asked her who the man was. She replied he was the Wandering Jew, had seen him in Florida. Then she sat near the wall and for an hour professed to be repeating what this man was telling her through the wall. During the afternoon she slept. Since the fire she has kept her trunks and property in the Fidelity Safe Deposit Company's building. In the beginning of the last week in April he called on her. She said that all Chicago was going to be burned, and she intended to send her trunks to some country town—to Milwaukee. Told her that Milwaukee was too near Oshkosh where there had been a terrible fire the night before. She said that witness's house, of all in Chicago, would be saved, and witness then suggested that was the best place to send the trunks. On the Saturday following she showed witness securities for $57,000 which she carried in her pocket. She has spent large sums of money lately; bought $600 worth of lace curtains; three watches costing $450; $700 worth of jewelry; $200 worth of Lubin's perfumeries, and a whole piece of silk. Witness had no doubt that she is insane. Had had a conference with her cousin Major Stuart, of Springfield, and Judge Davis, of the Supreme Court, as to the best thing to be done for her. They advised the present course.

Q. *Do you regard it safe to allow your mother to remain as she is, unrestrained?*

A. She has long been a source of much anxiety to me. [Again Mr. Lincoln was affected to tears.] I do not think it would be safe or proper. Have had a man watching her for the last three weeks, whose sole duty was to watch after her when she went on the street. She knew nothing about it. She has no home, and does not visit at witness's house because of a misunderstanding with his wife. Has always been exceedingly kind to witness. She has been of unsound mind since the death of father; has been irresponsible for past ten years. Regarded her as eccentric and unmanageable, never heeding witness's advice. Had no reason to make these purchases, for her trunks are filled with dresses and valuables of which she makes no use. She wears no jewelry and dresses in deep black.

After a few minutes of deliberation, the jury was satisfied that Mrs. Lincoln was insane and fit to be sent to a state hospital for the insane.

Among the Rest

Immediately following the verdict, Mrs. Lincoln tried to commit suicide. She was taken under the private care of Dr. R. J. Patterson at Batavia, Illinois, who after three months published his opinion that she was behaving normally. Then the President's widow was committed to the care of her sister in Springfield, and after nine months a panel judged her sane. She left for Europe, where she wandered for five years. In October 1880, Mrs. Lincoln returned to the United States from France on the steamer Amérique, *and among her fellow voyagers was Sarah Bernhardt, the French actress. The* New York Sun, *in describing the reception of the latter, incidentally mentions Mrs. Lincoln:*

A throng was assembled on the dock and a a greater throng was in the street outside the gates. During the tedious process of working the ship into her dock there was a great crush in that part of the vessel where the gangplank was to be swung. Among the passengers who were here gathered was an aged lady. She was dressed plainly and almost commonly. There was a bad rent in her ample cloak. Her face was furrowed, and her hair was streaked with white. This was the widow of Abraham Lincoln.

She was almost unnoticed. She had come alone across the ocean, but a nephew met her at Quarantine. She has spent the last four years in the south of France. When the gangplank was finally swung aboard, Mlle. Bernhardt and her companions, including Mme. Columbier of the troupe, were the first to descend. The fellow voyagers of the actress pressed about her to bid adieu, and a cheer was raised, which turned her head and provoked an astonished smile, as she stepped upon the wharf. The gates were besieged, and there was some difficulty in bringing in the carriage which was to convey the actress to her hotel. She temporarily waited in the freight office at the entrance to the wharf.

Mrs. Lincoln, leaning on the arm of her nephew, walked toward the gate. A policeman touched the aged lady on the shoulder and bade her stand back. She retreated with her nephew into the line of spectators, while Manager Abbey's carriage was slowly brought in. Bernhardt was handed inside, and the carriage made its way out through a mass of struggling longshoremen and idlers who pressed about it and stared in at the open windows. After it, went out the others who had been passengers on the *Amérique*, Mrs. Lincoln among the rest.

In her own memoirs, Sarah Bernhardt describes how on board she saved Mary Lincoln's life when she slipped on the stairs, realizing only afterward that this gesture was probably most unwelcome.

Pension

The first time a pension was ever suggested for the widow of an ex-president was, we are told, when William H. Harrison died one month after his inauguration. The death of Harrison peculiarly appealed to the sentiment of the Nation, and Mrs. Harrison was voted outright $25,000. Even this sum was not extravagant, for she had to live on it for the twenty-three years she survived her husband.

Widows

In the mid-1930s two of the seven widows of Presidents lived in Washington and took part in the social life of the Capital. Here is a study in contrast between Mrs. Wilson and Mrs. Taft, as recorded by George Abell and Evelyn Gordon, two prominent journalists of the time:

Mrs. Wilson plays a big role in unofficial society; at times even in official circles. The memory of the wartime President is still green in many hearts, and the once strikingly handsome "Widow Galt" who wooed and won him is surrounded by an aura of reverence. Democratic organizations of all types angle for her patronage. She is forever being pestered by committees who plead for the use of her name. She is often invited to the White House, and the Polish Embassy seldom gives a large party without having the widow of the man who insisted on Poland's independence. Enthusiastic Poles have decorated her with the order of Polonia Restituta. Many cranks write letters, too, making impossible demands for money and favors. Young Woodrow Wilson, a *Washington Daily News* photographer who is no relation whatsoever to the late President, often receives these letters by mistake. He always sends them on to Mrs. Wilson.

Instead of the brilliant colors she wore at the time of her marriage to Woodrow Wilson (her favorite shades were violet and turquoise blue), Mrs. Wilson today affects black with a corsage of purple orchids during the daytime. At night she frequently wears scarlet lace and ropes of pearls. All her jewels are distinctive and should be since her first husband was Norman Galt, an owner of Washington's oldest and most widely known jewelry firm. Despite her display of flowers and gems, however, Mrs. Wilson dislikes personal comments on her appearance. She avoids much of the publicity which would be showered upon her by Democrats and others by keeping an unlisted telephone. Whenever a newspaper reporter finds out the number, she has it changed.

Mrs. Taft, who during the years her husband served as President was a semi-invalid, has become the prize concertgoer of Washington. She goes to everything—musicales, teas, luncheons, and bridge parties. She takes cocktails but never smokes. Bridge games hold a great fascination for her, but she once trumped her partner's ace. Her pet bridge cronies are Mrs. William E. Borah, Mrs. Mark Sullivan, and Mrs. George Sutherland, wife of the Supreme Court Justice. Recently Mrs. Taft has taken to foreign travel. She goes about Europe carrying *Baedeker's*, thick sunglasses, and steamer rugs. She is still talking about eating papayas on a cruise she made to Mexico. Two annual itineraries of hers are as fixed as the Polar star; a spring jaunt to Charleston's azalea gardens and a late summer visit to her country home at Murray Bay, Canada.

Living alone with Mary, her housekeeper, in a roomy red brick mansion set among magnolia trees, she entertains seldom but goes out all the time. People are slightly bored with her sprightliness, but as the widow of the only man who has been both

President and Chief Justice, she is tolerantly accepted in lame-duck circles.

Pedestal

After her husband's murder, many people expected Jacqueline Kennedy to live as a widow. "But Jackie was more realistic," writes Helen Thomas, who knew her as well as any reporter was allowed to. "I was not surprised when she married Onassis. Before the big event, a friend cautioned her: 'But, Jackie, you're going to fall off your pedestal.' Her response was searing, logical, and pure Jacquelinian. 'That's better than freezing there,' she said."

Recognition

Fanny Holtzmann came on April 29 to Eleanor Roosevelt's cluttered little apartment overlooking Washington Square. Her hostess arrived late and in a pleasurable flutter. She had been riding by subway from the temporary UN headquarters at Hunter College in the Bronx—

"The rush-hour subway, on a clammy afternoon like this? Why didn't you take a taxi?"

"My dear Fanny, do you realize how much a taxi from the Bronx costs?" She resumed her story. There she was, hanging on to a strap in the crowded, steamy express, when a fellow voyager looked up from his newspaper and recognized her. "Until that moment I had been just another old lady in the jostling crowd, trying to stay on my feet and catch a breath of air. The instant he called out my name and offered me his seat, the whole car came to life. A path opened up for me like the Red Sea parting; everybody gathered around. It made me feel so good that people remembered Franklin!"

THEIR END

Till Death Did Them Part

On May 8, 1782, her fifth daughter was born (the infant was given the name of Lucy Elizabeth, to replace the first Lucy Elizabeth, who had died the previous year). Martha was now a very sick woman. Jefferson spent almost every waking moment at her side.

Four months later, without having left her bed, Martha Wayles Jefferson died, not quite thirty-four. The date was September 6, 1782. The moment of her death was recorded simply, and poignantly, in Jefferson's account book: "My dear wife died this day at 11:45 A.M."

Although he himself would never discuss it, Jefferson's grief over Martha's death was intense. The following description comes to us from his daughter Patsy:

"He kept to his room for three weeks, and I was never a moment from his side. He walked almost incessantly night and day, only lying down occasionally, when nature was completely exhausted. When at last he left his room, he rode out, and from that time he was incessantly on horseback. In those melancholy rambles, I was his constant companion, a solitary witness to many a violent burst of grief."

Shortly before she died, Martha copied a passage from Laurence Sterne's *Tristram Shandy*. She must have struggled on it laboriously, for any exertion, even a simple task such as putting a few words on paper, would have been almost beyond her.

These were the words she wrote:

> time wastes too fast: every letter
> I trace tells me with what rapidity
> life follows my pen, the days and
> hours of it are flying over our heads
> like clouds of windy day never to
> return—more everything presses on—

She could not continue. She stopped there, and Jefferson completed the quotation for her, without correcting some errors she had made:

> . . . and every
> time I kiss thy hand to bid adieu, every absence
> which follows it, are preludes to that eternal separation
> which we are shortly to make!

A persistent legend tells us that when Martha was dying she asked Jefferson never to remarry. He gave her his promise and remained a widower for the rest of his life.

Beyond the Grave

Rachel Jackson died just before her husband became President, and his mourning for her influenced the rest of his life. The following description of his abiding love is by his private secretary, Mr. Trist:

One evening after I parted with him for the night, revolving over the directions he had given about some letters I was to prepare, one point occurred on which I was not perfectly satisfied as to what those directions had been. As the letters were to be sent off early in the morning, I returned to his chamber door, and tapping gently, in order not to wake him if he had got to sleep, my tap was answered by "Come in."

He was undressed, but not yet in bed, as I had supposed he must be by that time. He was sitting at a little table, with his wife's miniature—a very large one, then for the first time seen by me—before him, propped up against some books; and between him and the picture lay an open book, which bore the marks of long use. This book, as I afterward learned, was her prayer book. The miniature he always wore next to his heart, suspended round his neck by a strong black cord. The last thing he did every night, before lying down to rest, was to read in that book with that picture under his eyes.

President Jackson's granddaughter was also called Rachel, in memory of his wife. Mrs. Rachel Lawrence lived well into the twentieth century and recalled the General's devotion in the years of his retirement:

It was Grandpa's daily custom to visit, just before nightfall, the tomb wherein his wife rested. He would come out on the piazza—standing for a moment looking out on the driveway of evergreens leading to the door—and would then slowly walk through the flowered paths of the garden to the tomb, where he stood with bowed, uncovered head in silence. As his health failed, my mother accompanied him upon this evening pilgrimage, he leaning heavily upon her for support.

I was starting for school on the Monday preceding his death [Mrs. Lawrence was thirteen years old at the time] and had gone into Grandpa's room to bid him good-bye. He stroked my hair and kissed me affectionately as usual, then tremblingly removed the ivory miniature of his wife from his breast, where he had worn it since her death. Placing it tenderly within my hand, he clasped them both within his own, and said: "Keep this, my baby, for her sake, whose name you bear, and for mine." To this hour this miniature is my most cherished possession.

Eulogy

Mrs. Letitia Tyler died in the White House on September 10, 1842. Her daughter-in-law, Mrs. Robert Tyler, remembered the sad event:

Nothing can exceed the loneliness of this large and gloomy mansion, hung with black, its walls echoing only sighs and groans. My poor husband suffered dreadfully when he was told his mother's eyes were constantly turned to the door, watching for him. He had left Washington to bring me and the children, at her request. She had everything about her to awaken love. She was beautiful to the eye, even in her illness; her complexion was clear as an infant's, her figure perfect, and her hands and feet were the most delicate I ever saw. She was refined and gentle in everything that she said and did; and above all, a pure and spotless Christian. She was my beau ideal of a perfect gentle-woman.

The devotion of father and sons to her was most affecting. I don't think I ever saw her enter a room that all three did not spring up to lead her to a chair, to arrange her footstool, and caress and pet her.

Not Eating Will Kill You

Housekeeper Elizabeth Jaffray had her own opinions, as usual, about the cause of Ellen Wilson's death:

One Sunday morning early in the second March that the Wilsons were in the White House, Mrs. Wilson came out of her room to go to church. The heel of her shoe caught in the taping of the carpet of her bedroom and she was thrown on her face. She seemed to be badly shaken and said that she would lie down instead of going to church. When Dr. Grayson came he found that she had strained her back, but apparently it was nothing serious. Shortly before this accident Mrs. Wilson had said to me: "I think I'll reduce ten or twelve pounds."

"That seems to me to be very foolish, Mrs. Wilson," I told her. "You have a lovely figure right now, and I think you would be silly to try to reduce."

"But I am going to take off at least ten pounds," she persisted—and diet she would.

Actually I think that this step had a great deal to do with her death. She was badly hurt by her fall, but by her self-inflicted diet she gave herself no chance to build up her strength.

Then, too, she apparently was in a rather unfortunate mental state at this time. Life in the White House seemed to her a little trying and hardly worthwhile. I don't believe that she really cared much about getting well. For months she simply gave up trying. President Wilson himself did everything he could to cheer her and get her to eat nourishing food.

Time and again I would go into her bedroom and find Mr. Wilson at her bedside.

"Please do eat just a little of this," he would beg. "You will soon get well, darling, if you try hard to eat something. Now please take this bite, dear."

But nothing seemed to be able to check the ebbing of Mrs. Wilson's strength. A slight operation failed to bring improvement. Without any apparent reason she continued to sink lower and lower, and for a week previous to her death it was only a question of hours until her remaining vitality would sink completely away.

Just a few minutes before five on the afternoon of August 6, 1914, I went into her bedroom. The nurse was having tea at a table in the doorway where she could watch her patient.

I stepped to Mrs. Wilson's bed and looked down at her. Her head moved gently to one side and she looked up at me and whispered, "Oh, Mrs. Jaffray," and her eyes closed.

These were the last words she uttered, and five minutes later, when the nurse approached the bed, she was gently breathing her last. She died just one year and five months after she had come to the White House.

The President was stunned and speechless. No other member of the family was as deeply affected. He refused to have the body put in a casket and held in state, as had been the custom in White House deaths. Instead, he had Mrs. Wilson laid on a sofa in her bedroom upstairs. With his own hands he placed around her shoulders a lovely white silk shawl. Her golden brown hair was braided and twisted around her head. She was a beautiful Madonna.

For two nights the President sat up alone in a chair by the sofa—a solitary and touching vigil.

Outside the bedroom door sat a Secret Service man, but the President was the only living person in the chamber of death.

On the third day the President permitted the body to be placed in a coffin, and it lay in state in the East Room of the White House until the funeral party started for Georgia, where it was interred.

I have often thought how queerly Fate twists things. The first Mrs. Wilson loved all flowers except orchids. Yet Fate so arranged it that the single floral piece on the coffin was a great wreath of orchids.

APPENDIX: WIVES OF
THE PRESIDENTS

MARTHA DANDRIDGE CUSTIS WASHINGTON
(b. June 21, 1731, New Kent County, Va.; d. May 22, 1802, Mount Vernon, Va.) Married Daniel Parke Custis in 1749; George Washington on January 6, 1759.

ABIGAIL SMITH ADAMS
(b. November 23, 1744, Weymouth, Mass.; d. October 28, 1818, Quincy, Mass.) Married John Adams on October 25, 1764.

MARTHA WAYLES JEFFERSON
(b. October 30, 1748, Charles City County, Va.; d. September 6, 1782, Monticello, Va.) Married Bathurst Skelton in 1766; Thomas Jefferson on January 1, 1772.

(DOLLEY) DOROTHEA PAYNE TODD MADISON
(b. May 20, 1768, Guilford County, N.C.; d. July 12, 1849, Washington, D.C.) She was a widow of John Todd when she married James Madison on September 15, 1794.

ELIZABETH KORTRIGHT MONROE
(b. June 30, 1768, New York City; d. September 23, 1830, Oak Hill, Va.) Married James Monroe on February 15, 1786.

LOUISA CATHERINE JOHNSON ADAMS
(b. February 12, 1775, London, England; d. May 15, 1852, Washington, D.C.) Married John Quincy Adams on July 26, 1797.

RACHEL DONELSON ROBARDS JACKSON
(b. June, 1767, Brunswick County, Va.; d. December 22, 1828, Nashville, Tenn.) She was separated from Lewis Robards when she married Andrew Jackson in 1791, then divorced from Robards and remarried to Jackson in 1794.

HANNAH HOES VAN BUREN
(b. March 8, 1783, Kinderhook, N.Y.; d. February 5, 1819, Albany, N.Y.) Married Martin Van Buren on February 21, 1807.

ANNA TUTHILL SYMMES HARRISON
(b. July 25, 1775, near Morristown, N.J.; d. February 25, 1864, North Bend, Ohio) Married William Henry Harrison on November 25, 1795.

LETITIA CHRISTIAN TYLER
(b. November 12, 1790, New Kent County, Va.; d. September 10, 1842, in the White House, Washington, D.C.) Married John Tyler on March 29, 1813.

JULIA GARDINER TYLER
(b. May 4, 1820, Gardiner's Island, N.Y.; d. July 10, 1889, Richmond, Va.) Married John Tyler on June 26, 1844.

SARAH CHILDRESS POLK
(b. September 4, 1803, near Murfreesboro, Tenn.; d. August 14, 1891, Nashville, Tenn.) Married James Knox Polk on January 1, 1824.

MARGARET MACKALL SMITH TAYLOR
(b. September 21, 1788, Calvert County, Md.; d. August 18, 1852, near Pascagoula, Miss.) Married Zachary Taylor on June 21, 1810.

ABIGAIL POWERS FILLMORE
(b. March 13, 1798, Stillwater, N.Y.; d. March 30, 1853, Washington, D.C.) Married Millard Fillmore on February 5, 1826.

CAROLINE CARMICHAEL MCINTOSH FILLMORE
(b. October 21, 1813, Morristown, N.J.; d. August 11, 1881, Buffalo, N.Y.) She was the widow of Ezekiel C. McIntosh when she married Millard Fillmore on February 10, 1858.

JANE MEANS APPLETON PIERCE
(b. March 12, 1806, Hampton, N.H.; d. December 2, 1863, Andover, Mass.) Married Franklin Pierce on November 19, 1834.

MARY ANN TODD LINCOLN
(b. December 13, 1818, Lexington, Ky.; d. July 16, 1882, Springfield, Ill.) Married Abraham Lincoln on November 4, 1842.

ELIZA MCCARTLE JOHNSON
(b. October 4, 1810, Leesburg, Tenn.; d. January 15, 1876, Greene County, Tenn.) Married Andrew Johnson on May 17, 1827.

JULIA BOGGS DENT GRANT
(b. January 26, 1826, St. Louis, Mo.; d. December 14, 1902, Washington, D.C.) Married Ulysses S. Grant on August 22, 1848.

LUCY WARE WEBB HAYES
(b. August 28, 1831, Chillicothe, Ohio; d. June 25, 1889, Fremont, Ohio) Married Rutherford Birchard Hayes on December 30, 1852.

LUCRETIA RUDOLPH GARFIELD
(b. April 19, 1832, Hiram, Ohio; d. March 14, 1918, Pasadena, Cal.) Married James Abram Garfield on November 11, 1858.

ELLEN LEWIS HERNDON ARTHUR
(b. August 30, 1837, Fredericksburg, Va.; d. January 12, 1880, New York City) Married Chester Alan Arthur on October 25, 1859.

FRANCES FOLSOM CLEVELAND
(b. July 21, 1864, Buffalo, N.Y.; d. October 29, 1947, Baltimore, Md.) Married Grover Cleveland on June 22, 1886.

CAROLINE LAVINIA SCOTT HARRISON
(b. October 1, 1832, Oxford, Ohio; d. October 25, 1892, in the White House, Washington, D.C.) Married Benjamin Harrison on October 20, 1853.

MARY SCOTT LORD DIMMICK HARRISON
(b. April 30, 1858, Honesdale, Pa.; d. January 5, 1948, New York City) She was a widow of Walter Erskine Dimmick when she married Benjamin Harrison on April 6, 1896.

IDA SAXTON MCKINLEY
(b. June 8, 1847, Canton, Ohio; d. May 26, 1907, Canton, Ohio) Married William McKinley on January 25, 1871.

ALICE HATHAWAY LEE ROOSEVELT
(b. July 29, 1861, Chestnut Hill, Mass.; d. February 14, 1884, New York City) Married Theodore Roosevelt on October 27, 1880.

EDITH KERMIT CAROW ROOSEVELT
(b. August 6, 1861, Norwich, Conn.; d. September 30, 1848, Oyster Bay, N.Y.) Married Theodore Roosevelt on December 2, 1886.

HELEN HERRON TAFT
(b. June 2, 1861, Cincinnati, Ohio; d. May 22, 1943, Washington, D.C.) Married William Howard Taft on June 19, 1886.

ELLEN LOUISE AXSON WILSON
(b. May 15, 1860, Savannah, Ga.; d. August 6, 1914, in the White House, Washington, D.C.) Married Woodrow Wilson on June 24, 1885.

EDITH BOLLING GALT WILSON
(b. October 15, 1872, Wytheville, Va.; d. December 28, 1961, Washington, D.C.) She was the widow of Norman Galt when she married Woodrow Wilson on December 18, 1915.

FLORENCE KLING DE WOLFE HARDING
(b. August 15, 1860, Marion, Ohio; d. November 21, 1924, Marion, Ohio) She was divorced from Henry De Wolfe when she married Warren Gamaliel Harding on July 8, 1891.

GRACE ANNA GOODHUE COOLIDGE
(b. January 3, 1879, Burlington, Vt.; d. July 8, 1957, Northampton, Mass.) Married Calvin Coolidge on October 4, 1905.

LOU HENRY HOOVER
(b. March 29, 1874, Waterloo, Ia.; d. January 7, 1944, New York City) Married Herbert Clark Hoover on February 10, 1899.

ANNA ELEANOR ROOSEVELT ROOSEVELT
(b. October 11, 1884, New York City; d. November 7, 1962, New York City) Married Franklin Delano Roosevelt on March 17, 1905.

ELIZABETH VIRGINIA WALLACE TRUMAN
(b. February 13, 1885, Independence, Mo.; d. October 18, 1982, Independence, Mo.) Married Harry S Truman on June 28, 1919.

MARIE GENEVA DOUD EISENHOWER
(b. November 14, 1896, Boone, Ia.; d. November 1, 1979, Washington, D.C.) Married Dwight David Eisenhower on July 1, 1916.

JACQUELINE LEE BOUVIER KENNEDY
(b. July 28, 1929, Southampton, N.Y.) Married John Fitzgerald Kennedy on September 12, 1953. Married Aristotle Onassis on October 20, 1968.

(LADY BIRD) CLAUDIA ALTA TAYLOR JOHNSON
(b. December 22, 1912, Karnack, Tex.) Married Lyndon Baines Johnson on November 17, 1934.

THELMA CATHERINE RYAN NIXON
(b. March 16, 1912, Ely, Nev.) Married Richard Milhous Nixon on June 21, 1940.

(BETTY) ELIZABETH BLOOMER WARREN FORD
(b. April 8, 1918, Chicago, Ill.) Married William C. Warren in 1942 (divorced in 1947). Married Gerald Rudolph Ford on October 15, 1948.

ROSALYNN SMITH CARTER
(b. August 18, 1927, near Plains, Ga.) Married James Earl Carter on July 7, 1946.

JANE WYMAN
(b. January 4, 1914, St. Joseph, Mo.) Married Ronald Wilson Reagan on January 25, 1940. They were divorced in 1948.

(NANCY) ANNE FRANCES ROBBINS DAVIS REAGAN
(b. July 6, 1921,* New York City). Married Ronald Wilson Reagan on March 4, 1952.

* Some sources say 1923.

SOURCES

1 WHAT WERE THEY LIKE?

PORTRAITS

Temper—Parton: *Daughters of Genius*

Neat as a Quaker—Holloway: *The Ladies of the White House*

Does She or Doesn't She?—Wharton: *Social Life in the Early Republic*; Holloway: *Ladies*

Plump Shoulders—Wharton: *Social Life*

Puritan Frigidity—Ellet: *Court Circles of the Republic*

A Daughter's Tribute—Ames: *Ten Years in Washington*

Actress—Caroli: *First Ladies*

Conspicuous by Her Presence—Ames: *Ten Years*

Diamonds Are a Girl's Best Friend—Pryor: *Reminiscences of Peace and War*

Typical Belle—Sandburg and Angle: *Mary Lincoln: Wife and Widow*

Careworn—Poore: *Perley's Reminiscences*

Reticence—Poore: *Perley's*

Everydayish—(Anonymous:) *Boudoir Mirrors of Washington*

Looking as She Should—J. B. West: *Upstairs at the White House*

CLOTHES

Recycling—Holloway: *In the Home of the Presidents*; Ames: *Ten Years*

Bird of Paradise—Wharton: *Social Life*

Exit the Bustle—*Boudoir Mirrors*

Terror—Jensen: *The White House and Its Thirty-two Families*

Watchdog—Parks: *My Thirty Years Backstairs at the White House*
Battle of the Underwear—McLendon and Smith: *Don't Quote Me!*
Recurring Nightmare—McLellan: *Ear on Washington*
Ill Will—McLellan: *Ear*

BELIEFS

Churchgoing—Hanscom: *The Friendly Craft*
Gentle Request—Willets: *Inside History of the White House*
Female Suffrage—Sandburg and Angle: *Mary Lincoln*
A Woman's Place—Weimann and Miller: *The Fair Women*
Split Persona—I. Ross: *Grace Coolidge and Her Era*
She Was Never Promised a Rose Garden—Johnson: *A White House Diary*
Ribbing—*McCall's*, September 1975
Seen and Heard—Ford: *The Times of My Life*
Reproach—Norton: *Rosalynn*; John and Abigail Adams: *Familiar Letters*

FOIBLES

First Ladies Are Human, Too—*Boudoir Mirrors*
Who Likes Whom—Jaffray: *Secrets of the White House*
Upset—Means: *The Woman in the White House*
The Green-Eyed Monster—Badeau: *Grant in Peace*
No Love Lost—McLellan: *Ear*
Equal Time—Ford: *Times*
Pandamania—Martin: *The Name on the White House Floor*
Mom the Klutz—J. Roosevelt: *Affectionately, F.D.R.*

2 BACKGROUND

PARENTAGE

Genes and Genealogy—Carnegie: *The Unknown Lincoln*
St. Patrick's Babe—Taylor: *The Book of Presidents*
Early Bloomer—Ford: *Times*
Nancy Davis's Eyes—Leamer: *Make-Believe*

The Ugly Princess—Lash: *Eleanor and Franklin*
The Black Prince—Buck: *The Kennedy Women*
Clash of Wills—Means: *Woman in White House*
Whatever Nancy Wants—Leamer: *Make-Believe*

CHILDHOOD

Perilous Voyage—Holloway: *Ladies*
Trauma—Lash: *Eleanor and Franklin*
Phobias—McLellan: *Ear*
Fat Kid—Ford: *Times*
Generosity—Holloway: *Ladies*
Sophomore—Logan: *Thirty Years in Washington*
Amour Propre—Buck: *Kennedy Women*
Rosalynn's Social Debut—Moorehead: *Entertaining in Washington*

ACCOMPLISHMENTS

But What Is It in English?—Logan: *Thirty Years*; Barzman; *The
First Ladies*
Danger of Meddling—Holloway: *Ladies*
Philosophy—Holloway: *Ladies*
A Writer—Holloway: *Ladies*
An Exception—Wharton: *Social Life*
Teacher—Logan: *Thirty Years*
An Intellectual—Ames: *Ten Years*; Wharton: *Social Life*
Training—Holloway: *Ladies*
A Linguist—Sadler: *America's First Ladies*
Wit—*Look*, July 1961

MANNERS

Up to Snuff—Holloway: *Ladies*; Logan: *Thirty Years*
Mob Scene—Holloway: *Ladies*
Graceful Gesture—Wharton: *Social Life*
Fancy That—Wharton: *Social Life*
The Second Mrs. Tyler—Wharton: *Social Life*
Hoops—Pryor: *Reminiscences of Peace and War*

No Gossip—Holloway: *Ladies*
But Can One Major in It?—*Look*, July 1961
Bedtime with Bonzo, or, *While Reagan Slept*—McLellan: *Ear*

3 ROMANCE

ATTRACTION

Mars and Venus—Holloway: *Ladies*
Charms—Brooks: *Dames and Daughters of the Young Republic*
Thy Neighbor's Wife—Holloway: *Ladies*; Wharton: *Social Life*
Searching for Mr. Right—Carnegie: *Unknown Lincoln*
Dancin'—Williams: *The Lincoln Story Book*
Her Ideal Beau—McAdoo: *The Priceless Gift*
Hot Pursuit—*Boudoir Mirrors*
Amazing Grace—I. Ross: *Grace Coolidge*
Rocks—Barzman: *First Ladies*; Sadler: *America's First Ladies*
The Real Tinsel—Reagan: *Where's the Rest of Me?*
Cross Purposes—D. Smith: *Peculiarities of the Presidents*

COURTSHIP

If Music Be the Food of Love—Robins: *Romances of Early America*
Tragedy and Romance—Willets: *Inside History*
Age of Consent—Frank: *The Presidents: Tidbits and Trivia*
The Time of Her Life—Starling: *Starling of the White House*
The Course of True Love—Means: *Woman in White House*; *Boudoir Mirrors*
Bread—I. Ross: *Grace Coolidge*
All in the Family—Lash: *Eleanor and Franklin*
Love at First Sight—Margaret Truman: *Bess W. Truman*
Kids—Norton: *Rosalynn*
Labor Negotiation—Reagan: *Where's the Rest*
Theatre—David: *The Lonely Lady of San Clemente*

WEDDINGS

The Minister's Daughter—Holloway: *Ladies*
Royal Sanction—Brooks: *Dames and Daughters*

Just Married—Holloway: *Ladies*
White House Wedding—Poore: *Perley's*
Silver Wedding—Holloway: *Ladies*
The Empty Nest—Willets: *Inside History*; Pendel: *Thirty-six Years in the White House*
Slashing the Cake—Willets: *Inside History*
The Shadow of Presidents—J. Roosevelt: *My Parents: A Differing View*
Get Me to the Church in Time—M. Smith: *The President's Lady: An Intimate Biography of Mrs. Lyndon B. Johnson*
Promised in the Rose Garden—Thomas: *Dateline: The White House*

4 RELATIONSHIPS

MARRIED LIFE

Newlyweds—Starling: *Starling*
After the Honeymoon—I. Ross: *Grace Coolidge*
His Dear Patsy—Holloway: *Ladies*; Logan: *Thirty Years*
So Much for History—*Time*, August 28, 1964
She Liked Ike—West: *Upstairs*
I Am Glad You Asked—*McCall's*, September 1975
Some Enchanted Evening—*McCall's*, September 1975
Chief Executive—*Saturday Evening Post*, May 10, 1962
Differences—*Newsweek*, November 5, 1979
The Cat Out of the Bag—*Ladies' Home Journal*, March 1979
Magic—*McCall's*, November 1985

DIFFICULTIES

Sensitive Monomaniac—Logan: *Thirty Years*
Jealousy—Carnegie: *Unknown Lincoln*
Little Wife—Caroli: *First Ladies*
In Sickness—Willets: *Inside History*; Logan: *Thirty Years*; Bryant: *Dog Days at the White House*
Unmerry Christmas—Means: *Woman in White House*
Mother-in-law—Parks: *My Thirty Years*
Let Them Eat Cake—Sparks: *The $20,000,000 Honeymoon: Jackie and Ari's First Year*

OTHER WOMEN

Father of His Country—Morgan and Tucker: *Rumor!*

Friendship—Miller: *Scandals in the Highest Office: Facts and Fictions in the Private Lives of Our Presidents*

Disgust—Miller: *Scandals*

Taboo—Brodie: *Thomas Jefferson: An Intimate History*

All in the Family—reprinted in Brodie: *Thomas Jefferson*

Presidents and the Ladies—Hoover: *Forty-two Years in the White House*

Campaign Issue—Boller: *Presidential Anecdotes*

Halo—Russell: *The Shadow of Blooming Grove: Warren G. Harding in His Times*

Harding's Luck—Russell: *Shadow*

Monkey Business—J. Roosevelt: *My Parents*

Crisis—Lash: *Eleanor and Franklin*

Solace—Faber: *The Life of Lorena Hickok*

Statue Therapy—Faber: *Lorena Hickok*

Ike Liked Her—K. Morgan: *Past Forgetting*

Sorry, No Sex, We're British—Dunleavy and Brennan: *Those Wild, Wild Kennedy Boys!*

Take Two, and Call in the Morning—Dunleavy and Brennan: *Those Wild*

The Prince and the Showgirl—Guiles: *Legend: The Life and Death of Marilyn Monroe*

Dirty Old Man—Howar: *Laughing All the Way*

Hypothetical Question—Friedman: *Washington Humor*

5 HOMELIFE

FAMILY

Children First—Ellet: *Court Circles*

Nagging Father—Wharton: *Social Life*

Her Father's Companion—Wharton: *Social Life*

A Great Favorite—Wharton: *Social Life*

Prodigal Son—Goodwin: *Dolly Madison*

Daredevil—Crook: *Memories of the White House: The Home Life of Our Presidents from Lincoln to Roosevelt*

Grandpa—Willets: *Inside History*
Kid Gloves:—*Boudoir Mirrors*
Eccentricities—*Boudoir Mirrors*
Where Mommies Come From—McAdoo: *Priceless Gift*
Ineligible—Truman: *Bess W. Truman*
Hail to the Little Chief—*Look*, July 1961
Where's Daddy?—Thomas: *Dateline*
And Give Them Ten Per Cent—*Time*, August 28, 1964
I Just Work Here—*National Review*, August 29, 1975
Bored Grandma—McLellan: *Ear*; Helen Thomas on CSPAN,
    November 12, 1986
Public Life—*Ladies' Home Journal*, March 1979

FUN

A Children's Party—Wharton: *Social Life*
Girls Will Be Boys—Willets, quoting Margaret B. Downing
Skittish—Faber: *Lorena Hickok*
You Do Know How to Whistle?—Truman: *Souvenir: Margaret
    Truman's Own Story*
Harry Gives Them Hell—terHorst and Albertazzie: *The Flying
    White House: The Story of Air Force One*
Just One of the Girls—*Life*, April 22, 1946
Soap Opera—West: *Upstairs*
Home Movies—Howar: *Laughing*
Being Herself—*McCall's*, September 1975
Dirty Stories—McLellan: *Ear*
The Nancified Joke—McLellan: *Ear*

AROUND THE HOUSE

Menagerie—Truman: *White House Pets*
Home Economics—Caroli: *First Ladies*
Undomesticated—Caroli: *First Ladies*
A Poor Housekeeper—Pryor: *Reminiscences*
Details—Crook: *Memories*
Paging Theodore—Hoover: *Forty-two Years*
Mistress of All That She Surveys—West: *Upstairs*

And So to Bed—Johnson: *White House Diary*
Oops!—Moorehead: *Entertaining*

6 AT WORK

A WOMAN'S DAY IS NEVER DONE

Always Knitting—Parton: *Daughters*
Housekeeping—Holloway: *Ladies*
Working Duchess—Barzman: *First Ladies; Boudoir Mirrors*
The *Paparazza*—McLendon and Smith: *Don't Quote Me*
Priorities—Sadler: *America's*

MISSIONS

Ambassadress—Holloway: *Ladies*
Guess Who Came to Dinner—Logan: *Thirty Years*
Royal Favorite—Holloway: *Ladies*
Constant Companion—Kelley: *Jackie, Oh!*
How to Be Popular—Baldrige: *Of Diamonds and Diplomats*
Under Fire—McLendon and Smith: *Don't Quote Me*
Whisper Campaign—*McCall's*, November 1985

IN TIME OF WAR

Dolley Rescues George—Wharton: *Social Life*; Hanscom: *Friendly*
Peace—Wharton: *Social Life*
Mrs. Jackson Lays Down the Law—Hanscom: *Friendly*
The Colonel's Wife—Holloway: *Ladies*
Mother of the Regiment—Logan: *Thirty Years*
Rover—Lash: *Eleanor and Franklin*

GOOD WORKS

Giving from the Heart—Willets: *Inside History*; Pendel: *Thirty-six Years*
Personal Attention—Willets: *Inside History*; Logan: *Thirty Years*
In the Presence of Greatness—Berkman: *The Lady and the Law*
Tribute—Johnson: *White House Diary*

Lassie Go Home—Carpenter: *Ruffles and Flourishes*
Clout—*Redbook*, April 1977
Drugs—McLellan: *Ear*

7 A HEARTBEAT AWAY

SUPPORTING CAST

At Valley Forge—Holloway: *In the Home of the Presidents*
Power Behind the Throne—Ames: *Ten Years*
Clipping Service—Caroli: *First Ladies*
Advocate—Holloway: *Ladies*
Behind Every Successful Man—Means: *Woman in White House*
Plus Ça Change—*Time*, August 28, 1964
Readiness Is All—I. Ross: *Grace Coolidge*
The President's Conscience—Lash: *Eleanor and Franklin*
A Tower of Strength—Lash: *Eleanor and Franklin*
Who Commands the Commander in Chief?—West: *Upstairs*
And Who Decides Who Is Right?—*Ladies' Home Journal*, March 1979
And That's the Truth—Friedman: *Washington Humor*

POLITICS

Advice—Hanscom: *Friendly*
Those Democrats—Wharton: *Social Life*
Repartee—Willets: *Inside History*
His Better Half—*Boudoir Mirrors*
Fish Story—Parks: *My Thirty Years*
Better Than Wyoming—*Time*, January 20, 1987
We Must Stop Meeting Like This—*Look*, July 1961
We're Also Holding Your Mother—*Look*, July 1961

CAMPAIGNS

Prayer—Ames: *Ten Years*
Disinterested Devotion—Logan: *Thirty Years*
Ambition Fulfilled—Holloway: *In the Home*
All the Way with LBJ—Carpenter: *Ruffles*

The Eyes of Texas—*Time*, August 28, 1964
Betty's Husband—*McCall's*, January 1977
Running Her for Office—*Ladies' Home Journal*, March 1979
And May the Best Man Win—*McCall's*, January 1977

8   THE PUBLIC ROLE

HOSTESS

Protocol—Holloway: *Ladies*
Gate-Crasher—Hansom: *Friendly*
Memory—Holloway: *Ladies*
Do as You Please—Holloway: *Ladies*
Wildflower—Holloway: *Ladies*
Duty—Poore: *Perley's*
Burden—Willets: *Inside History*
The Party Wasn't Over—*Boudoir Mirrors*
Shocking the Help—Fields: *My 21 Years in the White House*
Smoking—Fields: *My 21 Years*
Democracy—Fields: *My 21 Years*
Royal Visit—Johnson: *White House Diary*

MEETING PEOPLE

Identity Crisis—Fields: *My 21 Years*
Moving Right Along—*Boudoir Mirrors*
The People's House—Willets: *Inside History*
Workout—Willets: *Inside History*
Looking Back—Johnson: *White House Diary*
Equal but Separate—Hoover: *Forty-two Years*
Swept Away—Moorehead: *Entertaining*
Fame—Murray: *Family Laugh Lines*
Plain Speaking—Murray: *Family*

THE PRESS

Signs of the Times—I. Ross: *Grace Coolidge*
Women Only—Abell and Gordon: *Let Them Eat Caviar*
Glad You Asked—*Time*, November 10, 1947

Make This Cup Pass from Me—*Look*, July 1961
Wanderer—*Look*, July 1961
Wish—Johnson: *White House Diary*
Hue and Cry—*Time*, August 28, 1964
And That's a Promise—*McCall's*, September 1970
The Deep End of the Pool—McLendon and Smith: *Don't Quote Me*

CONTROVERSY

Criticism—Poore: *Perley's*
Exhibition—Poore: *Perley's*
Breach of Trust—McLendon and Smith: *Don't Quote Me*
Hopelessly Devoted to Him—*Redbook*, July 1981
Reversal—McLellan: *Ear*

TRAVEL

At Sea—Hanscom: *Friendly*
An American in Paris—Hanscom: *Friendly*
Indian Princess—Wilson: *My Memoir*
Voodoo Economics—*Saturday Evening Post*, May 10, 1962
Chinese Puzzle—*Time*, March 6, 1972

9 IN THE PRESIDENT'S HOUSE

REAL ESTATE

Finding the Spot—Poore: *Perley's*
What to Call It—Willets: *Inside History*
The First Occupant—Hanscom: *Friendly*
Drying Clothes—Ellet: *Court Circles*; Wharton: *Social Life*
Amen—Parks: *My Thirty Years*
Furnishings—Poore: *Perley's*

A Place Like No Home—Willets: *Inside History*
Enjoyment—Poore: *Perley's*
Attic—*Boudoir Mirrors*
Stuffed Moose—Fields: *My 21 Years*
Ghost Stories—Parks: *My Thirty Years*
Out Damned Spot—West: *Upstairs*
A Bargain—Kelley: *Jackie*

CHINA

The Problem Begins—Wharton: *Social Life*; Ames: *Ten Years*
Ogling the Spoons—Poore: *Perley's*; Wharton: *Social Life*
Fauna and Flora—Poore: *Perley's*
The China Connection—Willets: *Inside History*
Wayward China—McLellan: *Ear*
Legacy—*Ladies' Home Journal*, March 1975

THE STAFF

Touching—Pendel: *Thirty-six Years*
She Should Have Been a Realtor—Crook: *Memories*
Kindness—West: *Upstairs*
That Special?—*Vogue*, September 1974
How to Be Indispensable—Hoover: *Forty-two Years*
Recognition Scene—*Boudoir Mirrors*
Sign Language—Hoover: *Forty-two Years*
Supporting Role—Fields: *My 21 Years*
Into the Closet—Fields: *My 21 Years*
Secret Service—Hoover: *Forty-two Years*
Bang, Bang—Parks: *My Thirty Years*
Getting the Sack—Jaffray: *Secrets*

AT THE TABLE

Simple Martha—Ames: *Ten Years*
Simplicity—Wharton: *Social Life*
Incongruous Food—Wharton: *Social Life*
The Virginian—Brooks: *Dames and Daughters*

The State Dinner—Ames: *Ten Years*
Paying for It—Ames: *Ten Years*
Temperance—Holloway: *Ladies*
Lifesaver—Poore: *Perley's*
Logistics—Caroli: *First Ladies*
Playing for Their Supper—Hoover: *Forty-two Years*
Food for Thought—Lash: *Eleanor and Franklin*
Let Them Eat Crab—Leighton: *The Search for the Real Nancy Reagan*
Penny Wise—McLellan: *Ear*
Simple but Good—Fields: *My 21 Yearrs*
Leftovers—Fields: *My 21 Years*

10 AFTERMATH

LEAVING

Free at Last—Willets: *Inside History*
Miserable—Means: *Woman in White House*
Independence—A. E. Hotchner: *Choice People: The Greats, Near-Greats, and Ingrates I Have Known*
Disgrace and Dignity—*Ladies' Home Journal*, March 1975

TRAGEDY

Omens—Sadler: *America's*
Shock—Holloway: *Ladies*
The Final Moments—Sandburg and Angle: *Mary Lincoln*
Restraint—Willets: *Inside History*
Grandeur—Thomas: *Dateline*
Remembering Camelot—*Look*, 1964
Farewell—Willets: *Inside History*
Taking Over—Wilson: *Memoir*
Positively Pat—*McCall's*, October 1973
Ordeal—*McCall's*, May 1975
Holding On—*Good Housekeeping*, September 1981
Blame—Ames: *Ten Years*

ALONE

Waiting for the Call—Barzman: *First Ladies*
That Way Madness Lies—Sandburg and Angle: *Mary Lincoln*
Among the Rest—Holloway: *Ladies*
Pension—Willets: *Inside History*
Widows—Abell and Gordon: *Let Them*
Pedestal—Thomas: *Dateline*
Recognition—Berkman: *Lady and Law*

THEIR END

Till Death Did Them Part—Barzman: *First Ladies*
Beyond the Grave—Willets: *Inside History*
Eulogy—Ames: *Ten Years*
Not Eating Will Kill You—Jaffray: *Secrets*

BIBLIOGRAPHY

Abell, George, and Evelyn Gordon. *Let Them Eat Caviar.* New York: Dodge Publishing, 1936.

Adams, John and Abigail. *Familiar Letters* (ed. C. F. Adams). Boston, 1875.

Adler, Bill. *The Kennedy Wit.* New York: The Citadel Press, 1964.

———. *Ronnie and Nancy: A Very Special Love Story.* New York: Crown, 1985.

———. *The Washington Wits.* New York: Macmillan, 1967.

Ames, Mary Clemmer. *Ten Years in Washington. Life and Scenes in the National Capital, as a Woman Sees Them.* Cincinnati, 1874.

Anonymous. *Boudoir Mirrors of Washington.* Philadelphia: John G. Winston Company, 1923.

Badeau, Adam. *Grant in Peace.* Hartford, Conn., 1887.

Baldrige, Letitia. *Of Diamonds and Diplomats.* Boston: Houghton Mifflin, 1968.

Barzman, Sol. *The First Ladies.* New York: Cowles, 1970.

Berkman, Edward O. *The Lady and the Law.* Boston: Little, Brown, 1976.

Bernstein, Carl, and Bob Woodward. *All the President's Men.* New York: Simon & Schuster, 1974.

Boller, Paul F., Jr. *Presidential Anecdotes.* New York: Oxford University Press, 1981.

———. *Presidential Campaigns.* New York: Oxford University Press, 1984.

Britton, Nan. *The President's Daughter.* New York: Elizabeth Ann Guild, 1927.

Brodie, Fawn M. *Thomas Jefferson: An Intimate History.* New York: W. W. Norton, 1974.

Brooks, Geraldine. *Dames and Daughters of the Young Republic.* New York: Thomas Y. Crowell, 1901.

Bryant, Traphes (with Frances Spatz Leighton). *Dog Days at the White House.* New York: Macmillan, 1975.

Buck, Pearl S. *The Kennedy Women.* New York: Cowles, 1970.

Butterfield, L. H., Marc Friedlaender, and Mary-Jo Kline. *The Book of Abigail and John: Selected Letters of the Adams Family, 1762–1784.* Cambridge, Mass.: Harvard University Press, 1975.

Cameron, Gail. *Rose: A Biography of Rose Fitzgerald Kennedy.* New York: Putnam, 1971.

Cannon, Lou. *Reagan.* New York: Putnam, 1982.

Carnegie, Dale. *The Unknown Lincoln.* New York: Forest Hills Publishing Co., 1932.

Caroli, Betty Boyd. *First Ladies.* New York: Oxford University Press, 1987.

Carpenter, Liz. *Ruffles and Flourishes.* Garden City, N.Y.: Doubleday, 1970.

Crook, Colonel W. H. *Memories of the White House: The Home Life of Our Presidents from Lincoln to Roosevelt.* Boston: Little, Brown, 1911.

Dall, Curtis B. *F.D.R. My Exploited Father-in-Law.* Washington, D.C.: Action Associates, 1968.

Daniels, Jonathan. *Washington Quadrille.* Garden City, N.Y.: Doubleday, 1968.

Daugherty, Harry M. (with Thomas Dixon). *The Inside Story of the Harding Tragedy.* New York: Churchill Company, 1932.

David, Lester. *The Lonely Lady of San Clemente.* New York: Thomas Y. Crowell, 1978.

Dunleavy, Stephen, and Peter Brennan. *Those Wild, Wild Kennedy Boys!* New York: Pinnacle Books, 1976.

Ellet, Mrs. E. F. *Court Circles of the Republic; or the Beauties and Celebrities of the Nation.* Philadelphia, n. d.

Faber, Doris. *The Life of Lorena Hickok.* New York: William Morrow, 1980.

Fields, Alonzo. *My 21 Years in the White House*. New York: Coward-McCann, 1961.

Fisher, James Knox. *Our Presidents—Their Lives and History*. Chicago: M. A. Donohue and Co., 1910.

Ford, Betty (with Chris Chase). *The Times of My Life*. New York: Harper & Row, 1978.

Frank, Sid. *The Presidents: Tidbits and Trivia*. Maplewood, N.J.: Hammond, 1975.

Frederick, Pauline. *Ten First Ladies of the World*. New York: Meredith Press, 1967.

Freud, Sigmund, and William C. Bullitt. *Thomas Woodrow Wilson—A Psychological Study*. Boston: Houghton Mifflin, 1967.

Friedman, Philip. *Washington Humor*. New York: The Citadel Press, 1964.

Gallagher, Mary Barelli. *My Life with Jacqueline Kennedy*. New York: David McKay, 1969.

Goodwin, Maud Wilder. *Dolly Madison*. New York: Scribner's, 1896.

Guiles, Fred Lawrence. *Legend: The Life and Death of Marilyn Monroe*. New York: Stein & Day, 1984.

Hanscom, Elizabeth Deering. *The Friendly Craft—A Collection of American Letters*. New York: Macmillan, 1908.

Harris, Leon A. *The Fine Art of Political Wit*. New York: E. P. Dutton, 1964.

Holloway, Laura Carter. *In the Home of the Presidents*. New York, 1875.

————. *The Ladies of the White House: or, In the Home of the Presidents*. Cincinnati, 1881.

Hoover, Irwin Hood. *Forty-two years in the White House*. Boston: Houghton Mifflin, 1934.

Hotchner, A. E. *Choice People: The Greats, Near-Greats, and Ingrates I Have Known*. New York: William Morrow, 1984.

Howar, Barbara. *Laughing All the Way*. New York: Stein & Day, 1973.

Hurd, Charles. *The White House: A Biography*. New York: Harper & Brothers, 1940.

Jaffray, Elizabeth. *Secrets of the White House*. New York: Cosmopolitan Book Corporation, 1927.

Jensen, Amy La Follette. *The White House and Its Thirty-two Families*. New York: McGraw-Hill, 1958.

Johnson, Lady Bird. *A White House Diary*. New York: Holt, Rinehart & Winston, 1970.

Kellerman, Barbara. *All the President's Kin*. New York: The Free Press, 1981.

Kelley, Kitty. *Jackie Oh!* Secaucus, N.J.: Lyle Stuart, 1978.

Klapthor, Margaret Brown. *The First Ladies Cook Book*. New York: Home Library Press, 1965.

Lash, Joseph P. *Eleanor and Franklin*. New York: W. W. Norton, 1971.

————. *Eleanor: The Years Alone*. New York: W. W. Norton, 1972.

————. *Love, Eleanor*. Garden City, N.Y.: Doubleday, 1982.

Leamer, Laurence. *Make-Believe: The Story of Nancy & Ronald Reagan*. New York: Harper & Row, 1983.

Leech, Margaret. *Reveille in Washington (1860–1865)*. New York: Harper & Brothers, 1941.

Leighton, Frances Spatz. *The Search for the Real Nancy Reagan*. New York: Macmillan, 1987.

Logan, Mrs. John A. *Thirty Years in Washington; or, Life and Scenes in Our National Capital*. Hartford, Conn.: A. D. Worthington and Co., 1901.

Longworth, Alice Roosevelt. *Crowded Hours*. New York: Scribner's, 1933.

McAdoo, Eleanor Wilson. *The Priceless Gift—The Love Letters of Woodrow Wilson and Ellen Axson Wilson*. New York: McGraw-Hill, 1962.

McLellan, Diana. *Ear on Washington*. New York: Arbor House, 1982.

McLendon, Winzola, and Scottie Smith. *Don't Quote Me!* New York: E. P. Dutton, 1970.

MacPherson, Myra. *The Power Lovers: An Intimate Look at Politics and Marriage*. New York: Putnam, 1975.

Martin, Judith. *The Name on the White House Floor, and Other*

Anxieties of Our Times. New York: Coward, McCann & Geoghegan, 1972.

Means, Marianne. *The Woman in the White House.* New York: Random House, 1963.

Miller, Hope Ridings. *Scandals in the Highest Office: Facts and Fictions in the Private Lives of Our Presidents.* New York: Random House, 1973.

Moore, Charles. *Washington Past and Present.* New York: The Century Co., 1929.

Moorehead, Lucy. *Entertaining in Washington.* New York: Putnam, 1978.

Morgan, Hal, and Kerry Tucker. *Rumor!* New York: Penguin Books, 1984.

Morgan, Kay Summersby. *Past Forgetting: My Love Affair with Dwight D. Eisenhower.* New York: Simon & Schuster, 1976.

Murray, Kathryn. *Family Laugh Lines.* Englewood Cliffs, N.J.: Prentice-Hall, 1966.

Norton, Howard. *Rosalynn.* Plainfield, N.J.: Logos International, 1977.

Packard, Jerrold M. *American Monarchy: A Social Guide to the Presidency.* New York: Delacorte Press, 1983.

Parker, John F. *The Fun and Laughter of Politics.* Garden City, N.Y.: Doubleday, 1978.

Parks, Lillian Rogers (with Frances Spatz Leighton). *My Thirty Years Backstairs at the White House.* New York: Fleet Publishing, 1961.

Parton, James. *Daughters of Genius.* Philadelphia: Hubbard Brothers, 1886.

Pendel, Thomas F. *Thirty-six Years in the White House.* New York, 1902.

Poore, Benjamin Perley. *Perley's Reminiscences of Sixty Years in the National Metropolis.* Philadelphia, 1886.

Prindiville, Kathleen. *First Ladies.* New York: Macmillan, 1951.

Pryor, Mrs. Roger A. *Reminiscences of Peace and War.* New York: Grosset & Dunlap, 1904.

Rankin, Henry B. *Personal Recollections of Abraham Lincoln.* New York: G. P. Putnam's Sons, 1916.

Reagan, Ronald (with Richard G. Hubler). *Where's the Rest of Me?* New York: Duell, Sloan & Pearce, 1965.

Robins, Edward. *Romances of Early America*. Philadelphia: George W. Jacobs, 1902.

Roosevelt, Eleanor. *On My Own*. New York: Harper & Row, 1958.

————. *This Is My Story*. New York: Harper & Brothers, 1937.

Roosevelt, Elliott, and James Brough. *Mother R: Eleanor Roosevelt's Untold Story*. New York: Putnam, 1977.

Roosevelt, James (with Bill Libby). *My Parents: A Differing View*. Chicago: Playboy Press, 1976.

Roosevelt, James (with Sidney Shalett). *Affectionately, F.D.R.* New York: Harcourt, Brace and Co., 1958.

Roosevelt, Mrs. Theodore (with other Roosevelts). *Cleared for Strange Ports*. New York: Scribner's, 1927.

Ross, George E. *Know Your Presidents and Their Wives*. New York: Rand, McNally, 1960.

Ross, Ishbel. *Grace Coolidge and Her Era*. New York: Dodd, Mead, 1962.

Russell, Francis. *The Shadow of Blooming Grove: Warren G. Harding in His Times*. New York: McGraw-Hill, 1968.

Sadler, Christine. *America's First Ladies*. New York: Macfadden Books, 1963.

Sandburg, Carl, and Paul M. Angle. *Mary Lincoln: Wife and Widow*. New York: Harcourt, Brace, 1932.

Shulman, Irving. *"Jackie"! The Exploitation of a First Lady*. New York: Trident Press, 1970.

Smith, Don. *Peculiarities of the Presidents—Strange and Intimate Facts Not Found in History*. Van Wert, Ohio: Wilkinson Press, 1938.

Smith, Marie. *The President's Lady: An Intimate Biography of Mrs. Lyndon B. Johnson*. New York: Random House, 1964.

Sparks, Fred. *The $20,000,000 Honeymoon: Jackie and Ari's First Year*. New York: Bernard Geis Associates, 1970.

Starling, Edmund W. *Starling of the White House*. New York: Simon & Schuster, 1946.

Stimpson, George. *A Book About American History*. New York: Harper & Brothers, 1950.

Taylor, Tim. *The Book of Presidents*. New York: Arno Press, 1972.

Tebbel, John, and Sarah Miles Watts. *The Press and the Presidency*. New York: Oxford University Press, 1985.

terHorst, J. F., and Col. Ralph Albertazzie. *The Flying White House: The Story of Air Force One*. New York: Coward, McCann & Geoghegan, 1979.

Thomas, Helen. *Dateline: The White House*. New York: Macmillan, 1975.

Truman, Margaret. *Bess W. Truman*. New York: Macmillan, 1986.

———. *White House Pets*. New York: David McKay, 1961.

——— (with Margaret Cousins). *Souvenir: Margaret Truman's Own Story*. New York: McGraw-Hill, 1956.

Weimann, Jeanne Madeline, and Anita Miller, Publishers. *The Fair Women: The Story of the Woman's Building at the World's Colombian Exposition, Chicago 1893*. Chicago: Academy Chicago Publishers, 1981.

West, J. B. *Upstairs at the White House—My Life with the First Ladies*. New York: Coward McCann & Geoghegan, 1973.

Wharton, Anne Hollingsworth. *Social Life in the Early Republic*. Philadelphia: J. B. Lippincott, 1902.

White, Calvin Coolidge. *All the Things You Never Knew About Our American Presidents*. Louisburg, N.C.: The Franklin Times, 1974.

White House Historical Association (in collaboration with the National Geographic Society). *First Ladies*. Washington, D.C., 1981.

———. *The Living White House*. Washington, D.C., 1966.

———. *The White House: An Historic Guide*. Washington, D.C., 1962, and updated.

Whitton, Mary Ormsbee. *These Were the Women: U.S.A. 1776–1860*. New York: Hastings House, 1954.

Willets, Gilson. *Inside History of the White House*. New York: The Christian Herald, 1908.

Williams, Henry L. *The Lincoln Story Book*. New York: G. W. Dillingham, 1907.

Wills, Garry. *Reagan's America: Innocents at Home*. Garden City, N.Y.: Doubleday, 1987.

Wilson, Edith Bolling. *My Memoir*. Indianapolis: Bobbs-Merrill, 1939.

Wright, Louis B. *The Cultural Life of the American Colonies*. New York: Harper & Brothers, 1957.

MAGAZINES AND NEWSPAPERS:

Good Housekeeping, Ladies' Home Journal, Life, Leslie's, Look, McCall's, Munsey's, National Review, The New York Times, Newsweek, Redbook, Time, Vogue, World's Work

SELECTED MAGAZINE ARTICLES:

Braden, Joan. *Saturday Evening Post*, May 10, 1962.

Kennedy, Jacqueline. Kennedy Memorial Issue of *Look*, 1964.

MacPherson, Myra. Article in *McCall's*, September 1975.

Martin, Ralph G. *Rosalynn, Ladies' Home Journal*, March 1979.

McBee, Susanna. *Pat Nixon and the First Ladywatcher, McCall's*, September 1970.

Stroud, Mandy. *Pat Nixon Today, Ladies' Home Journal*, March 1975.

Weinraub, Bernard. *Mrs. President, McCall's*, November 1985.

West, Jessamyn. *The Real Pat Nixon, Good Housekeeping*, February 1971.

INDEX

FOR THE BEST IN PAPERBACKS, LOOK FOR THE (Ⓟ)

In every corner of the world, on every subject under the sun, Penguin represents quality and variety—the very best in publishing today.

For complete information about books available from Penguin—including Pelicans, Puffins, Peregrines, and Penguin Classics—and how to order them, write to us at the appropriate address below. Please note that for copyright reasons the selection of books varies from country to country.

In the United Kingdom: For a complete list of books available from Penguin in the U.K., please write to *Dept E.P., Penguin Books Ltd, Harmondsworth, Middlesex, UB7 0DA.*

In the United States: For a complete list of books available from Penguin in the U.S., please write to *Dept BA, Penguin*, Box 120, Bergenfield, New Jersey 07621-0120.

In Canada: For a complete list of books available from Penguin in Canada, please write to *Penguin Books Ltd, 2801 John Street, Markham, Ontario L3R 1B4.*

In Australia: For a complete list of books available from Penguin in Australia, please write to the *Marketing Department, Penguin Books Ltd, P.O. Box 257, Ringwood, Victoria 3134.*

In New Zealand: For a complete list of books available from Penguin in New Zealand, please write to the *Marketing Department, Penguin Books (NZ) Ltd, Private Bag, Takapuna, Auckland 9.*

In India: For a complete list of books available from Penguin, please write to *Penguin Overseas Ltd, 706 Eros Apartments, 56 Nehru Place, New Delhi, 110019.*

In Holland: For a complete list of books available from Penguin in Holland, please write to *Penguin Books Nederland B.V., Postbus 195, NL-1380AD Weesp, Netherlands.*

In Germany: For a complete list of books available from Penguin, please write to *Penguin Books Ltd, Friedrichstrasse 10-12, D-6000 Frankfurt Main I, Federal Republic of Germany.*

In Spain: For a complete list of books available from Penguin in Spain, please write to *Longman, Penguin España, Calle San Nicolas 15, E-28013 Madrid, Spain.*

In Japan: For a complete list of books available from Penguin in Japan, please write to *Longman Penguin Japan Co Ltd, Yamaguchi Building, 2-12-9 Kanda Jimbocho, Chiyoda-Ku, Tokyo 101, Japan.*

FOR THE BEST IN HISTORY, LOOK FOR THE ⓟ

☐ **THE FACE OF BATTLE**
John Keegan

In this study of three battles from three different centuries, John Keegan examines war from the fronts—conveying its reality for the participants at the "point of maximum danger."

366 pages   *ISBN: 0-14-004897-9*   **$6.95**

☐ **VIETNAM: A HISTORY**
Stanley Karnow

Stanley Karnow's monumental narrative—the first complete account of the Vietnam War—puts events and decisions of the day into sharp, clear focus. "This is history writing at its best."—*Chicago Sun-Times*

752 pages   *ISBN: 0-14-007324-8*   **$12.95**

☐ **MIRACLE AT MIDWAY**
Gordon W. Prange
with Donald M. Goldstein and Katherine V. Dillon

The best-selling sequel to *At Dawn We Slept* recounts the battles at Midway Island—events which marked the beginning of the end of the war in the Pacific.

470 pages   *ISBN: 0-14-006814-7*   **$10.95**

☐ **THE MASK OF COMMAND**
John Keegan

This provocative view of leadership examines the meaning of military heroism through four prototypes from history—Alexander the Great, Wellington, Grant, and Hitler—and proposes a fifth type of "post-heroic" leader for the nuclear age.

368 pages   *ISBN: 0-14-011406-8*   **$7.95**

☐ **THE SECOND OLDEST PROFESSION**
Spies and Spying in the Twentieth Century
Phillip Knightley

In this fascinating history and critique of espionage, Phillip Knightley explores the actions and missions of such noted spies as Mata Hari and Kim Philby, and organizations such as the CIA and the KGB.

436 pages   *ISBN: 0-14-010655-3*   **$7.95**

☐ **THE STORY OF ENGLISH**
Robert McCrum, William Cran, and Robert MacNeil

"Rarely has the English language been scanned so brightly and broadly in a single volume," writes the *San Francisco Chronicle* about this journey across time and space that explores the evolution of English from Anglo-Saxon Britain to Reagan's America.   *384 pages*   *ISBN: 0-14-009435-0*   **$12.95**

☐ **MOVE YOUR SHADOW**
South Africa, Black & White
Joseph Lelyveld

Drawing on his two tours as a correspondent for *The New York Times*, Lelyveld offers a vivid portrait of a troubled country and its people, illuminating the history, society, and feelings that created and maintain apartheid.

402 pages   *ISBN: 0-14-009326-5*   **$7.95**

☐ **THE PELICAN HISTORY OF THE WORLD**
Revised Edition
J. M. Roberts

This comprehensive and informative survey of the growth of the modern world analyzes the major forces of our history and emphasizes both their physical and psychological effects.

1056 pages   *ISBN: 0-14-022785-7*   **$11.95**